AF541732

THE CROSSROADS

THE CROSSROADS

Kashmir—India's Bridge to Xinjiang

KULBHUSHAN WARIKOO

RUPA

First published by
Rupa Publications India Pvt. Ltd 2023
7/16, Ansari Road, Daryaganj
New Delhi 110002

Sales centres:
Bengaluru Chennai Hyderabad
Jaipur Kathmandu Kolkata
Mumbai Prayagraj

P-ISBN: 978-93-5702-569-0
E-ISBN: 978-93-5702-570-6

First impression 2023

10 9 8 7 6 5 4 3 2 1

Printed in India

Contents

Preface

Kashmir, due to its close physical proximity and shared cultural affinity with Xinjiang, has been a hub for India's socio-economic exchanges with Central Asia since ancient times. During the British rule, the nature and extent of political and commercial interactions between Kashmir and Xinjiang were conditioned by the rivalry between the British and Russian empires (for control over Central Asia). The British were quick to realize the strategic importance of Kashmir, and used their influence in the Valley to restrain Russian designs on Central Asia. Kashmir and its frontier territories of Ladakh, Gilgit, Baltistan, Hunza and Nagar came to occupy a pivotal position in the British strategy of checkmating Tsarist Russia and later Soviet Russia.

The British kept a close watch on Russian activities. This 'great game' elevated the significance of Kashmir because the British utilized it as a frontier operational post to monitor Russian movements in the Pamirs, Xinjiang and Central Asia. It also served as a launching point for the strategic advances of the British.

Like Kashmir, Xinjiang also occupies a highly strategic position due to its coterminous borders with Kashmir, Ladakh, Hunza, Gilgit and Baltistan. Xinjiang, now an autonomous region in China, was the peripheral territory that had usually remained out of effective Chinese control. The Qing dynasty was able to secure control over this territory only in 1757. It is only since 1877 that China has held the region without any interruption.

As Ladakh enjoyed a central position in the network of caravan trails, and due to its linkage with the Silk Route passing through Xinjiang, it was a major gateway for the Indo-Central Asian exchange in matters of diplomacy, trade and culture. Xinjiang exported gold and silver; jade; fine *pashm* (wool); hides and skins; Khotan silks and carpets; and *charas* (cannabis) to

India, in exchange for Indian fabrics, books, sugar, medicines, dyes, spices and tea.

After taking control of Xinjiang, the Qing dynasty struggled to contain the political insurrections raised by the Muslim Khoja rebels in Kashgar. The Qing authorities in Kashgar even sought the support of the ruling chiefs in Ladakh and Hunza to prevent the entry of the Khoja rebels inside Kashmir's territory. In most cases, such cooperation was provided in exchange for concessions in matters of trade and landed property. Thus, we find that in the eighteenth century, the chief of Hunza was provided an estate at Yarkand (in Xinjiang). The chief was also allowed to cultivate Raskam lands and levy taxes on the Kyrgyz of Taghdumbash Pamir.

With the beginning of the Dogra rule in Jammu and Kashmir in 1846, the movement of trade and traffic between Kashmir, Ladakh and Xinjiang increased. The Dogras had a vested interest in the uninterrupted supply of shawl wool from Xinjiang and Tibet to Kashmir looms. The main aim of the Dogra General Zorawar Singh's expeditions to Tibet and his challenge to the chief of Yarkand in 1830s and 1840s was to secure physical control of the shawl wool production areas in and around western Tibet. However, the British were averse to the Dogra regime making inroads in Tibet and Xinjiang. The British had pinned their hopes on China serving as an obstacle to Russian advances in the Pamirs.

Gulab Singh, the founder of the Dogra dynasty, played his own game. In fact, the Dogras pursued an active policy towards Central Asia, much to the chagrin of the British authorities. Thus, when Yakub Beg wrested control of Kashgar from the Qing dynasty, direct diplomatic contact between Yakub Beg of Kashgar and Maharaja Ranbir Singh of Kashmir was established in the 1860s. This compelled the British to recalibrate their foreign policy. Then they used the Dogra contact in Kashgar to extend their 'friendly' contacts with Yakub Beg and encouraged him to play the role of a 'buffer' among Tsarist Russia, China and the British in India.

It was with this object in view that the British tried to play a peacemaker when Chinese forces attacked Yakub Beg in 1875–77.

With Yakub Beg dead and the Chinese having re-established their authority over Xinjiang, the British policy focussed on developing Indian trade with Xinjiang and on securing consular access to Kashgar in Xinjiang. Kashmir's geographical contiguity and close commercial ties with Xinjiang were used as a cover for extending political influence over that area. The main objective was monitoring the Russian movements in Central Asia and checking any possible extension of Russian influence in Xinjiang. In 1891, Macartney, a British officer, was posted at Kashgar, without any official recognition of his consular status by the Chinese authorities. Then ensued a determined effort to secure a consular status for Macartney, at par with the Russian consul, which was gained after several years of diplomatic manoeuvres. These manoeuvres often came at the cost of Kashmir's territorial claims on Shahidulla, Raskam and the Trans-Karakoram territory. The British were focussed on buying the goodwill of China and developing some diplomatic gains in Xinjiang vis-à-vis Russia. They neglected the demarcation of Kashmir–Ladakh–Xinjiang borders, thus leaving a troubled legacy for independent India to cope with.

Even after the signing of the Pamirs Boundary Agreement in 1895, the Anglo-Russian tug of war over this part of the Himalayan frontier did not recede. Instead, the focus shifted to the frontiers of Kashmir (in Hunza, Gilgit and Ladakh) abutting Xinjiang. The British induced China to occupy certain areas beyond the Muztagh–Karakoram range, over which the Chinese had not exercised any authority before. This was done with a view to forestall any future Russian expansion from their newly acquired vantage position in Bozai Gumbaz.

In 1930, with reports of the Russian success in exercising their influence over political affairs in Xinjiang coming in, the British policy was geared to consolidate their hold over the strategic frontier outposts of Gilgit, Hunza and Nagar. The British took the Gilgit Agency on a 60-year lease under an agreement signed with Maharaja Hari Singh of Kashmir in 1935. The volume of Indo-Central Asian trade that passed through Kashmir, Ladakh and Xinjiang witnessed a steady rise even with the Qing rule in Xinjiang till 1911; the advent of warlordism; and the subsequent Muslim rebellions there. As per official statistics, goods worth about ₹28.5 million were exported from India to Xinjiang through Kashmir and Ladakh between 1917 and 1931. European cotton goods and silks, dyed skins, indigo, spices and tea constituted the main items. During the same period, merchandise valued at about ₹33 million was imported from Xinjiang into Ladakh and Kashmir. Russian gold and paper roubles, charas, gold dust, raw silk, carpets and felts were the main items. From the late 1930s, internal disorders in Xinjiang began to act as a stumbling block for this overland trade that finally ceased to flow after 1949, following the communist takeover of Xinjiang and its subsequent closure to outside traffic. After the departure of the British from the subcontinent, the Indian Consulate at Kashgar was closed in 1949. With this, an era of productive Indo-Central Asian overland contacts through Kashmir and Xinjiang ended abruptly.

Presently, most parts of the vital frontier areas of Jammu, Kashmir and Ladakh are under the occupation of Pakistan (Gilgit, Baltistan, Hunza, Nagar, Yasin) and China (Raskam–Shimshal area and Aksai Chin). Taking full advantage of this ground reality and quite conscious of the traditional relationship between the people of Xinjiang and Kashmir, particularly in matters of trade and culture, Pakistan and China constructed the strategically important road linking Pakistan Occupied Kashmir, Gilgit and Baltistan with Xinjiang. Known as the Karakoram Highway (KKH), this road not only ensured direct access to China inside all the strategic points in Gilgit and Baltistan but also resulted in free and increased movement of men and materials between Xinjiang and Pakistan. As opposed to this, on the Indian side all connections between Ladakh and Xinjiang were snapped after China sealed the borders of Xinjiang in 1949. This stands in sharp contrast to the pre-1949 scenario when Ladakh hummed with activity for most part of the year, being the transit emporium of Indo-Central Asian trade.

Following the disintegration of the Soviet Union, the KKH became the direct overland corridor between Pakistan and the newly independent Central Asian republics through Gilgit, Baltistan and Xinjiang. Pakistan is thus placed on a firm footing to translate this physical advantage to pursue its strategic games in Central Asia. On the other hand, India has been besieged with the problem of lack of overland connectivity with Central Asia. Recently, China is reported to have built a 35 km road on the Shimshal highland (currently under the occupation of China) linking it with Pakistan occupied Gilgit region, thus overlooking Indian positions on the Siachen glacier and posing a serious challenge to Indian security in Ladakh. Moreover, the China–Pakistan Economic Corridor (CPEC) is being built with a massive $64 billion Chinese investment to widen, deepen and upgrade the China–Pakistan overland route connecting Xinjiang (through Gilgit) to Pakistan. The CPEC is a game changer from trade, political and strategic points of view and poses a direct challenge to Indian security in this frontier region. China has virtually extended its influence (political, economic and cultural) in Gilgit–Baltistan and rest of Pakistan through the CPEC by building multiple projects like hydel, thermal, rail, road, upgradation or widening of the KKH, posting of Chinese personnel along the CPEC, laying an optical fibre network from Tashkurgan (in Xinjiang) through the KKH to Pakistan, creating industrial and special economic zones, teaching of Chinese language and culture, etc.

It is against this background that this book examines, records and reflects upon such a rich and productive experience and its implications for the ongoing border dispute between India and China in the Ladakh–Xinjiang sector. China has not only brought the remote north-western frontier region of Xinjiang close to China's mainland by air, rail and road networks, but it has also turned Xinjiang into a bridge to extend its direct transportation links with adjoining Central Asia and also with Pakistan (via the KKH and the CPEC).

China's experience in this region offers important lessons for India, and this is what this book is all about. By Kashmir, we mean the undivided state of Jammu and Kashmir including Ladakh, Hunza, Gilgit, Baltistan and adjoining frontier territories. Throughout this book, the Chinese official name for Xinjiang (Xinjiang Uyghur Autonomous Region) has been used, which is interchangeable with Chinese Turkestan, Sinkiang, East Turkestan, Kashgaria and Alty Shahr. These are terms invariably used in the accounts of British officials, travellers etc. My experiences during field studies across the length and breadth of Xinjiang have been factored in the book, which focusses on the period beginning with mid-nineteenth century (i.e., the founding of Jammu and Kashmir State by Maharaja Gulab Singh) up to contemporary times. The study for the book has tapped all available archival sources at National Archives of India; J&K Government Archives; India Office Library & Records, London; and Nehru Memorial Museum and Library records, besides contemporary eyewitness accounts. The study offers important lessons for India to understand the pre-meditated Chinese strategy in Hunza, Gilgit and beyond, and offers Kashmir's perspective on the Sino-Indian border in the Ladakh sector. It lays bare unknown aspects of this subject so important for Sino-Indian, Sino-Pak and Indo-Pak relations.

The first chapter traces the historical and cultural links between Kashmir and Xinjiang since ancient times. Chapters two to four analyse the actual extent and pattern of trade, imports and exports between Ladakh and Xinjiang from 1860s to 1936, for which primary sources of Ladakh Trade Reports, Ladakh, Gilgit and Kashgar Dairies (available in National Archives of India) have been used.

Chapter five examines the state of diplomatic exchanges between Kashmir and Xinjiang authorities during the Dogra dynasty's rule. Since Hunza maintained a direct and complex relationship with the Chinese authorities in Xinjiang, this intricate issue has been comprehensively dealt with in Chapter six. The Raskam issue has been examined in the seventh chapter. The unfolding of Anglo-Russian rivalry in Central Asia and its impact on the region is explained in Chapter eight. Chapter nine offers a thorough analysis of the British policy towards Kashmir and its frontier territories of Ladakh, Gilgit, Hunza, Nagar, Yasin, etc., in the context of their overall imperial strategy in Central Asia. Chapter 10 brings to light the British action in preventing the Maharaja of Kashmir from reclaiming his territory in Shahidulla while also inducing the reluctant Chinese to occupy this Trans-Karakoram tract (in order to prevent Russia's forward moves in the Pamirs). It nails the Chinese lie of describing the Indian claims on the Himalayan frontiers as the legacy of British expansionism in India. Similarly, Chapter 11 examines the process of the establishment of the British Indian consulate at Kashgar (in south Xinjiang). It reinforces the view that the British prioritized their imperial interests in Central Asia and China, relegated the issue of demarcation of Kashmir–Xinjiang borders to the background and thus created a border dispute which was avoidable. Chapters 12 and 13, while discussing the fallout of the establishment of Russian power in Central Asia and their inroads in Xinjiang, lay bare the British strategy of wresting control of the vital Gilgit region from the control of Maharaja Hari Singh on a 60-year lease in 1935. Following the independence of India, when the Gilgit Agency was restored to the Maharaja of Kashmir, the British launched a secret mission called Operation Datta Khel, employing their officers posted in Pakistan, Peshawar and Gilgit to physically occupy Gilgit and hand it over to Pakistan. With this, the British strategy in Central and South Asia came full circle, with India licking its festering wounds.

Xinjiang witnessed disturbances and civil war during 1930s and 1940s, which resulted in mass exodus of refugees to Kashmir. Finally, another stream of refugees came to Kashmir following communist China's takeover of Xinjiang in 1949. This issue is dealt with in detail in Chapter 14. The construction of the KKH and its upgradation as part of the CPEC are explained in Chapter 15. Chapter 16 critically analyses China's policy in Xinjiang and draws parallels and contrasts with the Indian experience in Kashmir.

PART I

HISTORY, CULTURE AND TRADE

One

An Ancient Relationship

Due to its unique geographical position, Kashmir stood at the crossroads connecting mainland India with the neighbouring regions of Gandhara, Afghanistan, Xinjiang, Central Asia and China. Notwithstanding the lofty barriers of Pamirs, Karakoram and Hindu Kush ranges, there have existed since ancient times close cultural and socio-economic links between Kashmir (including its frontier territories of Ladakh, Baltistan and Gilgit) and the adjoining regions of Xinjiang, Tibet and Central Asia.

During the Kushan period (second century BC to third century AD), when Central Asia and north-western India were integrated into a single kingdom, various cities like Khotan, Kashgar, Balkh and Bamiyan had developed into important centres of Buddhism.[1] This is amply borne out by the archaeological finds at various sites in Kashmir and Xinjiang. The vast wealth of archaeological, epigraphic and other remains found in Xinjiang (in Khotan, Niya and other places) also testifies to the diffusion of culture and Buddhism from Kashmir in the Trans-Karakoram region.

The discovery of wooden tablets, manuscripts, seals, stucco reliefs, sculptural fragments and lotus flower motifs from Niya and other sites in Khotan, point to close historical links between Kashmir and Khotan. Bezeklik and Kizil caves, ruins of Buddhist temples at Gaocheng, Jiaohe, Khotan and other sites across Xinjiang are living testimony to the glorious Buddhist heritage of this region. The terracotta tiles found in Harwan (near Srinagar in Kashmir) depict figures dressed in Central Asian ethnic style and also contain Kharosthi numerals, pointing to the Central Asian imprint on Kashmir.

Kashmir was the cradle from which Buddhism spread to different directions in Xinjiang, Central Asia, Tibet, China and beyond. Gilgit, Chilas, Chitral, Baltistan, Ladakh, Zanskar and other frontier areas of Kashmir have been important mileposts of the famed Silk Route. The preponderance of carvings and inscriptions of prehistoric and Buddhist periods in the Gilgit–Baltistan region provide sufficient evidence of the prevalence of Buddhism in this region (in pre-Islamic times). The sites at Shaital, Thor, Thaplan, Shing Nala, Satpara, Kargah, Chilas, etc., that still exist today, have a high concentration of drawings of stupas, Buddhas, Bodhisattvas and jatakas besides thousands of inscriptions written in Kharosthi, Brahmi, Sanskrit, Sogdhian and Tibetan scripts. Some 80 per cent are in the Brahmi script.

The famous Gilgit manuscripts (containing the Lotus Sutra), written on birch bark, were first discovered by chance in a ruined stupa near Gilgit in 1931. These manuscripts contain Buddhist texts dating back to fifth and sixth centuries AD. The second lot of these manuscripts was discovered by Pandit Madhusudhan Kaul during his excavations in Gilgit in 1938. A major part of the Gilgit manuscripts is in the possession of the National Archives of India, which released the facsimile edition of its work on the Lotus Sutra series on 3 May 2012, in association with Soka Gakkai International.

Professor (Prof.) Karl Jettmar and his Pak-German Study Group did pioneering work on rock carvings and inscriptions in this region. The diversity and density of rock carvings (about 50,000 carvings and 5,000 inscriptions) in Gilgit–Baltistan turned the area into one of the most important petroglyph sites in the world. Unfortunately, over 30,000 carvings and inscriptions are doomed to be inundated due to the ongoing construction of the Diamer-Bhasha dam. According to Prof. Harald Hauptmann of Heidelberg, who has worked on the heritage of this area for many years, 37,051 carvings on 5,928 boulders will be inundated.[2] Hauptmann added that some 3,000 stupas and a number of drawings would also be submerged under the dam.[3] Obviously, it was through this region—which acted as the crossroads of ancient routes and cultures, and attracted travellers, traders and pilgrims—that Buddhism was transmitted to Xinjiang and beyond.

Buddhism reached Xinjiang during Ashoka's reign in third century BC. According to ancient Khotanese beliefs, a son of Ashoka named Kustana founded Khotan in around 240 BC. His grandson, Vijaya Sambhava is reported to have introduced Buddhism in Khotan. This Indian dynasty is said to have ruled Khotan for several generations, during which Buddhism was the religion of the state.[4]

Small colonies of Indians had come up in parts of Southern Xinjiang, along the Silk Route. Chinese scholars confirm that a Kashmiri monk Virochana built a Buddhist shrine in Khotan in 80 BC, 'which became the first Buddhist temple in Chinese history, and was worshipped mainly by Indian immigrants'.[5] They also affirm that 'Buddhist art, as an arm of the religion, was introduced in Yutian (Khotan) in Xinjiang from Kashmir, soon after the founding of the Yutian state'.[6]

Buddhism spread from Khotan to Kashgar, Niya, Cherchen, Loulan, Aksu, Kucha, Karashahr, Turfan and other parts of China. The Kushans, particularly Kanishka who had extended his rule to Xinjiang, spread Buddhism far and wide in Xinjiang, Central Asia and China. Kanishka organized the fourth Buddhist Council in Kashmir, in which around 500 Buddhist scholars are said to have participated. The proceedings of their debates were engraved on copper plates, put in a box and buried somewhere in Kashmir. Archaeologists are yet to locate this treasure trove buried somewhere in the Kashmir valley. A Chinese scholar, Prof. Liu Shiu Lin, noted the legacy of Kashmir's cultural relations with China. He stated:

> People of China know about Kashmir since ancient times. China has had a tradition of history writing since ancient times. Same tradition existed in Kashmir in the Indian sub-

continent. Historiographical tradition of Kashmir is very ancient. The tradition of friendly and cultural relations between China and Kashmir is over 2,000 years old. These ties flourished during the Buddhist period. Chinese monks would come to Kashmir to learn Buddhist philosophy and literature. They have left a valuable record about Kashmir. Chinese have translated many such works.[7]

KASHMIRI SCHOLARS/MONKS IN XINJIANG/CHINA

As mentioned previously, Kashmir was an eminent centre of Buddhist learning and attracted Buddhist scholars, monks and pilgrims from Xinjiang and adjoining territories. Kashmiri scholars and monks were held in high esteem in Xinjiang and China. Young men from Kashgar, Khotan, Kucha and other places would come to Kashmir for higher learning.

A long line of Kashmiri monks and scholars, 'who combined at the same time a high standard of learning, both linguistic and exegetic, with the audacity of explorers',[8] played a pivotal role in spreading Buddhism in Xinjiang, Central Asia and China through the translation of Buddhist teachings and texts into Chinese. They introduced and propagated Buddhist art and literature through translations of scriptures in China.

The Mahavibhasa (The Great Exegesis) is a 'compilation established by teachers in Kashmir'.[9] Its summary was translated into Chinese in AD 383 by a Kashmiri named Sanghbadra, whose name in Chinese transcription is given as Chi-to-panni.[10] The first Chinese translation of *gathas* was made by a Kashmiri scholar Dharmatrata in AD 221–23. Harivarman, a famous Sarvastivadi scholar of Kashmir composed his work Satyasiddhi Shastra in AD 253.

Sanghabhuti is said to be the first Buddhist scholar who went to China in AD 381 and remained there till his death.[11] His name in Chinese transcription is given as Seng-kia-pocheng, and in translation it is Chang Hien. His most important work is the commentary on Vinaya Pitaka of the Saravastivada school.[12]

Gautama Sanghdeva was a Kashmiri Buddhist scholar specializing in Abhidharma. He reached China in AD 383, when Sanghbhuti was still working there.[13] He later went to South China and translated several texts into Chinese, with the assistance of his Chinese and Kashmiri followers.

Punyatrata was a Buddhist scholar from Kashmir, who reached China around AD 399–415.[14] He worked in Kucha with Kumarajiva and translated several important works.

Dharmayasas was another Kashmiri Buddhist, known as Fo-Cheng in Chinese. He was a pupil of Punyatrata. He went to Xinjiang and onwards to China somewhere between AD 397–401. He was in Changan during AD 405–414 and translated several works into Chinese. He is reported to have returned to Xinjiang later.

Kumarajiva was the most eminent Buddhist scholar, who broke geographical, cultural, linguistic and political barriers for propagation of Buddhism. He was the son of a Kuchean princess (Jiva) and a Kashmiri Brahmin (Kumarayana). His father had renounced his ministership in Kashmir to become a monk and had left Kashmir for Kucha. Kumarajiva was named by combining the names of his parents. He was taken to Kashmir by his mother at the age of nine to study Buddhist literature and philosophy. He stayed there for three years studying Madhyama Agama and Dirgha Agama under a well-known master named Bandudatta. He then returned to Kucha along with his mother. Many Kashmiri monks and scholars are reported to have accompanied Kumarajiva to Kucha. En route, he reportedly stayed at Kashgar and studied Abhidharma. He went to Kucha and learnt Sarvastivada Vinaya from his Kashmiri master Vimalaksha.

Within a few years, Kumarajiva attained fame as a scholar and attracted other Buddhist scholars from Kashgar, Khotan, Yarkand

and other parts of China. When Kumarajiva was in Kucha, the Chinese emperor Fu-Kien sent an envoy to the Kuchean ruler, requesting him to send the celebrated monk to China. On the refusal of the Kuchean ruler, the Chinese emperor sent forces to subdue him. Kumarajiva was taken to the Chinese capital Changan in AD 401. He was warmly received by the Chinese emperor. Kumarajiva organized the Sutra Tanslation Bureau (*Yyingyuan* in Chinese) at Changan, where Buddhist scriptures were translated into Chinese. Over 800 scholars were attached to this bureau and a mammoth task of translation was undertaken under Kumarajiva's leadership. He had deep knowledge of Buddhist philosophy and its various schools, besides having command over Sanskrit and Chinese. He had a large following among the Chinese Buddhists. He died in AD 413. Kumarajiva is a bridge between Kashmir and Xinjiang, and a strong symbol of cultural cooperation between India and China.

Vimalaksha was a famous Kashmiri *sramana,* who is known as Wu Ke yen in Chinese. He went to Kucha and studied in the Miracle Monastery, also known as Royal Vihara. Here he became known as the Vinaya master. He taught Vinaya to Kumarajiva. Vimalaksha stayed at Changan from AD 406–413, working with Kumarajiva. He translated a number of works. After Kumarajiva's death, Vimalaksha went to South China where he spent the rest of his life preaching Buddhism.[15]

Buddhayasas was a Kashmiri scholar who went to Kucha. He is known by the Chinese name of Fo-to-She. He first went to Kashgar at the invitation of its ruler, who had invited Buddhist monks on a religious occasion. Buddhayasas stayed at Kashgar for several years. Here he came in contact with Kumarajiva, who was travelling back from Kashmir to Kucha. Later, he joined Kumarajiva at Changan and helped translate several works into Chinese. It is believed that Buddhayasas returned to Kashmir after Kumarajiva's death.[16]

Dharmamitra was another Kashmiri Buddhist monk who first went to Kucha and then travelled to other areas of Xinjiang. His name is mentioned in Chinese transcription as Tan-mo-muts and in Chinese translation as Fa Siu. He went to Dunhuang in AD 424 and founded a monastery there.[17]

CHINESE PILGRIMS VISIT KASHMIR

Kashmiri monks, missionaries and scholars would visit the Buddhist centres in various towns in Southern Xinjiang and mainland China. Similarly, Chinese pilgrims and scholars also traversed long distances through the inhospitable desert and high mountains to reach Kashmir in their quest for knowledge. This vibrant exchange of erudition between Kashmir and Xinjiang continued at least till tenth century AD, before the Arab and Turk invaders destroyed Buddhism in Xinjiang.

Chinese scholars who felt the dearth of authentic Indian texts for the propagation of Buddhism in China travelled to India in search of these texts. Prof. Tan Chung has pointed out that 'Hiuen Tsang (Xuan Zhang's) self-appointed mission is for ever remembered in China as *Xitiunqujing,* i.e. "obtaining sutras from the Western Heaven-India"'.[18] Chinese pilgrims played a key role in the exchanges between ancient India and China, and introduced Indian texts and doctrines to the Chinese monks.

Fa-Hien (Fa Xian, AD 338–423) was born in Shanxi. He was a Buddhist monk since his early years. He embarked upon a pilgrimage to India, the land of Buddhism, 'to seek the truth of Buddhist moral principles'.[19] Accompanied by 10 other prominent monks, Fa-Hien left Changan in AD 399 for Khotan in Xinjinag, from where they crossed the mountain passes to reach Kashmir frontiers at Kia-Chha, near Ladakh and Baltistan. Kia-Chha, mentioned in Fa-Hien's *Fe-Ku-Ki* (*Account of Buddhist Kingdoms*), has been identified with Ladakh by Alexander Cunningham. However, some Sinologists like Kalparoth equate it with Skardu (Baltistan). Thomas Watters agrees with Kalparoth.[20] What is important is that Fa-Hien came along the Silk Route to Khotan, thence to Tashkurghan and must have crossed the Pamirs to reach Gilgit, Baltistan and Ladakh (which already had strong trade and cultural connections with Xinjiang).

Fa-Hien mentioned two relics of Buddha which he found in Kia-Chha. One of them was a bowl made of stone and the other was a tooth of the Buddha, which was preserved in a stupa. Fa-Hien also recorded the existence of over 1,000 monks of the Hinayana school attached to this stupa.[21] Fa-Hien later moved on to Swat, Taxila, Gandhara and onwards to central India, where he stayed for three years. He travelled widely, seeking Buddhist texts, studying religious rituals, practices and Sanskrit. In AD 410 Fa-Hien went to Ceylon (Sri Lanka) and then returned to China via the sea route. He carried with him the valuable Buddhist scriptures he had brought from India. Fa-Hien had a Kashmiri associate named Buddhajiva, who accompanied him on his return to China.

Che-Mong followed Fa-Hien and started his journey along with 14 companions from Changan in AD 404 to Xinjiang and across the Pamirs to Kashmir.[22] Only six of his associates are believed to have survived in this strenuous journey.[23] Che-Mong and his colleagues stayed in Kashmir for a long time, after which they started on a pilgrimage to Buddhist shrines in India.[24] He returned to China in AD 424 via the same route.

Fa-Yong was another Chinese monk who came in AD 420, accompanied by a group of 25 monks. He travelled via Turfan, Kucha, Kashgar then over the Pamirs to reach Gilgit, from where he went to Kashmir.[25] Fa-Yong and his colleagues spent a year in the Valley studying Sanskrit and Buddhist traditions.[26] He then returned to China by sea, also visiting the holy places in India on his way back.

Hiuen Tsang (Xuan Zhuang), the eminent Chinese Buddhist scholar came to India in search of further knowledge. He started his journey in AD 631 by the Silk Route and entered Kashmir via Hazara (Urusa).[27] He stayed in the Valley for two years studying Buddhist scriptures and literature. He was received with full honours by the then ruler of Kashmir, who sent his nephew to escort Hiuen Tsang from Baramulla to his palace in Srinagar. The ruler himself, followed by a number of Buddhist monks and people, led Hiuen Tsang into the capital (where he lodged in the Jayendra Vihara). He was provided with 20 assistants to copy the sacred texts. Hiuen Tsang visited various Buddhist monasteries and stupas. He mentioned the existence of 100 monasteries in Kashmir with 5,000 monks. He crossed into Poonch over the Tosa Maidan route and went to Rajouri, Akhnoor, Sialkot and onwards to Nalanda. Hiuen Tsang returned to Changan, China in AD 645 carrying with him a huge collection of Buddhist scriptures, statues, flower and plant seeds. He recorded his experiences and description of the territories visited by him in his book *Da Tang Xi Yu Ji* (*Records of the Western Regions in the Tang Dynasty*).

Ou-Kong came to Kashmir via Kabul and Gandhara in AD 759. He stayed in the Valley for four years and learnt Sanskrit and Vinaya from Kashmiri scholars. He has mentioned the existence of several *viharas* namely MongTe, Amitab Bhawan, Anand Bhawan, Ki-tche, Nao-ye-le, Jo-Jo, Yeli-Li-Te-Lo, Ko-toon etc., in Kashmir. He found over 300 shrines and stupas in Kashmir.

Wu-Kong, another Chinese pilgrim, had come to Kashmir in AD 751 during the Tang period. He spent several years in Kashmir studying the Buddhist texts.[28] He returned to China in AD 790. Even after the decline of Tang rule in China, the exchange of monks and pilgrims between India and China continued. According to Song dynasty sources, 'in the tenth and eleventh centuries about 80 Indian monks arrived in China, 38 Chinese monks returned after visiting the Indian sub-continent, a total of 1,028 Indian texts were procured, and 564 scrolls of Buddhist *sutras* were translated into Chinese'.[29]

KASHMIR–CHINA ALLIANCE DURING TANG PERIOD

Close political and cultural contacts between Kashmir and Xinjiang were witnessed during the rule of Karkota dynasty (AD 625–855) and Tang dynasty (AD 618–690, AD 705–907) in China. Facing hostilities from the Arabs and Tibetan incursions in seventh century AD, the Tang court had established 'diplomatic contacts with at least three important kingdoms in the southern Hindu Kush area, Jibin (Kapisa, around the present day Kabul region), Xieyou (Zabulistan, present day Ghazni region) and Gushimi (Kashmir)'.[30] Under the Karkota dynasty, Kashmir rose to be a formidable power, 'incorporating adjoining areas, conquering several Himalayan tracts and acquiring considerable territories in north India'.[31]

According to Chinese records, between AD 650–750,

> [...] a quadrangular fight was being fought between the Turks, Turfans, Arabs and the Chinese, for possession of Central Asia. Kashmir assisted China in her enterprise in that region. Chandrapida fought with the Arabs. When China came in conflict with Tibet, Lalitaditya blocked all routes to Tibet. He also carried out expeditions against the Tukhars and Dards, to assist in the establishment of Tang supremacy in the region.[32]

Ahmad al-Biruni wrote of a victory obtained by Lalitaditya Muktapida over the Turks and that Kashmiris continued to celebrate this victory even in his time. Tang annals inform that in the eighth century AD, ambassadors were exchanged between Kashmiri rulers Chandrapida (or Tchen-To-lo-pi-li in Chinese), Lalitaditya (or Muto-pi in Chinese) and Tang rulers. In AD 720, the Tang court is reported to have dispatched an envoy to Kashmir to bestow the title of 'King of Kashmir' on Chandrapida.[33]

In AD 733, the new Kashmiri ruler Lalitaditya sent his envoy to the Chinese emperor with a letter informing him about his military victory over the Tibetans, and his offer of continued support to

China. To quote Prof. Tansen Sen, 'Elated by Lalitaditya's offer of support, the Chinese emperor praised the Kashmiri king and bestowed the title of "King" on him.'[34]

It is clear that Kashmir played an important role in Tang China's military victories against its foes in the Hindu Kush–Pamirs region. However, after the decline and defeat of Tangs by the Arabs in mid-eighth century AD, the Islamic conquest of Xinjiang in tenth century AD and the advance of Arabs in South Asia, there was a great setback to the fruitful contacts between Kashmir and Xinjiang. Khotan was the last citadel of Buddhism, which fell to Islamic invaders in early eleventh century AD. It had a colony of Kashmiri monks and settlers. Aurel Stein, during his archeological expedition in Khotan, was 'struck with the resemblance of features between the Khotanese and the Kashmiris, a resemblance difficult to define yet all the more noteworthy on account of unmistakable peculiarity of type presented by the Kashmiris'.[35]

I noticed the similarity in the ethnic features of indigenous Khotanese and Kashmiris, during my visit to Khotan over two decades ago. I also noticed *mandala/yantra* symbols engraved on the wooden false ceiling of my hotel in Khotan. This clearly indicates that the Khotanese people have retained the memory of their pre-Islamic heritage.

After the consolidation of Islam in Central Asia and Xinjiang, contacts with the Hindu kingdom of Kashmir took a new shape. Lalitaditya is reported to have inducted a Turk Chief Minister, Cankuna, into his court. Cankuna was described by Kalhana as having built stupas and viharas in Kashmir.[36] Kalhana referred to the hospitality provided by King Kalasa (AD 1063–89) to *Turuska* (Turk) artists and to the grant of favours upon hundreds of Turuska captains by King Harsa (AD 1089–1101).[37]

When Islam came to Kashmir in fourteenth century AD[38], Central Asian mercenaries and *syeds* entered Kashmir. One Syed Sharif-ud-Din (popularly known as Bulbul Shah) of Turkistan[39] and Shah Mir (who is believed to have been of Turkish origin)[40], introduced Islam in Kashmir. They were followed by a series of syeds and mercenaries who put Islam on a firm footing with the support of the rulers. It was during the rule of Zain-ul-Abidin (AD 1420–70) that master craftsmen from Central Asia were invited to Kashmir. Numerous arts such as window cutting, stone cutting, shawl and carpet weaving flourished in the Valley during his reign. Later, Mirza Hyder Dughlat—a Chagatai Turkic-Mughal military general, governor of Kashmir, and author of *Tarikh-i-Rashidi*—is reported to have introduced Central Asian style of dress, food and musical instruments like lutes, dulcimers and harps in Kashmir.[41] Musical instruments from Xinjiang like *dotar, sarangi, rabab, surnai* and *santoor* are still in vogue in Kashmir, used in Sufiana Kalam. This classical music is quite similar to the famed Muqam of Xinjiang, which too has 12 *muqams* or suites.

With the introduction of the Islamic mode of government and Persian as court language in Kashmir under the Sultanate, a large number of Persian and Turki words got assimilated in the Kashmiri language. Kashmiri artisans acquired fame in the arts art of wood carving, making *panjras* (door and window panels), *khatam bandi* (ornamented ceilings), papier-mâché, and brick and tile works of Central Asian style. Even today, the Kashmiri carpet manufacturers find it convenient to introduce their goods in the market as Khotan, Bukhara and Samarkand carpets. Numerous such signboards are displayed by Kashmiri shops. The people of Kashmir and Xinjiang drink the same hot tea in the same type of *piala* (a big porcelain cup) and relish the same *pilau* (rice with meat). A large number of Kashmiri families bearing such surnames as Pirzada, Akhun, Beg, Kashgari, Turki, Nakshbandi, Mirza, Baba etc., are a living example of the cultural impact of immigration of Central Asians into Kashmir in medieval times.

During the nineteenth century AD the Nakshbandis maintained close links with Xinjiang. The Nakshbandi family in Kashmir not only maintained close contacts with their *murids* (followers) in Xinjiang but also remained quite active in the sociopolitical life of the region. They provided intelligence regarding the state of affairs in Xinjiang and Central Asia to the British, at a time when

British sources in the region were quite negligible. The British missions to Xinjiang would secure letters of recommendation from the Nakshbandi brothers (Muhammad Shah and Ahmad Shah) for their numerous followers in Xinjiang to facilitate their travels and adventures in that land.[42] Similarly, the pilgrims from Central Asia and Xinjiang during their transit journey from Yarkand and Leh to Srinagar (en route Bombay [now Mumbai] and Mecca or back home) would not miss their appointment with their Nakshbandi pirs in Kashmir and would often stay with them.[43]

Syed Yakub Khan Tora, the official envoy of the ruler of Kashgar, stayed in Gafur Shah Nakshbandi's house during his visits to Kashmir in 1872 and 1875. The ongoing overland trade between India and Xinjiang via the Kashmir–Leh–Yarkand route kept these contacts alive till this traffic of men and materials came to a close after the incorporation of Xinjiang into the People's Republic of China in 1949.

Two

Ladakh: Entrepôt of India-Xinjiang Trade

The huge mountain ranges of western Himalayas, Karakoram, Kuen Lun and Hindu Kush could not deter the overland trade that existed between India and Central Asia since ancient times. With the passage of time and after the establishment of urban cultures in Central Asia, this trade developed further. In effect, the caravan traders not only became the instrument of transmission of culture between the two regions but also assisted the process of urbanization. Many areas along the trade routes became famous for their specific products. For instance, Khotan was famed for jade, carpets and silken fabrics. Samarkand became known for its paper and cotton fabrics. Bukhara was noted for its carpets; Badakhshan for Lapis lazuli and rubies; Tibet for musk and pashm; Turfan for pashm; and Kashmir for its saffron, fine shawls and calligraphy books. In short, these areas developed into important transboundary trading centres connected to the famous Silk Route. Starting from the Chinese terminus, Luoyang, this trade route ran up to Dunhuang where it bifurcated into northern and southern routes (to circumvent the Taklamakan desert) to join again at Kashgar.[1] Several tracks branched off the southern route at Khotan and Yarkand, towards the Karakoram or Pamir passes, on the way to India through Ladakh and Kashmir.

Due to its geographical contiguity with Xinjiang and Tibet, Ladakh played an important role in cultural interaction, overland trade and communication in the region. Enjoying a central position in the network of caravan routes that were linked to the Silk Route,

Ladakh acted as a gateway to the India–Xinjiang exchange of men, materials and ideas. Undaunted by numerous physical obstacles, the Kashmiri, Arghun, Hoshiarpuri, Yarkandi, Povindah (Afghan) and Andijani traders peddled across the lofty Himalayan and Karakoram mountains and the barren deserts, displaying indomitable mercantile enterprise and unique adventurous spirit. Ladakh's place in India–Xinjiang trade was only that of a transit emporium, as it did not produce or consume much to make any indigenous trade of importance. Traders from Tibet, Xinjiang and India gathered in Ladakh's capital (Leh) to exchange their merchandise. This commercial intercourse sustained the poor and backward economies of the semi-closed systems in these remote and high-altitude areas. They also provided the essential raw materials for the flourishing shawl and carpet industry of Kashmir. It also lent strong support to the local trade passing between Leh and Skardu (Baltistan), which formed a *tehsil* (sub-district) of the Ladakh *Wazarat* (Administration) of the State of Jammu and Kashmir during the Dogra rule (1846–1947).[2]

Some Western and Chinese sources have confirmed the movement of trading caravans between Ladakh and Xinjiang, from at least the seventeenth century. Ippolito Desideri—an Italian Jesuit missionary and early European traveller, who spent two months in Leh in 1715 en route from Srinagar to Lhasa—reported that 'occasionally merchants come from the kingdom of Kotan with well bred horses, cotton goods and other merchandise'.[3] Luciano Petech has referred to some documents from 1740s and 1750s related to trade across the Karakoram between Ladakh and Yarkand.[4] This trade, which stabilized after the Qings conquered Xinjiang in 1759, was strengthened with the posting of British officers in Ladakh in 1867 and in Kashgar in 1890. The 11 *aksakals* (elders) in 1916 who resided in the southern towns of Xinjiang (in Keria, Khotan, Goma, Karghalik, Yarkand, Yangi Hissar, Kashgar, Faizabad, Aksu and Kucha), besides one in Ili (north of Tien Shan) to look after Indian trading interests, testified to the presence of Indian traders in the southern oasis cities of Xinjiang.[5]

TRADE ROUTES

From the Indian side, the bulk of trade passed through the Srinagar–Leh–Yarkand route. Although, the traders from Skardu, Kishtwar, Kullu, Lahoul, Spiti, Nurpur and Bushahr carried on their business with Ladakh directly through the Khapalu–Chorbat–Nobra, Kishtwar–Zanskar and Kullu-Rohtang Pass–Lahoul–Key Long-Bara Lacha Pass–Rupshu-Longa Lacha Pass–Thung Lung La and Leh routes, respectively. To the east of Ladakh, a caravan trail passed through Gartok towards Lhasa (the capital of Tibet). In the north, Ladakh stood connected with the Silk Route at Yarkand by a caravan route running across the Karakoram Pass. The Leh–Yarkand route was about 350 miles long, passing over high passes and enduring the intense cold. From Leh there existed three paths leading to Yarkand—the nearest big trading centre of Xinjiang. Those traders and passers-by who opted to travel to Yarkand in winter would cross Digar La and follow the narrow and winding valleys of the Shayok River. The Shayok, which remained frozen during winter, had to be crossed and re-crossed several times. After negotiating the Karakoram Pass, traders would start their descent towards Yarkand, passing through Kugiar and Karghalik. But it was usual for traders from India and Xinjiang to bring their caravans to Ladakh in summer and start their return journey homewards in autumn.

The summer route from Leh to Yarkand passed through Khardung La, Nobra Valley, Saser La, Karakoram Pass and the Suget Pass. Yet another route ran across the Changla Pass, the Chang Chenmo Valley and Lingzithang plains to join the Leh–Yarkand summer route at Shahidulla. The Chang Chenmo Valley route to Xinjiang was improved considerably after the conclusion of a treaty between the Kashmir Durbar and the British Indian government in 1870. Under the treaty, this route was also declared a free highway. Efforts were made to establish this track as the main trade route between Leh and Yarkand, as it was easier than those going through the Shayok River or Saser Pass. But as it was relatively longer in distance, used more fuel and as grass and water was not so abundantly available on this route, it did not become so popular with traders, except with those using camels to transport their goods.

Another route started from Gilgit and passed through Nomal, Chalt, Aliabad, Baltit, Atabad, Gulmit, Pasu, Misgar, Kilik (or Mintaka Pass), Mintaka Ghazi, Beyik (a Chinese post), Dafdar, Tashkurghan, Karasu, Karakul, Tashmalik, Opal and Kashgar. It covered a length of over 420 miles. This route was less frequented than the Leh–Yarkand–Kashgar route. It has now been built into a modern KKH connecting Pakistan overland with China. In 1936, total trade carried via the Gilgit route was only ₹0.1 million as against over ₹2 million traded via the Leh–Yarkand route, i.e., less by 20 times.[6]

Those traders who conducted small business in Chitral, Gilgit, Hunza, Nagar, Skardu etc., thus bypassing Leh and Kashmir, used other caravan mountainous tracks like the Ferghana–Kashgar–Tashkurghan–Hunza–Gilgit track, Bukhara–Kabul–Chitral–Peshawar track and the Ferghana–Pamirs–Wakhan–Chitral track. The volume of Indian trade with Central Asia via the above-noted channels was considerably lesser in value than what passed through the Punjab–Afghanistan–Central Asia or the Bombay–Batumi–Caspian Sea routes. But the importance of overland trade routes between India and Central Asia lies in the fact that they also acted as channels of communication between the two sides before the discovery of sea routes.

Notwithstanding its physical difficulties, the Srinagar–Leh–Yarkand route was the most important and long-established thoroughfare between India and Xinjiang. Even though British authorities took numerous steps to improve the Kullu–Leh route with a view to encourage direct trading between British India and Xinjiang, traders continued to use the Srinagar–Leh route, as it was 'the easiest and best supplied as to grass, provisions etc. and thoroughly open for two or three months longer than the Kullu route'.[7] It was through this route that the Kashmir shawl industry received its supplies of pashm that was imported into Ladakh from Tibet and Yarkand.

Soon after his conquest of Ladakh (1834–42), the Dogra general, Wazir Zorawar Singh, improved this route to make it an easy passage for mounted travellers.[8] The Srinagar–Leh–Yarkand route, which was declared a Treaty Road in 1870, was kept in excellent condition throughout the Dogra rule in Kashmir. As a sequel to the treaty concluded between Maharaja Ranbir Singh and T.D. Forsyth in April 1870, the Kashmir government allocated a yearly sum of ₹1,500 for the maintenance of roads and *sarais* in Srinagar, Dras, Kargil, Leh etc., along this trade route from Zoji La to Karakoram Pass. In the late nineteenth century, an extra annual grant of ₹5,000 was made available by the Kashmir Durbar for this purpose.[9] There were two big caravanserais, one each at Leh and Srinagar, for accommodating the traders and Central Asian pilgrims. Besides that, godowns, stables, dak bungalows and inns were established at various stages of the route where traders received shelter and supplies of grain and forage for their ponies at subsidized rates. Similarly, the villagers living in and around a particular stage of the trade route in Ladakh were responsible for supplying pony and coolie transport to traders and travellers at reasonable rates. It became known as the Res system under which 15 to 20 ponies would always be available at each stage for use of the traders, public servants and travellers enjoying official patronage.[10] Such was the safety of this route that in the event of unfavourable weather or death of ponies, traders would march on to the next safer stage leaving behind their goods. These goods would then be fetched after the climate became favourable or substitute transport became available. As a result, the Srinagar–Leh–Yarkand route became the most important thoroughfare between India and Xinjiang during the Dogra rule in Kashmir.

Local Trade with Baltistan

Domestic trade between Leh and Skardu (Baltistan) was similar in nature to what was carried between Leh and adjoining areas like Nobra, Zanskar, Puring and Chang Thang. It passed through two channels, (i) Leh–Indus Valley–Skardu and (ii) Leh–Nobra–Chorbat–Khapalu. A substantial number of Baltis would visit Leh throughout the year. Balti peasants and petty traders brought the produce of their farms and households such as apricots, apricot oil, butter, grapes, almonds, barley, tea cups, stone vessels for cooking, woollen cloth and coarse shawls for sale to Ladakh. They took back in exchange Indian cotton cloth and other piece goods, tea, gold and silver thread, Yarkandi leatherware, sheep wool and also some quantity of Yarkandi and Tibetan wool (which was used in the manufacture of Balti Shawls). From Leh, these apricots and coarse shawls were transmitted to Lhasa and Yarkand. Between 400–500 *maunds* (about 150 quintals) of dried apricots were exported to Tibet each year from Baltistan until the early 1870s. Later, its quantity increased to about 1,500 maunds (about 450 quintals) per year.[11] Some adventurous Baltis went to Jammu, the plains of Punjab and even as far as Yarkand in search of livelihood and stayed there for a few years to work as manual labourers or to do small trade. Unemployed Baltis would earn their livelihood by working as porters and pony drivers for traders. The Trans-Himalayan trade of Ladakh further integrated its economy with that of Baltistan, which was already under its administrative jurisdiction (1846–1947). Many Kashmiris set up shops in Skardu Bazaar and engaged themselves in weaving shawls for which pashm was brought from Ladakh.[12]

Trade with Tibet

Tibet's trade with Ladakh and Kashmir was regulated by the Treaty of Tingmosgang, concluded between Ladakh and Tibet in 1684, under which Ladakh had monopoly over the shawl-wool produced in Tibet, and the Tibetans acquired the exclusive right to the brick-tea trade with Ladakh.[13] The treaty also provided for dispatch of periodic missions by Ladakh to Lhasa carrying presents for the Dalai Lama.[14] Since bearers of this religious mission were allowed to carry merchandise, it soon acquired a commercial character. The shawl wool that was imported from Tibet and Xinjiang into Ladakh was exclusively exported to Kashmir through the agency of Kashmiri merchants. Brick-tea imported from Tibet was almost entirely consumed within Ladakh and some was also sent forward to Kashmir. Such trade ties between Ladakh and Tibet were reinforced by the Treaty of 1842, concluded between the Dogra and Tibetan officials. Under this treaty, semi-official trade missions were exchanged at intervals between Leh and Lhasa.[15] The triennial mission that left Leh for Lhasa carrying presents and merchandise was known as the Lapchak Mission. The annual Tibetan caravan coming to Leh with brick-tea and other goods was called Chaba. Just as the Ladakhi traders were entitled to free transport and accommodation during their travel and stay in Tibet, traders from Tibet enjoyed similar facilities during their sojourn in Ladakh.

After the final annexation of Ladakh by the Dogras in 1842, the Lapchak Mission lost its religious character, as it was then managed by professional traders. These traders were mainly Kashmiri Muslims settled in Leh, who earned large profits in the transactions. When Sven Anders Hedin—a Swedish geographer and explorer of Central Asia—visited the well-known Muslim merchant Haji Nazer Shah at Leh (during a stopover in his journey to Tibet in 1906), he was astonished to see in the merchant's commercial house 'chests full of silver and gold dust, turquoise and coral, materials and goods'[16] to be sold in Tibet. Hedin soon found that the source of this wealth was the professional traders monopoly over the Lapchak Mission which fetched them an annual profit of about ₹25,000.[17] This Muslim family of about 100 members, headed by Nazer Shah, was entrusted the duty of carrying out the Lapchak Mission by the Maharaja of

Kashmir. At the time of Hedin's visit in 1906 they had retained this confidential post for some 50 years.[18] The close involvement of Kashmiri Muslim settlers in Ladakh's trade with Tibet can be gauged from the fact that even as late as 1959, about 129 such families (with a total of about 600 members) were residing in the Lhasa–Shigatse area of Tibet.[19]

Leh was the starting point of a trade route that followed the course of the Indus upstream and passed through Demchok, Gartok and Lake Mansarowar to reach Shigatse and Lhasa. Its cultural affinity with Tibet in terms of religion, language, dressing and food habits facilitated the vibrant exchange between Ladakh and Tibet. Western Tibet was the main source for the supply of shawl-wool. Ladakhis engaged in regular trade with the adjoining areas of Guge, Rudok and Gartok in western Tibet. Gartok was the main trading mart of western Tibet, where a trade fair was held each year during the summer months. Merchants from the neighbouring areas of Ladakh, Koonawar, Rampur, Kumaon, Xinjiang and even from Russian Central Asia attended this fair to exchange their wares and local raw materials such as borax, salt, shawl wool and gold.[20] Ladakhi imports from Tibet comprised fine pashm, coarse wool, brick-tea, salt, silver, gold, turquoises, tea cups, paper and musk.[21] Henry Strachey extensively surveyed western Tibet in 1840s, and visited Ladakh in 1847 in his capacity as member of the Boundary Commission of Jammu and Kashmir. He estimated the value of such imports as one and a quarter of ₹1 lakh.[22]

Ladakh's exports to Tibet included *yambus* (silver ingots), gold, China silk and coarse cotton goods received from Xinjiang, glass-ware, coral, silver coins, cotton cloths, chintzes, brocades, goatskin and furs imported from British India, saffron and rice from Kashmir, apricots and barley from Ladakh and Baltistan.[23] Apricots, Chinese silver, cotton goods and silk cloth (made in Turkestan), Kashmir saffron and grains constituted the bulk of Ladakhi exports to Tibet. Much of this trade was generated by the heavy demand for pashm in Kashmir, which had developed into the main centre for shawl production. The assured supplies of pashm from Tibet not only sustained Kashmir's shawl industry, but also provided new avenues of employment for skilled and unskilled workers in Ladakh and Kashmir.

Silver ingots, jade, gold, cotton and silk fabrics and carpets produced in Kashgar and Khotan were imported into Ladakh, from where they were exported to Tibet through Ladakhi and Kashmiri Muslim traders leading the Leh–Lhasa caravans. William Moorcroft—a British official employed by the East India Company (EIC) who travelled extensively in the Himalayas, Ladakh and Central Asia—mentioned silver ingots from Yarkand as the principal export from Leh to Lhasa.[24] Even a century later, Radhus (the leading caravan leaders) were known to carry jade, gold and carpets from Yarkand in their Leh–Lhasa caravans.[25] There existed no direct communication between western Tibet and Xinjiang till early 1950s, when China built a road connecting Xinjiang with Tibet (through Aksai Chin). The annual turnover of Ladakh's trade with Tibet during the Dogra rule amounted to several lakh rupees. This trade suffered heavily after the incorporation of Tibet into the People's Republic of China in 1950. However, it continued to operate even under strains, until it came to a standstill in 1959 following disturbances in Tibet.

India–Xinjiang Trade in Ladakh and Kashmir

The bulk of Indian trade with the towns of Yarkand, Kashgar and Khotan in Xinjiang was carried through Kashmir and Ladakh. Xinjiang's exports to Ladakh and Kashmir comprised gold and silver, hemp drug, shawl wool, carpets and felts, Chinese teacups, leatherware, coarse cotton cloths, raw silk and ponies. Out of these items, bullion, charas, raw silk and shawl-wool constituted the major imports. The Yarkandi and Andijani traders used to bring these goods to Ladakh, where they exchanged the same with their Indian counterparts. Occasionally, these traders would move forward to Kashmir and Punjab in the hope of making better profits. Similarly, Indian traders would also proceed beyond Ladakh towards Yarkand to make direct purchases at relatively lower prices. Indian traders brought to Leh, Indian- and British-made cotton cloths, brocades, Kashmiri shawls, indigo, spices, dyed goat skins, opium, preserved fruits, coral, indigenous medicines, sugar and books. Even though most of the Indian imports were exported to Yarkand, part of it also went to Lhasa. Maharaja Ranbir Singh of Kashmir had been organizing a trade fair at Leh annually since September 1868, which used to be well attended.

In the late 1840s, merchandise valued at about ₹7.5 lakh was reported to have exchanged hands in Ladakh each year.[26] Out of this figure, the imports from Yarkand and India via Kishtwar, Nurpur, Kulu and Bushahr represented amounts of ₹1.75 and ₹4.50 lakh, respectively.[27] Another contemporary estimate of trade passing through Ladakh has been provided by Alexander Cunningham, a British official heading the Boundary Commission to fix the Ladakh–Tibet boundary and a historian who visited Leh twice during 1846–47. According to him, annual Indian imports into Ladakh averaged ₹220,000, whereas Xinjiang's exports to India via Ladakh were valued at ₹238,000.[28] This meant an annual trade turnover of little more than ₹4.5 lakh. Though Cunningham's estimate is much less than that of Henry Strachey, we get a rough assessment of the volume of annual trade passing through Ladakh in the 1840s, which can be safely put between ₹6–7 lakh. However, the extent and pattern of overland trade carried through Ladakh fluctuated from time to time due to the changing political situation in and around Xinjiang. In the early nineteenth century, when relations between Omar Khan (ruler of Kokand [presently in Uzbekistan]) and Chinese authorities in Xinjiang became strained, all Andijani traders left Yarkand for their country and abandoned their business trips to Ladakh.[29] This led to considerable decrease in Yarkandi exports to Ladakh.[30] Such disruptions in trade occurred later as well, when Xinjiang was rife with turmoil caused due to Khoja uprisings against the Chinese rulers.

The volume of trade between India and Xinjiang registered a steady increase after the Chinese were driven out of the country by Yakub Beg in 1867. This was owing to the stoppage of all Chinese imports into Xinjiang and due to development of harmonious relations between Yakub Beg and the British Indian authorities. The abolition of all transit duties on merchandise passing to and from Xinjiang (through Kashmir and Ladakh) by Maharaja Ranbir Singh also encouraged this trade. During the rule of Yakub Beg in Kashgaria, the export of Indian tea to that quarter increased considerably. Even the Chinese tea imported into Ladakh (via Lhasa and Punjab) was exported to Xinjiang to meet the shortages caused there by the cessation of its trade with China. British-manufactured cotton and silk cloths began to substitute Indian cotton prints and silks. However, charas, pashm and ponies continued to be imported into Ladakh from Xinjiang as before. Indian exports to Xinjiang shot up to an unprecedented figure of more than ₹8 lakh during 1874.[31] This included arms and ammunition worth over ₹120,000 imported by Yakub Beg for his army.[32] Such an unusual increase in Indian exports was largely due to the fact that a British merchant Russell took large quantities of English cotton goods and silks to Xinjiang for sale via Ladakh.[33] However, Ladakh's import and export trade with Xinjiang decreased by over ₹4 lakh in 1877, when unsettled political conditions prevailed there on account of war between Yakub Beg and the Chinese forces.[34]

Yakub Beg's death in 1877 and the subsequent reoccupation of Xinjiang by Chinese forces did not have any adverse impact on the Indo-Xinjiang trade. Several factors were responsible for continuance of this trade even after Xinjiang became a Chinese possession in 1878. Firstly, Chinese authorities did not interfere in the long-established trade. Their restrictions on import of Indian tea and opium also proved ineffective in the face of smuggling of these commodities, in connivance with the Chinese customs officials. Second, Xinjiang did not possess an industrial base to cater to the demand for manufactured and other piece goods imported mainly from Russia through the Kokand–Kashgar route and partly from India through the Srinagar–Leh–Yarkand route. Third, Indian trade with Bukhara, Kokand and other parts of Russian Central Asia, hitherto carried through the Peshawar–Kabul–Bukhara route was partly diverted to the Srinagar–Leh–Yarkand route after Russians imposed strict restrictions on import of British Indian goods into Russian Central Asia. Fourth, the arrival of Central Asian pilgrims (en route their Haj pilgrimage to Mecca via India) at Leh also contributed to increased Central Asian imports into Ladakh. This was because they brought along with them a large quantity of bullion, silks and ponies for sale in Leh or Srinagar. Fifth, the complete security of the Srinagar–Leh–Yarkand route (as it was devoid of robbers), along with the facilities available at various stages of this route (as far as the supply of ponies, transporters, food and fodder was concerned) helped in the development of Ladakh as an important trading centre.

After the conclusion of the Russo-Chinese treaty at St Petersburgh in 1881, bilateral overland trade between Xinjiang and Russia scaled new heights. This further affected Indian trade with Xinjiang in more than one way, as it now had to face stiff competition from Russia in that quarter. Then the import of Khotanese gold dust and Chinese silver ingots into Ladakh was substituted by that of Russian gold and paper roubles. The Yarkandi felts and Khotanese carpets became dearer in Ladakh and Kashmir, as their prices appreciated due to increased demand in Russian markets. And lesser quantity of Turfani fine wool was imported into Ladakh, as the same was being supplied to Russian Turkestan in large quantities. Import of coarse wool and pashm from Xinjiang dropped considerably in value from 1930 onwards. But the prosperity of the Russo-Xinjiang trade also meant a corresponding increase in Indian trade with Xinjiang. Since Xinjiang's exports to Russia far exceeded the imports from that end, balance was met by rouble payments which ensured a regular and abundant supply of Russian currency in the markets of Xinjiang. This led to increased imports from India, which was now paid back largely in Russian gold and paper roubles and raw silk. At the close of the nineteenth century, Russian currency began to occupy an important place in Indian imports from Xinjiang. Indian traders resorted to using rouble imports as forced medium for sending back their sale proceeds to India. Russian gold and paper roubles worth about ₹8 million were imported into India via Ladakh during 1897–1919. However, charas continued to be imported into Ladakh despite its heavy taxation in India. An average of 3,000–3,500 maunds (1 maund=37.32 kg or 82.28 lb) of charas was annually imported into Ladakh from Xinjiang during 1882–1932. Most of this charas was consumed in Punjab and Oudh, whence it was carried by Indian traders via the Leh–Kullu route.

With the establishment of Soviet power in Central Asia (1917–22), bilateral trade between Xinjiang and Russian Turkestan received a setback. It was then diverted to Ladakh and Kashmir. This resulted in an unusual increase in Indian exports to Xinjiang through Ladakh. As per official trade statistics recorded by the office of the British Joint Commissioner at Leh, goods worth about ₹28.5 million were exported from India to Xinjiang through Kashmir and Ladakh during 1917–1931, of which European cotton goods and silks, dyed skins, indigo, spices and tea constituted the main items. In the same period, merchandise valued at about ₹33 million was imported from Xinjiang into Ladakh and Kashmir of which charas, Russian gold and paper roubles, gold dust, raw silk, carpets and felts were the main items. Balance of trade thus stood in Xinjiang's favour. However, this official trade figure must also include significant amount of high value and lightweight items like gold, silver, silk etc., which were not reported by the importing traders and pilgrims. India–Xinjiang trade through Kashmir and Ladakh, which had scaled an unprecedented height of more than ₹6.8 million during 1920–21[35], began to decline in value soon after the opening of Russian overland trade with Xinjiang. From the late 1930s onwards, internal disorders in Xinjiang began to act as a stumbling block to this trade, which finally ceased to flow in 1949 following the communist takeover of Xinjiang and subsequent closure of the region to outside traffic. This deprived Ladakh and Kashmir of their importance as emporiums of Indo-Central Asian overland trade, passing through a network of caravan trails criss-crossing Ladakh and Kashmir. In quantitative terms, this trade (officially recorded figures of total imports and exports from 1868 to 1936 are given in Table 1) was substantial to meet the local demands, but due to modest prices of commodities traded its overall value may look small.

IMPACT OF TRADE ON SOCIETY AND CULTURE

The lucrative trade between India and Xinjiang through Ladakh and Kashmir left a distinct impression upon the local society and economy there. Leh acquired a cosmopolitan character during the trading season when merchants of different nationalities coming from Bukhara, Andijan, Kashgar, Yarkand, Kabul, Badakhshan, Tibet, Amritsar, Hoshiarpur, Kullu, Nurpur, Bushahr and Kashmir arrived at Ladakh to sell their goods. The sparsely populated town of Leh suddenly hummed with activity, which lasted throughout the summer months. This trade brought economic prosperity to those involved in it in one way or another. However, Ladakhis only partially benefitted from this trade because very few of them had their own business. Most Ladakhis, being poor and illiterate, contented themselves to act as pony-drivers, porters and as suppliers of pack animals and forage to traders. Arghuns and Kashmiri settlers in Leh who traded with Xinjiang and Tibet turned into a richer and affluent class as compared to the majority of Ladakh's population, which remained poor. Buddhist *skudrags* of Ladakh generally engaged in domestic trade. As opposed to this, Muslim traders of Leh were involved in trade on all routes and they maintained family in Skardu, Kashmir, Lahaul, Nurpur, Yarkand and Tibet. They wielded considerable influence in Ladakh, quite disproportionate to their small numbers.

Due to the circumstances of trade, several Yarkandi, Hoshiarpuri and Kashmiri merchants were obliged to take up their abode in Leh. Most of these traders got into marriages of convenience with the local Ladakhi girls and became an inseparable part of Ladakhi society. Among them were Kashmiri Muslims who traded with Tibet and exported pashmina wool and tea to Kashmir. Similarly, some merchants from Xinjiang (Yarkandi, Kashgari, Khotanese) would stay back in Ladakh in times of political uncertainty in their homeland, or owing to the closure of passes, and take temporary Ladakhi wives. As a result, new hybrid class of Arghuns came into being. They were the offspring of traders from Kashmir or Xinjiang who had taken Ladakhi wives, temporary or permanent. By and large, the Arghuns continued the tradition of trading with Xinjiang or Tibet. Some of them also acted as carriers of merchandise that belonged to traders.

The movement of trade through Ladakh and Kashmir influenced the dressing, eating and drinking habits of its people. Machine-made cloth brought by Indian traders, velvets, otter skin hats, Khotanese or Chinese silk fabrics and Yarkandi cotton cloths were increasingly used by the local people (particularly from the elite classes) as their dress material. Similarly, Yarkandi pilau became an important addition to the Ladakhi cuisine. The use of steamed dumplings of meat locally called *momo* also became common in Ladakh. Brick-tea, *sattu* and apricots became their favourite diet. Similarly, they used the same articles like saffron, *nabat* and yak tails for worship and presented them as religious offerings. Affluent sections of Ladakhi society used to wear long leather boots that were imported from Yarkand. Some items of Yarkandi dress such as *pichak tungyu* (conch-handled knife) and *kosa masi* (long calf-leather footwear with a separate pair of leather slippers) became fancy items in Ladakhi dressing as well. The use of Chinese tea cups, jade articles from Khotan, Yarkandi steamers and teapots was also introduced in Ladakh and Kashmir. Central Asian visitors and Arghuns who frequented between Xinjiang and Ladakh introduced certain dance forms prevalent in Xinjiang such as tall-man, dragon, *kishti* (lion and boat) in Leh.[36]

The farmers in Leh and its surrounding villages (like Stok, Shey, Spitok, Chushot, Choglamsar and other villages situated along the trade routes) took to extensive cultivation of lucerne grass. Large-scale introduction of a perennial variety of this grass called Yarkandi Ol is clearly the direct result of Ladakh's commercial intercourse with Yarkand.[37] The agriculturists profited by leasing out their grass fields to traders and pony drivers to feed their ponies on. But this trade drained the food resources of Ladakh. During the Dogra rule, an average quantity of 3,000–4,000 maunds of barley grain was collected as land revenue from Ladakhi peasants.[38] It amounted to less than half of the actual requirements of traders.[39] The deficit was partly met by forced procurement of barley from Ladakhi cultivators at prices much lower than the actual market rates.[40] The result was that Ladakhi agriculturists faced immense hardships, as they were also required to deliver grains at the godowns. State granaries were located at Leh, Saspol and Lamayuru, where barley was supplied to traders at fair prices.

Ladakhis indulged in large-scale weaving of coarse woollen cloth and blankets. They also manufactured sacking, which was in constant demand from the traders who required the same to pack their goods. According to Alexander Cunningham, the quantity of blanketing and sacking annually consumed in Ladakh in connection with the carrying trade amounted to about 120,000 yards of 1 ft width in the manufacture of which about 6.5 lakh lb of wool were consumed.[41] Except for this homemade wool, Ladakhis were almost wholly dependent upon imports for their day-to-day requirements such as manufactured cotton cloths and silks, tea, spices, utensils, leather goods, felts, carpets etc. These commodities were abundantly available at cheaper prices in the Leh market.

The continuation of a traditional trade relationship between Ladakh and Tibet under the Dogras was matched by the strengthening of cultural ties between the people of Ladakh and Tibet. Apart from the frequent exchanges of Buddhist monks, this trade resulted in the settlement of some Ladakhi Muslim trading families in Tibet. Kashmiris, Baltis, Ladakhis and Tibetans had similar eating and drinking habits.

The movement of pilgrims, books, Kashmiri shawls, gold coins, Central Asian silk, Indian tea and spices, coral, etc. formed an essential ingredient of the socio-economic intercourse between Xinjiang and Kashmir till the early twentieth century.

Traditional and historical trade linkages between India and Xinjiang via Kashmir and Ladakh ceased to be functional after 1949. Therefore, the time has come to reflect upon the legacy of such a rich and productive experience and revive these linkages and trade relations on a new and dynamic footing. On its part, China has developed Xinjiang as a land corridor between mainland China and its neighbouring Central Asian republics, Pakistan, Afghanistan and even beyond. In response to China's offer to join the Belt and Road Initiative (BRI), India can pursue its alternative of reviving the traditional trade routes from Ladakh to Xinjiang through the Leh–Karakoram Pass–Yarkand–Kashgar route and the Leh–Chang Chenmo–Yarkand route; and to Tibet via the Leh–Demchok–Gartok–Lhasa route. This will give both India and China huge opportunities in terms of overland trade and travel, besides being a big confidence-building measure. Table 1 shows the trade figures drawn from the Ladakh Trade Reports.

Table 1
Trade Figures from Ladakh Trade Reports

Year	Imports from Xinjiang to Ladakh (In INR)	Exports from Ladakh to Xinjiang (In INR)
1868	158,057	123,999
1869	278,799	193,323
1870	262,000	346,545

Year	Imports from Xinjiang to Ladakh (In INR)	Exports from Ladakh to Xinjiang (In INR)
1872	321,762	322,944
1873	330,690	255,660
1874	381,802	802,563
1875	372,707	403,547
1876	779,121	437,784
1877	353,126	393,052
1878	576,960	271,729
1879	550,517	470,625
1880	636,642	581,421
1881	580,224	839,401
1882	722,615	761,324
1883	821,145	565,387
1884	920,434	507,680
1885	880,608	502,195
1887	747,647	7,23,916
1888	414,028	5,60,003
1889	563,495	6,72,934
1890	623,028	6,20,762
1893	757,112	1,017,029
1894	1,274,700	1,440,599
1895	1,293,246	1,508,074
1896	1,172,697	1,435,667
1897	647,947	1,110,723
1898	656,578	1,032,114
1899	695,424	854,592
1900	920,287	756,954
1901	1,134,132	1,029,236

Year	Imports from Xinjiang to Ladakh (In INR)	Exports from Ladakh to Xinjiang (In INR)
1902	869,169	892,958
1903	803,221	973,041
1904	1,409,494	991,469
1905	1,183,408	1,015,963
1906	1,322,238	1,025,385
1907	1,545,782	1,680,812
1909	1,499,199	1,066,552
1910	1,193,021	1,046,866
1911	1,358,580	1,599,444
1912	1,182,554	1,410,206
1913	1,335,524	1,614,949
1914	1,138,831	1,341,824
1915	970,041	1,263,133
1916	2,047,590	1,114,276
1917	3,025,899	2,819,554
1918	3,887,540	3,530,256
1919	3,307,608	4,487,129
1920	3,511,949	4,351,292
1921	1,947,238	2,199,989
1922	1,963,802	2,206,654
1923	2,324,995	2,434,493
1924	2,610,448	1,416,742
1925	2,356,582	1,823,232
1926	3,281,464	2,398,259
1927	2,014,565	1,186,848
1928	1,165,742	926,129
1929	1,904,129	999,091

Year	Imports from Xinjiang to Ladakh (In INR)	Exports from Ladakh to Xinjiang (In INR)
1930	1,446,353	778,239
1931	1,236,439	409,767
1932	874,587	450,127
1933	1,012,586	344,865
1934	1,247,097	614,840
1935	1,337,198	982,107
1936	1,367,455	1,172,686

Three

Imports from Xinjiang

Since the economy in Xinjiang was underdeveloped, there was practically little—barring few commodities like raw wool, silk, carpets, numdas, charas, gold and silver—for which the Indian traders could barter away their goods. Besides, due to the prevailing instability and fluctuations in the local currency, Indian traders had no other profitable means to sustain their exports to Xinjiang.

A few hundred ponies were usually brought in by traders and travellers for their own use and carriage of goods. Haj pilgrims would also bring some ponies with them for sale. While some were sold, in many cases, these were taken back by these traders and travellers on their return journey from Ladakh to Yarkand. Besides, some piece goods like China cups, porcelain, jade stone and leatherware were also brought in by traders, though in small quantities.

HEMP DRUG (CHARAS)

The hemp (cannabis) plant was widely cultivated in the districts of Kashgar, Yangi Hissar, Yarkand and Karghalik (in the southern part of Xinjiang). However, when the local governments imposed restrictions on its regular cultivation, it was grown in single rows around other crops like maize. This was done in order to escape detection and punishment for breach of law. The plant, which would be 8–10 ft high, was locally called *kandir*. It was grown chiefly for extraction of the drug called charas in India and *nasha* in Turk. After extraction, the drug was made into small balls, and packed up first in a coarse cloth and then in raw hide for export to India. While the good quality charas used to be exported to Bukhara and Kokand, it was the adulterated version that came to Ladakh. The adulteration was done by mixing pounded green leaves with the resin extracted from hemp. Owing to this, the price of charas in Yarkand bazaar was three-fourth of the actual prices. The local peasantry twisted ropes out of the fibres of stalks of hemp plants after the drug was extracted.

During the 1860s and 1870s, on an average 2,000 maunds of charas were imported annually from Xinjiang into Ladakh. This rose to 4,000 maunds per year during 1890s. Almost all of the import was taken to Punjab and North West Provinces (Agra, Delhi, Oudh) of India.[1] Charas was not consumed in Kashmir. Bihari Lal Parashar—who looked after the business of Shadi Lal Dwarkanath of Hoshiarpur in Yarkand during the 1930s and 1940s—estimated that 2,000 horseloads carrying about 5,000 maunds of charas were exported from Yarkand to Ladakh each year.[2] The trading was generally done by Indian traders from Hoshiarpur and Amritsar, who bartered away their Indian and British manufactured goods in Xinjiang in exchange for charas. The price per maund of charas varied between ₹40 to ₹100 depending upon the supply and demand factors. As it was small in volume, had more value and was easily portable as a pony-load with no risk of damage on the way, charas provided the Indian traders easy means of transferring capital earned out of their exports to Xinjiang.

Import of charas, despite the negative consequences for its consumers, had assumed importance for sustaining Indian trade with Xinjiang. This trade was considered crucial in promoting British interests in Central Asia. Whenever import of charas into Ladakh was adversely affected by any circumstances—be it the prohibition imposed by local Xinjiang authorities on cultivation of hemp and trading of its drug, or the levying of heavy import duties by the Punjab government—the net result was the dislocation of India–Xinjiang trade through Ladakh. Charas imports constituted about 20–35 per cent of the total imports into Ladakh each year.

However, the restrictions imposed by Yakub Beg (1867–76) on the cultivation of the hemp plant in Xinjiang, resulted in some decline in its exports to Ladakh. Soon after the death of Yakub Beg and resumption of Chinese authority in Xinjiang, charas exports to India through Ladakh registered an increase and attained their previous levels. From 1882 onwards, charas exports to Ladakh increased substantially. This increase was due to curbs imposed by Russian authorities on import of charas into Russian Turkestan in late 1881, which resulted in the diversion of all charas exports to India. The exports were so much that during 1882, 3,579 maunds of charas, valued at ₹304,289, were brought to Ladakh[3], which comprised more than 40 per cent of total imports into Ladakh. And this level was maintained throughout 1893–94, when the prices of charas rose sharply in Indian markets due to the Punjab government's proposal to levy import duty.

The negative consequences of increasing the use of hemp drug, on the society as a whole and on the mental and physical health of the drug addicts, led the British Indian government to appoint a commission in 1893, under the Presidentship of W. Mackworth to 'examine the subject and to propose measures for controlling the cultivation of the hemp plant and the manufacture, sale and taxation of hemp drugs'.[4] Commenting on the evils generated by using charas, James Edward Tierney (J.E.T.) Aitchison, the British Joint Commissioner in Ladakh, wrote in 1874: 'Half the insanity of Sikhs in Punjab is due to this and many of the crimes which they have committed can be traced back to its influence.'[5] He also referred to the murder by a person 'under the influence of *charas,* of his intended wife and mother, for which crime he was later hanged'.[6] Aitchison urged the government to impose heavy import duties on charas trade to make it extinct. The Hemp Drugs Commission ascribed the increase in consumption of charas in Punjab to the development of India–Xinjiang trade.[7] It noted that nearly one maund of charas was consumed in a population of 10,000, particularly in Ludhiana district.[8] The commission found that on an average 4,000 maunds of charas was imported from Xinjiang through Ladakh into Punjab during 1880s, out of which nearly three-fourths passed on to the states of Oudh and Rajputana.[9] The commission recommended that a duty of not less than ₹80 per maund be levied on all charas imported into Punjab.[10]

Accepting the recommendation, the Punjab government levied the import duty of ₹80 per maund of charas imported into Punjab, with effect from 1 April 1896.[11] This upset the British Residency in Kashmir, which took the stand that 'this duty would damage the general trade with Xinjiang, because until their *charas* is sold, traders have no means for purchasing return consignments for Central Asia'.[12] However, the Punjab government partially modified its order so that a duty of ₹80 was imposed with effect from 1 January 1897.[13] Indian excise authorities collected average taxes of ₹1.5 million on charas imported from Xinjiang each year.[14] For the financial years 1932–33 and 1933–34, the duty collected in British India amounted to ₹2.45 million and ₹2.7 million respectively.[15] Traders dealing with charas were in for yet another blow when the Chinese authorities in Kashgar prohibited the charas trade in 1898, due to rise in local crime under the evil influence of this drug.[16] But the British Officer on Special Duty (OSD) in Kashgar, Macartney, influenced the Kashgar authorities to allow export of charas to India.[17]

Obviously, the British Indian officials' opinion was divided on the issue of charas import. On the one hand, the British Indian government committed itself to eliminate the menace of increasing drug addiction by imposing heavy prohibitive duties on charas in Punjab and North–Western Provinces, to discourage its consumption. On the other hand, the British officers posted in frontier outposts, like Ladakh and Kashgar, were desperately trying to ensure that charas exports to Ladakh continued as before to maintain a steady level of Indian trade with Xinjiang. G. Macartney, the British consul at Kashgar persuaded the *Taotai* (Chinese provincial governor) of Kashgar in April 1898 to remove the restrictions on export of charas to Ladakh.[18] They seemed to be convinced that any reduction of the charas imported into India would lead to a proportionate decrease in demand for Indian and British-manufactured goods in Xinjiang, thereby causing a decline in general trade. Though Macartney persisted in his efforts to persuade the Chinese authorities in Xinjiang not to stop the cultivation of the hemp plant and trading of its drug, the British Indian government finally decided in 1909 not to discourage the policy of the Chinese government.[19]

The government policy of imposing heavy duties led to a progressive decline in the consumption of this drug. Besides, the step ultimately helped in restoring equilibrium to Indian trade with Xinjiang, as Indian traders now looked for other means of transfer of capital to India. The importance of charas in India–Xinjiang trade can be seen from the fact that subsequent to the imposition of 100 per cent duty (₹80 per maund) on charas imports in 1896, there was a general depression in the trade that persisted for a few years. However, from 1923 onwards, charas imports into Ladakh declined.

SILK CLOTH AND RAW SILK

The small quantity of fine silk cloth made in Bukhara, Kokand, Andijan and Khotan reached Ladakh through its usual trade connection with Xinjiang. Among such silk imports were soft, thin, silken handkerchiefs known as *rumals,* which were produced in Bukhara; *darya* (a mixture of cloth and silk in various coloured designs) and *shahi* (fine silk cloth); *tavar* (Chinese satin), silk velvets; and satin.[20] According to an official estimate, Bukhara and China silks worth about ₹4,000–5,000 a year used to be imported into British India via the Yarkand–Ladakh–Kullu route before and during 1850.[21] Aitchison has recorded that silk cloths worth about ₹34,411 were imported into Leh from Yarkand between 1867 and 1872[22], most of which was exported to Tibet and India via Kullu and Rampur. In 1875, 200 pieces of Kokandi silks (darya and shahi) valuing about ₹1,125 were imported into Ladakh from Xinjiang.[23] There was a sudden spurt in the value of such imports from Yarkand during and after 1883. This was because Kokandi and Andijani traders, who personally came to Ladakh to buy Indian tea[24] for consumption within Russian Central Asia, brought large quantities of silk cloth for selling purpose. Overall, the import of silk cloth, whether made in Khotan (in Xinjiang), Kokand or Bukhara declined steadily in value from 1890 onwards.[25] However, from 1916 till 1936, 792 maunds of Khotanese silk cloth, valued at over ₹0.8 million, was imported into Ladakh. Such small imports of Central Asian silk goods into Kashmir, however, stood nowhere close to the large export of Indian silk goods like brocades, velvet and satin to Xinjiang. The import of Bukharan and Kokandi silks into Ladakh and Kashmir was not only insignificant in value but also irregular and fluctuating.

Raw silk was the main item of import into Ladakh. Khotan and Yarkand had developed as main centres of silk production. As per the annual Ladakh Trade Reports, 44,531 maunds of raw silk valued at ₹23.4 million was imported into Ladakh from Xinjiang between 1869 and 1936. This silk, which went to Kashmir and Punjab for manufacture of silk goods, was a convenient and lucrative medium for Indian traders to bring back their sales.

GOLD

Gold coins, nuggets and dust were traditional items of import into Ladakh and Kashmir from Xinjiang. Several factors were responsible for such import. The hazardous journey over the high altitude and the tedious Leh–Yarkand route made it incumbent upon traders to carry such goods, as they were light and easily transportable. The Central Asian Haj pilgrims—who annually travelled through Ladakh, Kashmir and India en route Mecca—brought sufficient quantities of bullion to meet their travel and other expenses. However, quantum of gold imports into India (via Ladakh and Kashmir) varied in accordance with the nature of political and economic conditions prevailing in Central Asia from time to time. During the first half of the nineteenth century, gold *tillas* (coins) from Bukhara[26] and Kokand flowed into Ladakh and Kashmir almost regularly. But with the extension of Russian control over these Central Asian Khanates, this trade was seriously disrupted. Gold tillas from Bukhara and Kokand, each of which weighed about two-fifths of an Indian tola (about 11.56 g) of nearly pure gold, bore the titles of the Khans of Bukhara and Kokand.[27]

According to a British officer, H. Strachey, who was in Ladakh during 1849–50 in connection with survey work, Kokandi gold coins were more common in Ladakh and the Bukharan coins contained the best gold.[28] All such coins were sold as merchandise rather than used as coins. According to Strachey, these coins were sold in India at the rate of ₹6.5–7.[29] The fact that these were being valued at ₹5.5–6 in the Ladakh market becomes clear from the value quoted for each coin in Ladakh Trade Reports. As per the statistics recorded in the annual Ladakh Trade Reports during 1867–1900, 159,336 *tolas* (over 1,858.4 kg) of gold dust and 76,449 gold coins worth over ₹4.3 million were imported into Leh from Xinjiang.[30] This gold was re-exported mostly to Kashmir and to Punjab via the Kullu route. Yakub Beg is reported to have issued his own gold coins in his kingdom in 1874.[31] That is why gold coins imported into Ladakh via Yarkand from 1875 onwards were of Kashgarian[32] rather than of Kokandi or Bukharan origin. Because of these gold coins getting overvalued[33] by Yakub Beg, their imports into Ladakh decreased considerably. But from 1883 onwards, the import of gold coins and dust registered a sharp increase. This was due to the arrival of Shikarpuri merchants from Bukhara and other towns in Russian Central Asia via the Kashgar–Yarkand–Leh caravan route. These traders, whose money-lending activities had been strictly restricted by Russian authorities in Central Asia, were forced by the changed conditions there to return to India. So, they brought along their accumulated capital and profits (earned during their long stay in Central Asia) in the form of gold coins and dust. Due to such increased imports, prices of gold in Kashmir fell.[34] In 1898, the government of Xinjiang prohibited all trading in gold by the traders, which led to stoppage of gold exports from Xinjiang to Ladakh.[35] Though Russian gold and paper roubles constituted major bullion imports from 1901 onwards, travellers and Haj pilgrims brought a substantial quantity of gold dust (about 677 kg), valued at ₹1.43 million to Ladakh between 1901 to 1936, which was meant to cover their travel and other expenses.

RUSSIAN GOLD AND PAPER ROUBLES

Import of Russian gold *ducats* (roubles) and copper *kopeks* (coins) into the Leh market from Yarkand as a trading commodity was occasional during the nineteenth century. G.T. Vigne, who visited Kashmir and Ladakh in the late 1830s, records that Russian gold ducats were brought into India via Yarkand and Leh as part of the merchandise imported from that end.[36] Strachey, who happened to be in Ladakh in 1850, found that such gold ducats were locally called *budki*.[37] The availability of budki and *bugh-i-ruski* (copper coins) in the Leh market has also been indicated by Aitchison.[38] But at the close of the nineteenth century, Russian currency began to occupy an important place in the Indian imports from Xinjiang. The tendency of Indian traders to transmit their earnings from Kashgaria to India (in Russian currency) continued, subject to minor fluctuations till 1919 when the British authorities in India prohibited such imports as part of their anti-Bolshevik measures.

Several factors—like the easy availability of Russian roubles in Xinjiang due to increased earnings from Xinjiang's exports to Russia, the advantageous position held by roubles vis-à-vis local Chinese currency in exchange value and the British Indian policy to restrict import of hemp drug into India by imposing high taxes on the same—were collectively responsible for the increased export of Russian roubles to India. The quantity and value of this import altered with the change in the overall trade climate ushered in by any shift in any of the aforementioned operational factors.

The raw materials exported from Xinjiang to Russia via Ferghana (in present day Uzbekistan) were paid back in Russian manufactured goods and roubles. Since Xinjiang's exports to Russia far exceeded the imports from the latter[39], the balance was met by rouble payments. As a result of the conclusion of the St Petersburgh Treaty in 1881[40], Russo-Xinjiang trade scaled new heights thereby ensuring a regular and abundant supply of Russian roubles in the market of Kashgaria. Due to the unusually large Kashgarian exports to Russian Turkestan in 1900–01, the value of rouble dropped to seven *tengas* in Kashgar[41], which encouraged Indian traders to purchase roubles in bulk. Any slump in this bilateral trade produced an adverse effect on the Indo-Xinjiang trade. When, in 1909, the export from Xinjiang to Russian Turkestan and Russia proper decreased in value, the year (April 1909–March 1910) witnessed a corresponding depression in the export trade of roubles to India from Xinjiang.[42] This was due to the fact that roubles became scarce in the Kashgarian markets and their high prices[43] rendered them unprofitable as a commodity for Indian traders. A similar situation had arisen earlier in 1905–06[44] due to the Russo-Japanese war and arose later in 1915–16[45] on account of the First World War.

Russian institutions operating in Kashgar, like the Kashgar branch of the Russo-Chinese Bank and the Russian Consulate, were actively encouraging brisk trading in Russian paper currency. The bank provided facilities to Indian traders in Kashgaria to transmit their money to India at fixed exchange rates, which in 1905 was ₹154 per 100 roubles.[46] Indian traders would deposit roubles with the bank in Kashgar and receive their payments in Bombay at approved exchange rates. Such measures helped in restricting the tendency to export Russian gold coins to India. They also acted as stimulants for Indian traders to balance their increased imports into Xinjiang with a corresponding export of their earnings. When the Russian banks and post offices stopped issuing drafts and money orders for India during 1914–16 (due to the First World War), there was a consequent spurt in the import of roubles into India through Ladakh. By the end of the nineteenth century, Russian currency had nearly substituted Chinese *yambus* and Khotan gold dust as treasure imports into India through Ladakh, mainly because of its higher profitability. However, the British imposed a prohibition on any rouble imports into India as part of their anti-Bolshevik campaign. This put a sudden halt to trading in Russian gold and paper currency. Even possession of the rouble invited punishment. During 1901–16, Russian gold coins were imported in considerable quantities into Ladakh from Xinjiang. Besides, Central Asian pilgrims desirous of making a Haj pilgrimage brought in sufficient quantities of gold coins to meet their expenses. This ensured a regular supply of Russian bullion to the Indian market.

Import of Russian roubles into India far exceeded the estimates as recorded in the annual Ladakh Trade Reports. Remittances made in cash by traders to India through the Russian banks and post offices at Kashgar were not listed in trade figures registered at Ladakh. As a result of British prohibition on trading in roubles, about 3 million roubles were deposited in government treasuries at Srinagar and Leh in a short period of three months in 1920.[47] Besides, more than 26 lakh roubles were re-exported to Xinjiang from Ladakh during April 1920–March 1921.[48] During 1932–34, 360,000 Russian gold roubles valued at over ₹0.9 million were imported by Haj pilgrims and immigrants from Xinjiang into India via the Chitral route.[49] During the same period, 460,000 gold roubles and gold dust valued at ₹1.2 million were brought by Haj pilgrims and immigrants from Xinjiang into India via the Gilgit route.[50] During the disturbed situation in Xinjiang, wealthy traders, immigrants and Haj pilgrims brought this gold treasure to India. But with the Xinjiang government promulgating the prohibition on the export of ready gold (bullion), gold, silver wares and currency on 21 November 1934, such imports from Xinjiang into Ladakh stopped.[51] Increasing rouble imports into India via the Yarkand–Ladakh route were a result of depression in the export trade of Xinjiang, which did not have the capacity to supply alternative goods to India.

SILVER

Chinese yambus or *kurus* were largely exported to Ladakh and Kashmir where these were melted and manufactured into silverware. In the 1870s, these were abundantly available in Ladakh at the rate of about ₹160–170 each. Later by 1900, their value declined to about ₹110–120. According to C.B.V. Hugel, an Austrian traveller who visited Kashmir in the 1830s, these silver ingots bearing Chinese stamp markings were made into coins in Kashmir.[52] About 500 yambus valued at ₹75,000 were reported to have been imported into Amritsar from Yarkand via the Leh–Kullu route in 1850.[53] The yambus were boat-shaped with a cavity so that it could be piled up, with one filling into the rim of the other. Each yambu weighed about 5 lb. Besides the yambus, silver coins and dust were also exported from Xinjiang to Ladakh as part of usual trade. 2,600 yambus worth ₹144,000 and 5 maunds of silver valued at ₹12,500 were imported into India via the Chitral route, during 1932–34.[54] In the same period, 2,300 yambus and 50 maunds of silver were imported via the Gilgit route.[55] This treasure was brought in by Haj pilgrims and immigrants from Xinjiang into India.

SHAWL WOOL/PASHM

Shawl wool formed the main item of export from Tibet to Ladakh. It was cleaned in Tibet, which reduced its gross bulk by half. Then, the cleaned, fine goat wool called pashm (used to make fine Kashmir shawls) was taken by Kashmiri traders to Kashmir. As per treaties, Ladakh and Kashmir maintained a monopoly over wool imports from Tibet, the whole being sent to Kashmir. It was in the early nineteenth century that Turfan and Yarkand wool began to be imported into Ladakh, after some Kashmiri traders taught the Yarkandi traders the process of cleaning this wool to suit the demands of Kashmir shawl manufacturers. From 1867–72, 2,331 maunds of fine wool from Yarkand, valued at ₹128,914, were imported into Ladakh.[56] During the same period, 3,451 maunds of pashm from Tibet, valued at ₹183,814, were imported into Ladakh.[57] Kashmiri traders purchased 5,348 maunds of this wool at Leh, valued at ₹288,814. Only 433 maunds of Yarkand wool valued at ₹24,028 went to Punjab.On an average, 600 maunds of wool were imported from Xinjiang each year during 1872–1925, after which there was a steep decline in such imports. As per the annual Ladakh Trade Reports, about 25,000 maunds of wool, valued at about ₹1.2 million was imported from Xinjiang into Ladakh during 1873–1936. The price of such uncleaned Yarkandi wool ranged between ₹40–50 per maund. While the fine wool was sent to Kashmir for shawl making, rough wool went to Baltistan for making blankets etc.[58]

FELTS AND CARPETS

Large quantities of *numdas* (felts made of wool) and carpets were imported from Xinjiang into Ladakh. Nearly all were exported to Kashmir, Punjab and Tibet. Yarkandi felts were dyed and embroidered in Kashmir and some were even exported as far as Europe. The tradition of using embroidered woollen numdas by Kashmiri households exists even today. One woollen felt cost just ₹2 between 1860s and 1880s. After that their prices rose, as there was a huge demand for wool and felts in Russian Turkestan. Woollen carpets called *gilim* in Yarkand were used extensively in Ladakh and Kashmir.

COTTON CLOTH

Russian-made cotton goods like drill-cloth, broadcloth and chintzes used to be imported into Ladakh and its frontier areas almost steadily during the nineteenth and early twentieth centuries, albiet in small quantities. These goods reached Ladakh through the medium of traders who operated on the Leh-Yarkand route. William Moorcroft, who was present in Ladakh in 1820, mentioned Russian broadcloth as one of the commodities imported by the trading caravans into Ladakh from Yarkand.[59] Aitchison states that Russian broadcloth, linen and long cloth (locally known as *banat, lanka* and *latha* respectively) used to be imported from Yarkand into Ladakh wherefrom these were also exported to Kashmir and Kullu.[60] From the late 1870s, an increased quantity of goods manufactured from cotton was imported from Xinjiang. Russian-made cloth was preferred by Buddhist lamas of Ladakh to that made in England, as it was cheap and durable. It was even exported to Tibet from Ladakh for the same reason. Russian-made chintzes and cloaks sold readily in the frontier areas of Kashmir like Gilgit, Hunza and Chitral. While the Bajaori and Badakhshi traders (operating between Chitral and Badkhshan via Dorah or Zebak passes) brought these goods into Chitral[61], Kashgari, Yarkandi or Gilgiti traders imported the same into Hunza[62] and Gilgit through the Pamirs, Tashkurghan and Kilik Pass. According to G. Macartney, at least ₹4,000 worth Russian cotton prints were exported to Hunza from Yarkand via Sarikol in 1910.[63] Yarkandi cotton cloth (*chakman*) was regularly imported into Ladakh during the nineteenth and early twentieth centuries, though in modest quantities. Being cheap, chakman had ready consumers in Ladakh and surrounding areas. During 1921–36, about 7,600 maunds of such cotton goods valued at over ₹0.5 million were imported into Ladakh.

Four

Exports to Xinjiang

Indian exports to Xinjiang via the Leh–Yarkand route comprised tea, indigo, dyes, paints, muslin, brocades (*kimkhab*), velvet, cotton goods (both Indian and European), red-dyed goat skins (*lakhi*), otter skins and furs, sugar, spices, indigenous medicines, Kashmiri shawls and corals. There existed a good demand among the people of Central Asia for these goods. Indian goods were consumed in the southern oasis cities of Yarkand, Kashgar, Khotan, Maralbashi, Yangi Hissar, Karghalik and Aksu in Xinjiang. Except for the direct export of its shawl produce, Kashmir's involvement in the India–Xinjiang trade was limited to being a transit station for the transmission of Indian goods to Xinjiang. Handmade books, mainly religious and historical in character and produced by Kashmiri calligraphists, were also exported. Some books, which were printed in Bombay, were also exported. Between 1869–85, over 37,000 books, valued at over ₹103,000, were exported to Yarkand.

In the early nineteenth century, opium produced in Kishtwar and Bushahr was exported to Xinjiang, where it was consumed by the Chinese traders and by the civil and military officials. Despite the Chinese prohibition on the import of opium, imposed in 1839, this drug was exported to Xinjiang by Indian traders to the extent of 210 maunds per year with the connivance of Chinese customs officials.[1] However, the export of opium declined due to the Kashmir government restricting the issuance of licences to traders for dealing in opium.

Sugar (both refined and unrefined) formed another item of export to Yarkand. Some quantities were exported to Tibet. Indian spices were exported to Yarkand in large quantities, from where some were re-exported from Xinjiang to Russian Turkestan.

TEA

The people of Central Asia harboured a special liking for Indian tea, which explained the increasing export of this commodity from India to Central Asia via the Punjab–Kabul–Bukhara and the Kashmir–Ladakh–Kashgar–Kokand overland trade routes. Nearly the whole of tea brought into Ladakh from India (Palampore and Calcutta [now Kolkata]) was exported to Yarkand. Part of the tea imported from Tibet into Ladakh was also exported to Yarkand. A considerable portion of this trade was later diverted to the Bombay–Batumi sea route after the extension of railway communication in Russian Turkestan. Part of the tea exported to Xinjiang from India found its way to Russian Central Asia, as Andijani traders came personally to Leh to purchase tea for consumption in their markets.[2] The Chinese authorities in Xinjiang had imposed no such curbs on Andijani traders if they imported Indian tea via the Leh–Yarkand route, on the condition that it would be sold only within Russian parts of Central Asia. Consequently, the value of Indian tea exported from Ladakh to Yarkand fell from ₹104,600 in 1887 to ₹12,000 in 1888.[3] The whole of it was bought by Andijani traders for sale in Russian Turkestan. The Chinese would detail a force to accompany such traders carrying Indian tea up to the frontier at Irkeshtam to ensure that no part from the consignment was sold in Chinese territories along the way.[4] This trade soon assumed considerable proportions. Since the Chinese had prohibited the sale of Indian tea for consumption within Xinjiang, the export of Indian tea was limited to the quantity required for export from Yarkand to Russian Turkestan. As this commodity could be exported to Russian Central Asia from India via the Afghanistan and Persia routes at cheaper rates than possible through the Leh–Yarkand route, the export of Indian tea to that quarter (via the latter route) dropped from the early twentieth century.

INDIGO, DYES AND PAINTS

Apart from its export to Central Asia via the Kabul–Bukhara route, indigo found its way to Xinjiang from India via Kashmir and Ladakh. The weavers in Yarkand and Kashgar used Indian indigo to dye the blue cloth, which was worn by Chinese citizens in Xinjiang. A fraction of this dye was later re-exported to Russian Turkestan from Kashgar. Macartney reported, in early 1895, that a large quantity of indigo imported into Xinjiang via Kashmir was being exported to Russian Turkestan via Osh.[5] But when indigo began to reach Russian Turkestan from India via Persia in large quantities, the re-export of this dye from Kashgar to the Russian side ceased in the closing years of the nineteenth century.[6]

HIDES AND OTTER SKINS

Large quantities of red-dyed goat skins called lakhi were exported from Punjab and Kashmir to Yarkand. These were used in making of long boots (*kafash massi*) worn by well-to-do classes in Xinjiang. Otter skins and furs from Bengal and Assam used in the lining of hats and coats for men and women were exported to Xinjiang.

COTTON CLOTH/GOODS

Indian cotton cloth, piece goods like chintzes, latha and sheets were exported to Xinjiang in large quantities. However, after 1880s, European cotton goods substituted the Indian cotton goods by over 90 per cent.

BROCADES, VELVET, SATIN

Brocades, (kimkhab [silk with gold pattern, made in Benaras]), satin and *makhmal* (velvet) used to be exported to Xinjiang in large quantities. About one-fourth of these went to Tibet.

SHAWLS

Shawl signifies an intricately woven and embroidered dress material made of fine pashm. It continues to be one of the celebrities of Kashmir. Used as a body-covering, scarf or turban, the shawl was a part of the attire of the kings, queens and the nobility. As in the Western countries, shawls were popular among the affluent sections of society in Central Asia. There existed a tradition among the Central Asian ruling nobility to present Kashmiri shawls to an honoured guest or to any superior in rank and authority as a mark of esteem. Central Asia, which maintained close commercial ties with Russia, acted as a transit station in the forward transmission of Kashmiri shawls to markets in Russia, Persia and Constantinople. While Kashmiris went as far as Orenburgh to trade their goods, Central Asians used to come to Ladakh and Kashmir to make on-the-spot purchases of the shawl. During his visit to Kashmir in 1783, George Forster—a British civil servant of the EIC and a traveller in Kashmir, Afghanistan, Central Asia and Russia—noticed several merchants and commercial agents who had come to the Valley from far-off places like Georgia, Turkey, Persia and Tartary.[7] Abdul Kerim, a Bukharan by birth, visited Kashmir towards the close of the eighteenth century. He was witness to several Kashmiri merchants travelling from Kashmir to Ladakh to sell their packages of shawls in Central Asia.[8] When Moorcroft visited Kashmir in 1820, he saw numerous merchants of Turkestan, Kabul and Persia getting shawl goods prepared in Kashmir in conformity with the requirements of their customers.[9] According to him, the demand for shawls in Russia was great at that time and a big trading house in Yarkand had sent its representative to Kashmir for the sole purpose of purchasing shawls suited to the Russian market.[10]

All available evidence suggests that Kashmiri shawls used to be exported to Central Asia and from there to Russia, mainly during the first half of the nineteenth century. After that, such trade dropped in value considerably. Bukhara had developed into a main transit centre to receive shawls from the direction of Kabul and from there it was forwarded for consumption in Russia. According to Burnes, approximately 120–300 pairs of Kashmiri shawls made of finest texture were annually exported to Russia through Central Asia.[11] Kashmiri shawls reached the Central Asian markets through the Leh–Yarkand–Kashgar–Kokand and the Srinagar–Amritsar–Kabul routes.

That Kashmiri shawls were imported into Kokand was revealed by the Kokandi envoy, Shahzada Sultan Muhammad Khan, during his visit to India in 1854.[12] According to another eye-witness account, Bukharan authorities used Kashmir shawls in *khilats* and presents to Russian authorities in Central Asia.[13] This created a reasonable demand for such goods in Central Asia. During 1867–72, shawl goods comprising pashmina shawls, *chadar* (sheets), *alwan* (pashmina cloth) for making *chogas* (gowns), scarfs and turbans—valued at ₹113,545—were imported into Ladakh from Kashmir. Most of these goods were exported to Yarkand and the remaining went to Tibet and Punjab.[14]

A study of the annual Ladakh Trade Reports, from 1867–1920, shows that the export of Kashmiri shawls from Kashmir to Central Asia via the Leh–Yarkand trade route became insignificant in quantitative terms after 1877, when the Chinese reoccupied Xinjiang. Evidently, the shawls of Kashmir (used as turbans by Andijanis and Kokandis[15]) were in demand in Kashgar during the rule of Yakub Beg. A part of such shawl goods also reached Russian Central Asia via Kashgar. But such trade appears to have dwindled after the extermination of Khoja rule in Xinjiang in 1877–78. However, the Kokandi and Andijani merchants, who personally came to Kashmir till the later years of the nineteenth century, used to take small quantities of Kashmir shawls for their own consumption.

CORAL

There existed a strong tradition among the Central Asian people to use coral ornaments. A steady and sizeable demand for coral ornaments among the Central Asians led to the increased export of coral beads to Russian Turkestan from India (via Ladakh) and Xinjiang. About half of the coral exported to Xinjiang was re-exported from there to Russian Turkestan. Though coral was equally popular among the people of Ladakh, Tibet and Xinjiang, its export to Xinjiang registered a sharp increase after the bilateral Russo-Xinjiang trade was put on a regular and firm footing (as a result of the signing of the St Petersburgh Treaty in 1881). This facilitated the export of coral to Xinjiang from India for consumption in Russian Central Asia. The Russian authorities had imposed duties of 4–5 roubles per 1b of coral[16] imported into Russian Turkestan as part of their policy to restrict Indian exports to that area. Owing to this, smuggling of coral into Ferghana through the mountain passes of Irkeshtam and Osh flourished. About half of the total quantity of coral imported into Russian Turkestan was estimated to have been smuggled.[17] As per the data available with the Russian Consulate in Kashgar, about ₹40,000 were collected by the Russian Customs House as duty on coral worth about ₹1 lakh exported to Russian Turkestan from Kashgar in 1901–02.[18] Similarly, 21,600 roubles were collected as duty on this item of trade alone during 1904–05.[19] In view of the high duties levied by the Russian customs authorities and the consequent smuggling of coral into Russian Turkestan, coral export to Russian Central Asia from India (via Kashgar) was actually more than what had been recorded at the Russian Consulate in Kashgar. As per the Ladakh Trade Reports, 1893–1908 saw an unusual increase in coral exports from Ladakh to Xinjiang, mainly because the Chinese were buying coral in large quantities. During this period, coral worth about ₹24 lakh was exported from Ladakh. This trade reached its lowest point in 1918, when coral worth ₹180 was exported from Ladakh to

Xinjiang.[20] It was possibly due to increased supplies from Russia. All such coral trade was entirely in the hands of British Indian traders who found it both profitable and easy to transport. This coral was imported from Italy into India and was re-exported to Xinjiang via Ladakh. Indian exported coral must have been selling at cheaper rates in Russian Turkestan than what had been imported via a more direct route of Batumi. A higher duty of 10 roubles (per lb) was chargeable on the latter route.[21] Despite such heavy odds, due to the restrictive duties imposed by the Tsarist government and the circuitous and hazardous nature of the Leh–Yarkand–Kashgar–Ferghana route, coral exports from India to Russian Central Asia flourished for more than a quarter of a century.

PART II

DIPLOMACY

Five

Diplomatic Contacts

During the nineteenth and early twentieth centuries, the extent and pattern of the exchanges between Kashmir and Xinjiang were conditioned by diplomatic relations at two different levels. In the wider international arena, they depended on relations between the three great empires of the world—Britain, Russia and China. Additionally, they were also influenced at a regional level by the degree of influence maintained by the Dogra rulers of Jammu and Kashmir in Xinjiang and adjoining territories.

Maharaja Gulab Singh of Jammu (1842–57) and his military commander General Zorawar Singh looked beyond the frontiers of Ladakh to safeguard trade routes from Kanjuti raiders based in Hunza. They also ensured the steady flow of trade, particularly the lucrative shawl wool trade from Tibet and Xinjiang, into Ladakh and Kashmir. Gulab Singh retained these concerns after becoming the maharaja of Jammu and Kashmir in 1846, as did his successor Ranbir Singh who ascended the throne in 1857. Although the Qing dynasty conquered Xinjiang in 1757, their authority remained weak. They faced successive Khoja uprisings, culminating in a full-scale rebellion by Yakub Beg. While the Qing authorities in Kashgar remained pre-occupied with the task of consolidating their authority in the face of political insurrections by Khoja rebels and other local chiefs, they even sought the support of the chiefs of Ladakh and Hunza to prevent such rebels from entering their territories. In most cases, this cooperation was provided in exchange for trade concessions or property rights.

William Moorcroft, who was in Leh during 1820–21, claims to have seen a letter from the Chinese Emperor, sealed with the Imperial Signet addressed to the Raja of Ladakh (around 1740s to 1750s) 'requesting the Raja to forward details of any military movements of the Khojas of Kashgar to Lhasa'.[1] The letter was also accompanied by presents of dresses, silk cloth and vases made of precious stones. This testifies to the respect and importance shown by Chinese high authorities to Ladakh.[2] The Chief of Hunza was given an estate at Yarkand (in south Xinjiang) in the eighteenth century. He was allowed to cultivate lands at Raskam (north of the Karakoram) and to levy taxes on the Kyrgyzs of the Taghdumbash Pamir.

The British Indian government's increasing interest in Central Asian affairs from 1840s onwards, impacted the ongoing traditional contacts between the Dogra rulers of Kashmir and the authorities in Xinjiang (particularly in Kashgar). The British remained determined to stall Kashmir ruler's contacts with Kashgaria to promote their direct political linkages with Xinjiang and Central Asia.

ZORAWAR SINGH'S AMBITIONS TOWARDS YARKAND AND TIBET

By 1840, Raja Gulab Singh, had firmly established his authority over Ladakh and Baltistan. He ruled these regions on behalf of the Sikh empire, while retaining a high degree of autonomy. During this period, Zorawar Singh—a trusted general who was also the *wazir* (governor) of Ladakh—considered the possibility of sending military expeditions to Yarkand and Tibet. The wool trade lay at the heart of the Dogra ambitions. Kashmir had emerged as the centre of shawl production, and depended on imports from western Tibet and Xinjiang for its raw materials. However, the 1830s saw a rapid rise in the export of shawl wool from across the Himalayas to Rampur in Bushahr (controlled by the British) instead of via the established route through Ladakh to Kashmir. With Ladakh in his hands, Gulab Singh and Zorawar now directed their efforts towards stopping direct trade between Tibet and the British-controlled territory.

The British authorities in India were monitoring Zorawar's communications beyond the boundaries of Ladakh. George Clark, the British political agent at Ludhiana, secured a copy of Zorawar's correspondence with the Yarkand ruler and forwarded it to the British Indian government on 25 August 1840. Zorawar had written to the Yarkand Chief informing him about the extension of Khalsa (Sikh) government to Punjab, Kashmir, Multan and Ladakh, and also about the submission of local rajas and chiefs to the Sikh power. Zorawar went on to invite the Yarkand chief to 'adopt the right road of submission and depute a qualified Agent to attend on that government according to an engagement, remit an annual tribute, without causing a disturbance and bloodshed in your country'. Zorawar warned that 'the neglect of this advice will entail shame and ruin on your country and your comforts and you will then repent'.[3]

In his reply, the Yarkand chief had informed Zorawar that their country was one of the dependencies of China and asked him first to 'depute his Agent to demand a tribute from China, and after having fixed the amount of that tribute with the ruler of the empire we then shall have no objection to follow his example'. He went on to advise the 'Sikhs to desist from vain boasting and remain satisfied with their place'.[4]

This was a period when the Chinese had successfully re-established their authority in Xinjiang. As part of their law enforcement measures in Yarkand, they had seized and destroyed opium worth ₹8–9 lakh, belonging to Indian traders.[5] The Dogras heard about this episode from Kashmiri and Punjabi merchants and, since their morale was particularly high following their conquest of Ladakh and Baltistan, used the destruction of the Indian traders' property as an excuse to put pressure on Yarkand. Thus, on 2 January 1841 Clark wrote to inform H. Maddock (the secretary to the British Government of India), reporting: 'Raja Gulab Singh is intent on an ambitious scheme of conquest of Yarkand, using the seizure and destruction of opium at Yarkand belonging to traders (subjects of the Sikh government) as a means of inciting the Durbar to authorise his scheme. His Wazir Zorawar Singh has considered it as an easy accomplishment.'[6]

Eventually, Zorawar took military action against Tibet rather than Yarkand. In early 1841, he wrote to the *Garpon* (local Tibetan leader) of Gartok, forbidding him from supplying pashm to any other area except Ladakh. He also demanded a tribute, thereby seeking to enforce Ladakh's old territorial claim to west Tibet.[7] Dissatisfied with the response from Gartok, he marched with his forces towards western Tibet in the summer of 1841. One immediate consequence was a dramatic fall in the value of Tibetan wool imports at Rampur, which dropped to only ₹17,766 in 1841.[8] News of the Dogra invasion of Tibet prompted Clark to write to the Lahore Durbar (the centre of the Sikh empire) asking it to 'put a restraint on Zorawar's activities'.[9] When reporting the matter to Maddock, Clark also expressed the view that 'the Jammu Rajahs have an eye upon Gilgit and Kashgar'.[10] The Lahore Durbar responded by claiming that they had no information about Zorawar's encroachments within the Chinese boundary, but at the same time pointed out that 'the country between the Chinese and the Ladakh frontiers being inhabited by various savage tribes of thieves and robbers, the pests of the trading classes, it is probable that such refractory tribes may have been punished'.[11] The Durbar, therefore, sought 'redressal for the merchants, Khalsa subjects who have lost lakhs of rupees worth of their merchandise on that frontier'.[12] The British Governor General of India concurred with Clark's analysis, and expressed his concern about 'the ambitious projects of the Jammu family in the direction of Kashgar'.[13]

Ultimately, it was a series of military setbacks—rather than British diplomacy—that put an end to the Dogra military exploits beyond Ladakh's northern and eastern borders. After initial successes in conquering Tibetan territory up to Taklakot, the Dogra army suffered a crushing defeat in December 1841 and Zorawar was killed. This defeat was mainly due to heavy snowfall. The Tibetans then invaded Ladakh. However, following the arrival of Dogra reinforcements, the Tibetans and Dogras signed a peace treaty in Leh on 17 September 1842. Under the terms of the treaty, the Tibetans accepted the Dogras as the legitimate authority in Ladakh and the 'old established frontiers' were reaffirmed.[14] The Tibetans also committed to not exporting shawl wool to any place other than Kashmir via Ladakh. The Ladakhi merchants could freely travel to Rudok, Gartok and any other place in Tibet, and the Tibetan traders had free access to Ladakh.

Four years later, following the defeat of the Sikhs in the First Anglo-Sikh War (1845–46), the British formally made over the territories of Jammu and Kashmir (including Ladakh) to Raja Gulab Singh. He had already controlled Jammu and Ladakh as a feudatory to the Sikh ruler. From then on, he became a maharaja of an Indian state subject to British paramountcy. In 1853, the Tibetan and Kashmiri authorities signed a second agreement confirming existing trade relations between their two territories.[15] Ladakh's trade with Tibet, therefore, continued throughout the Dogra rule, and by the early twentieth century, was worth ₹100,000 a year.[16] The traditional overland trade ceased after the extension of Chinese communist rule over Tibet in 1950.

DOGRA RULERS' POLITICAL CONTACTS WITH KASHGARIA

The Dogra rulers of Jammu and Kashmir, though subject to British paramountcy, remained determined to maintain their relations with Central Asia and Tibet. In contrast, the British Indian authorities took all possible steps to erode the Dogra Maharaja's political influence outside the borders of Jammu and Kashmir. As Anglo-Russian rivalry gained momentum in the mid-nineteenth century, the British became highly averse to any direct diplomatic contacts between the Kashmir Durbar and the Central Asian chiefs. For their part, the Dogra rulers of Kashmir sought to retain their influence in Xinjiang and, therefore, regularly exchanged envoys with the region (often without the knowledge of the British). The Kashmir Durbar kept itself abreast of developments in Central Asia by securing information through agents and traders. They even tried to prevent direct contact between British officers and Central Asian visitors to Ladakh and Kashmir.

Nobility, chiefs and envoys from Kokand and East Turkestan visited Ladakh and Kashmir intermittently, along with regular visits by traders and Haj pilgrims. The Dogra rulers of Kashmir did not miss any opportunity to provide appropriate hospitality to such important visitors. Occasionally, Central Asian fugitives would flee to Ladakh and Kashmir to escape reprisals from their rivals at home, to bring their wealth (gold, silver, etc.) out of East Turkestan safely to Ladakh and Kashmir or to seek moral and material support from the Maharaja of Kashmir and his representatives.

In 1837, Captain Wade (the British Political Agent at Ludhiana) received authentic information about the arrival of an envoy of the ruler of Kokand (en route India) in Leh.[17] This envoy was forced to adopt the guise of a merchant through Yarkand, owing to the hostile relations between the ruler of Kokand and the Chinese in Xinjiang. He had been deputed by the Khan of Kokand to present a pair of horses to the governor general of India with a view to establish friendly relations with the British government.[18] It was a strange coincidence that at about the same time, Haji Mohammad Ali of Yarkand had been maltreated by Raja Gulab Singh's representative at Leh for his friendly conversations with G.T. Vigne.[19] The Dogra Chief was keen to prevent the friendly intermingling of British travellers with any visitors from the neighbouring Central Asian Khanates and Xinjiang. Alarmed at the treatment meted out to the Yarkandi visitor, the Kokand envoy sold off his property in Leh and burnt the letter charged to his custody. He then returned to Kokand through Yarkand and Kashgar without attaining his objective.[20] Thus, Raja Gulab Singh's political prestige in the neighbouring Central Asian territories as a ruler powerful enough to reject the requests of British travellers like Vigne rose high.

Finding himself unable to resist the Russian occupation of Fort Ak-Masjid in 1853, Khuda Yar Khan (the ruler of Kokand) made efforts to obtain succour from the British to enable him to safeguard the remaining portion of his territory. It was in August 1854 that an accredited envoy from Kokand, Shahzada Sultan Mohammad Khan, arrived at Peshawar bearing letters for the Governor General of India and the Commissioner of Peshawar Division, H.B. Edwardes.[21] The Kokand ruler wanted the British government to loan the services of some of its officers for training his undisciplined forces to withstand any future Russian onslaught.[22] This envoy came to India through Oxus, Badakhshan, Zebak and Chitral, crossing the Malakand pass to reach Peshawar. He chose to return to Kokand via Abbotabad, Kashmir, Ladakh and Yarkand. He preferred it to the Kabul route on account of its being safe and free from turmoils and robbers. Shahzada's visit to Kashmir on his way back to Kokand enabled Gulab Singh to establish direct rapport with the Kokandi ruler, and also to make a show of strength before his Central Asian guest. When Shahzada arrived at Srinagar on 10 September 1855, he was not only received personally by the ruler of Kashmir but was also presented a purse of ₹500.[23] Besides that, ₹20 was provided as daily allowance for each day of the envoy's stay in the Valley.[24]

The British government had sent a trained local surveyor, Baboo Shuja, along with this envoy to explore the route to Kokand and ascertain the position of Russians on the Kokand border.[25] But owing to his anxiety to keep his territory free from any British influence, Gulab Singh managed to dissuade Baboo Shuja from undertaking his mission. The Maharaja's agent at Leh, Bulla Joo, was reported to have misrepresented the intention of the Kokand envoy to the Yarkand authorities. They then took precaution by detaining the Kokandi envoy and his companion at the frontier.[26] According to Faiz Buksh, the British native agent deployed in Central Asia, Rasul Mir (the Kashmiri agent) at Yarkand had instigated the Chinese *Amban* (Magistrate) at Yarkand against the establishment of friendly relations between the British Indian government and the ruler of Kokand, as it would have revealed the true state of affairs in Xinjiang to the British. Thereupon the Amban detained Shahzada at Yarkand for two months.[27] Gulab Singh's policy was to maintain direct and friendly contacts with the neighbouring Central Asian territories, and to prevent any type of British activity in the frontier regions in and around Ladakh.

OVERTURES FROM KHOTAN

In 1865, Haji Mohammad Habibullah (the chief of Khotan) sent several emissaries to Ladakh and Kashmir in the hope of securing military assistance against attacks by Tungan and Chinese forces. In June 1865, Mirza Mahmud (the first such emissary) brought a letter addressed to the *Thanedar* (Governor) of Ladakh. According to the letter, Habibullah offered '...the allegiance of Khotan state to the British government, with a view to receiving in return assistance against the advancing power of Russia and the oppression of Tungans, in the shape of a supply of muskets and military accoutrements'.[28] The Maharaja of Kashmir referred the matter to the Lieutenant Governor of Punjab seeking advice as to how he should reply. The Lieutenant Governor advised the Maharaja to write that 'while the British government was glad at all times to cultivate friendly relations with neighbouring states, it was not prepared to take any part in their disputes with other countries'.[29] The British Governor General of India concurred with the course taken by the Lieutenant Governor of Punjab.[30]

Another such emissary, Mohammad Alam, arrived in Ladakh from Khotan on 4 July 1865, bringing a letter from Habibullah to the British authorities and Ladakh officials. While referring to the earlier mission of Mirza Mahmud, the Khotan chief asked the British authorities to 'listen to our representations, send their Mohtamids (confidential agents) to Khotan, easily take possession of the territories of the Khakan-i-Chin (Emperor of China), stop the progress of Russia, prevent their encroaching upon this territory and relieve the Musalmans from the tyranny and oppression of the Tunganis'. He continued by pleading that 'we Musalmans may be freed from the hostilities of the Tunganis. The road may be made open to trade, and the intercourse of caravans ensured. Indian and European goods may pour in abundance and both parties benefit thereby'. Habibullah also asked for '12,000 European muskets with bayonets and accoutrements and 12,000 European units of military clothing'.[31]

In September 1865, Juma Khan, an Afghan merchant, arrived at Ladakh bringing yet another letter from Habibullah. This was dated 8 July 1865, and was also signed by Mohammad Ibrahim Ghazi (Habibullah's eldest son), Bahauddin Bahadur Ghazi (his nephew), Mohammad Masoom (his younger son) and Saifulla (his younger brother). In the letter, Habibullah mentioned the earlier dispatch of his three emissaries to India, with letters describing the state of affairs in Khotan. Claiming that none of these emissaries had returned, Habibullah authorized Juma Khan to 'conclude a Treaty of Mutual Friendship with the British government on condition that he was acknowledged to be the sovereign of Khotan and its dependencies; there should be no interference with the law of Mohammad obtaining in his territories; and the British would undertake not to invade countries such as Kokand or Bukhara, which were held by Muslim rulers'. Habibullah also wanted the 'traders of both sides to be allowed free access to each other's territories, and that Hajis be allowed to pass through the British territory'. He further requested the British Indian authorities to send through Juma Khan 'weapons of war and men skilled in military tactics and engineering'.[32]

Juma Khan was hospitably entertained by the Kashmir Durbar before he went on to Lahore. He arrived there on 25 November 1865 and met the then Lieutenant Governor of Punjab two days later and presented him a gift of silk carpets and other Khotan products.[33] Juma Khan was well received, and the Punjab government provided him with a daily allowance and took care of the expenses for his journey from Lahore to Calcutta where he had an audience with the Viceroy.[34] However, the British Indian government stuck to its previous stand of 'maintaining amicable relations with other states and encouraging trade, but without getting involved in their internal affairs'. The Lieutenant Governor of Punjab was authorized to send a reply to this effect to the Khotan Chief. It stated that the British Indian government 'is quite ready to be on friendly terms with him and to encourage trade between the two countries, but cannot enter into any treaty with the Chief of Khotan, because of the great distance between the two countries and the difficulties of the way'.[35] Therefore, Juma Khan left Ladakh for Khotan in early August 1866 without accomplishing his objective.

Habibullah persisted in making such overtures, despite the British Indian government's refusal to establish direct relations with him. In 1877–78, when Yakub Beg was suffering defeat at the hands of Chinese forces, the Khotan Chief again sent an envoy to Ladakh. This time he sought to establish direct relations with the Maharaja of Kashmir.[36] The Maharaja sought an opinion on this matter from P.D. Henderson, the British OSD. Henderson told him that 'since Khotan was integral part of the dominions of Kashgar, no person styling himself to be Wali of Khotan or his representative could be recognised'.[37] Thus, the British followed a consistent policy of discouraging the Kashmir Durbar from having any direct dealings with the Central Asian chiefs. This did not, however, prevent the Central Asian nobility from using the Kashgar–Yarkand–Leh–Kashmir–Punjab route on their way to Mecca. For instance, Mohammad Sadik (Habibullah's nephew) arrived at Leh on 23 September 1880 on his way to Mecca.[38] The Central Asian nobility, particularly those who had lost their positions of power, would find their first refuge in Kashmir while looking for greener pastures elsewhere, mainly in Central Asian Khanates or Turkey.

CONTACTS BETWEEN YAKUB BEG AND RANBIR SINGH

Yakub Beg exchanged a series of letters with Maharaja Ranbir Singh regarding the need to secure the borders of Ladakh from the Kanjuti raiders of Hunza (who disrupted trade by plundering caravans). The first such letter, dated 18 July 1866, was sent by hand through the Yarkandi envoy Badal Bai Meerakhor who presented it personally to Ranbir Singh in Srinagar.[39] In his letter, Yakub Beg briefed Ranbir Singh about his successes in 'recovering Kashgar, Yangi Hissar, Yarkand, Yuran Kash, Khotan, Aksu and other territories from the Chinese, Tunganis and Koocharis'.[40] Pointing to the great obstacles to trade posed by the Kanjuti robbers, Yakub Beg informed Ranbir Singh about the dispatch of an armed detachment, which brought Sanju, Sarikol and Tashkurghan under Kashgar's control. Yakub Beg also informed Ranbir Singh about the steps taken to repair and build the forts at Tashkurghan and Sarikol in order to keep the trade route safe from robbers. While communicating his intention to subjugate and extricate the Kanjutis, he proposed to establish a friendly alliance with the Kashmir Durbar. The Yarkandi envoy was to return to Yarkand in five months with a response. He had already spent two months on the journey to Srinagar and was prepared to stay there for another month.[41]

Ranbir Singh got worried about Yakub Beg's hostile designs on Hunza, which was a feudatory of Kashmir, and rushed a *parwanah* (letter) to Dewan Nihal Chand (*vakil* [envoy/agent] in the court of the Lieutenant Governor of Punjab). He sent along a copy of Yakub Beg's letter and expressed concern over his intentions.[42] He informed the Lieutenant Governor about the positive role played by the Kashmiri *aksakal* (traders' leader) at Yarkand in advising the ruler of Kashgaria to send a vakil to Srinagar before dispatching a force against the Kanjutis. Ranbir Singh also forwarded a copy of his reply to Yakub Beg.

In his letter dated 16 October 1866, Ranbir Singh acknowledged the receipt of Yakub Beg's letter and stated: 'It is the sole wish of the Maharaja to see tranquillity and peace prevail everywhere, travellers and traders secure from the depredations of robbers, and commerce free from molestation.' Reiterating that Raja Ghaznafur, the former chief of Kanjut (Hunza), was his subject, he informed Yakub Beg that since his son Ghuzan Khan (the Kanjuti chief) had 'deviated from the path pursued by his father, it has been determined to punish him and accordingly troops have been sent against him from three sides in order that he may receive condign punishment, and travellers and traders may be freed from the depredations and enjoy security and comfort'. Ranbir Singh expressed the hope that 'when Ghuzan Khan is attacked by the Maharaja's forces, the Yarkand ruler would refuse to give refuge to any of the rebel's party (Kanjutis) who may fly for protection to the Yarkand territory'. Ranbir Singh's prompt action in sending his letter through Sadikulla Hakim to the Yarkand ruler, pre-empted the latter's move to make an incursion towards Hunza. Yakub Beg was quick to acknowledge the receipt of Ranbir Singh's reply.[43]

Khoja Buzarg Khan (brother of Walli Khan Tora and son of one of the descendants of the old Khoja rulers of Kashgar) arrived in Leh in 1868, ostensibly on a Haj prilgrimage to Mecca but actually to escape from the country after he was dispossessed of power by Yakub Beg in Kashgaria.[44] In fact, Yakub Beg sought to exile the rival Khoja chief from his kingdom by sending him on a pilgrimage to Mecca via Kashmir. But Buzarg Khan chose to return to Kokand via Kashmir, Punjab and Bukhara, rather than go to Haj.[45] Mahomed Akhoond and Khasum Akhoond, reported to be vakils of Yakub Beg, arrived at Leh in August 1869.[46] They were deputed by the *Dad Khwah* (Governor) of Yarkand with letters of introduction to Henry Cayley (the British OSD at Leh), informing him about the objective of their visit to purchase arms (rifles, revolvers, etc).[47] Another important visitor Mirza Alam, reported to be Yakub Beg's nephew and the governor of Maralbashi district, arrived in Leh in September 1869 en route Mecca (via Kashmir, Punjab and Bombay).[48] He was provided 3,000 gold tillas by the Kashgar ruler for building inns at Medina and Mecca. During August and September 1869, around 300 pilgrims—all well-off men of standing from Yarkand, Kashgar and Aksu—arrived in

Leh to make their Haj pilgrimage through Kashmir, Punjab and Bombay.[49]

In October 1871, Ghafur Shah Nakshbandi—who was well known in Yarkand and would keep the British Indian authorities informed about the proceedings in Kashgaria and Kashmir—reported the arrival of an official named Mulla Baki in Ladakh, bearing letters for the Kashmir Durbar.[50] According to Nakshbandi, as the communication between the emissary and Kashmiri authorities was kept secret, Mulla Baki was sent back to Yarkand from Ladakh and his letters were forwarded to the Kashmir Durbar.[51] Yakub Beg was reported to have sent other emissaries (Kari Hamid and Syed Ahrar Khan Torah) to meet the Maharaja of Kashmir.[52] Kari Hamid (reported to have come in the winter of 1869) returned from Jammu to Leh in mid-1870 on his way back to Yarkand. He met Cayley at Leh on 1 July 1870. Kari Hamid and another emissary Mirza Shadi were invited to dinner by Cayley on 2 July 1870 to meet T.D. Forsyth's party (who were on a mission to Yarkand).[53] Mirza Shadi had been deputed by Yakub Beg to visit India to purchase arms. He bought 400 muskets and ammunition, and brought 15 artificers/mechanics from India and Kashmir to accompany him on his way back to Kashgar.[54] According to Faiz Buksh, both Kari Hamid and Mirza Shadi met Ranbir Singh. Mirza Shadi reportedly showed Ranbir Singh a letter written by Yakub Beg addressed to the Viceroy of India (before he left for Calcutta to meet the Viceroy). The Kashmiri ruler is reported to have offered to supply any number of guns and ammunition. He even provided some armourers and guns to Kari Hamid on his way back to Yarkand.[55]

Mirza Shadi met the British Viceroy of India in Calcutta on 28 March 1870 and requested him to send a British officer on a friendly visit to the court of Yakub Beg.[56] This opportunity was immediately availed by the British. They decided to send the T.D. Forsyth mission to Kashgar to obtain full and reliable information regarding the prospects of trade and resources of Yarkand and Kashgar; and to open direct, friendly communication with the Kashgarian ruler. Forsyth was accompanied by Robert Shaw, Dr Henderson, Tara Singh (Punjabi merchant) and Faiz Buksh (of the G.T. Survey of India) on this mission.[57] Forsyth reported to the Punjab government that Ranbir Singh was not in favour of the friendly relations between Yakub Beg and the British.[58] He alleged that 'messages were sent to Yarkand to create misgivings about the British intentions and to lower the British prestige in Kashgaria'.[59] Forsyth made a particular mention of the obstructions caused by Akbar Ali Shah, the wazir of Ladakh, in making arrangements, as 110 horses out of 220 were reported to have died within a week's journey.[60]

In view of the seriousness of the charges, which were also levelled by Cayley, the Lieutenant Governor of Punjab took up the matter with Ranbir Singh on 15 August 1870. He requested Ranbir Singh to make necessary arrangements for the return journey of Forsyth and his mission.[61] Ranbir Singh was prompt enough to reply on 19 August 1870, informing Cayley of the deputation of Mehta Sher Singh (governor of Anantnag) and Lala Rammohan so that they could do the needful.[62] In another letter dated 29 August 1870, the Maharaja informed that Akbar Ali Shah was suspended from his office of wazir of Ladakh.[63] In yet another letter, dated 17 September 1870, Ranbir Singh reported about the appointment of Mehta Sher Singh as the new wazir of Ladakh.[64]

Several Kashmiri Muslim traders—namely Khaliq Dar, Rasul Mir, Mahomaed Shah, Kabir Shah, Kamal Joo, Qadir Joo, Sadik Shah and Ahmed Shah—functioned as agents of the Dogra rulers of Kashmir in Yarkand and would report all events of importance to the Kashmir Durbar. Ranbir Singh would advance them money for trading purposes. He would send valuable gifts to the rulers of Yarkand and Kashgar through these agents, in a bid to maintain his friendly relations and also to demonstrate the power and independence of his kingdom. Many a time, they would indulge in rumour-mongering with the local authorities in Yarkand and Kashgar (both Chinese and Kashgarian) against the British Indian authorities. This was done with a view to demonstrate their loyalty to their host authority, to conduct their trading activities smoothly and to thwart the British attempts to reconnoitre the areas around Kashmir's frontiers and in Xinjiang by instigating the Kashgar authorities.[65]

In January 1878, Haji Nur Mohammad arrived at Leh from Yarkand with 800 silver yambus (equivalent to £12,000). This money belonged to Beg Kuli Beg, the son and successor of Yakub Beg, the former chief of Kashgar who had fled to Kokand after the reoccupation of Xinjiang by the Chinese in 1877. Nur Mohammad gave a written statement at the office of the British Joint Commissioner, Leh, giving details of the treasure valued at about ₹132,600 that had been entrusted to him by Kuli Beg for safe keeping.[66] Kuli Beg was anxious to establish friendly relations with Ranbir Singh, possibly to prepare the way for his settlement in Kashmir. But when he sent some presents to Ranbir Singh from Lahore, the latter returned them. Ranbir Singh treated the former ruler of Kashgaria as an exile and a mere traveller.[67] Following this, the fugitive Kashgar Chief retreated to Kokand. Nur Mohammad visited Amritsar along with his family and later returned to Kokand. Meanwhile, Kuli Beg wrote to A. Lyall (the British Indian foreign secretary), informing him about his arrival at Constantinople in August 1881 and expressing his wish to travel to India to recover his money from Nur Mohammad.[68]

YAKUB KHAN TORAH'S KASHMIR CONNECTION

Syed Yakub Khan Torah was a close confidante of Yakub Beg. He had gone as envoy to Constantinople, India, Afghanistan etc., to forge friendly relations for Yakub Beg's newly acquired kingdom in these countries. That Yakub Khan had a strong connection with Kashmir is borne out by the fact that he was the inheritor of several villages/landed estates in the Valley, which had been acquired earlier by his father Syed Ali. This factor and the geographical proximity between Kashmir and Kashgar placed Yakub Khan as a key figure in the conduct of diplomatic contacts, firstly of the Maharaja of Kashmir and later of the British Indian government with Yakub Beg.

Yakub Khan arrived in Ladakh from Yarkand as Yakub Beg's envoy on 3 December 1872, along with 24 followers and 50 horses.[69] He brought along a letter for Ranbir Singh from Yakub Beg with a message for consolidation of friendship. The envoy planned to go from Srinagar to Jammu to meet Ranbir Singh and to deliver the letter to him personally. But he did not take the Srinagar–Jammu route and instead proceeded via Muzaffarabad. At Hasan Abdal, Yakub Khan was received by T.D. Forsyth, which resulted in the postponement of his visit to Jammu to meet Ranbir Singh.[70] However, he sent Yakub Beg's letter to Ranbir Singh through Mulla Artuk Panjakbashi and also sent a horse as a present. Mulla Artuk was received well in Jammu and was granted a dress of honour (*khillat*). Ranbir Singh also sent a courteous reply to Yakub Beg, acknowledging his letter of October 1872, and sent his compliments and good wishes for health and prosperity.

The Foreign Secretary of the British Indian government had instructed the Secretary to Punjab government on 7 January 1873 that 'no separate negotiations should be entered between the Maharaja of Kashmir and the Envoy, and the Maharaja should report fully to the Punjab government all communications that may take place with the Envoy'.[71] However, Wazir Pannu, the governor of Kashmir, organized a grand reception in honour of Yakub Khan at Srinagar on 26 December 1872. As mentioned previously, T.D. Forsyth waited for Yakub Khan at Hasan Abdal and escorted him to meet the Lieutenant Governor of Punjab.[72] The Lieutenant Governor received Yakub Khan on 3 February 1873. A guard of honour was also presented to him on his arrival. The envoy explained to the Lieutenant Governor that 'though Kashgar had entered into a commercial treaty with Russia, it would in no way weaken the friendship between Yarkand and England. Besides, the Russians will not interfere in Yarkand, after latter's friendship with England'.[73] Yakub Khan also revealed that Yakub Beg had instructed him to first go to Jammu to meet the

Maharaja, but he proceeded to India via Muzaffarabad, as 'he was conscious of the advantage of abstaining from communication with a subordinate power and direct dealing with the British Indian government'.[74] He also carried with him a letter, dated 5 October 1872, from Yakub Beg, addressed to the British Viceroy of India, expressing his desire to strengthen the friendship with the British Indian government.

Yakub Khan had a detailed meeting with the Foreign Secretary of the British Indian government on 27 February 1873. He again explained that he had been deputed by Yakub Beg 'to strengthen the bonds of amity and relations between Kashgaria and England'.[75] Kashgaria offered full facilities for the promotion of Indian trade with Yarkand. They desired to 'have an envoy/representative of Yarkand stationed at the headquarters of the British government, and also requested for permanent stationing of the British representative in Kashgaria'.[76] Yakub Khan also requested for a British mission to accompany him on his return to Yarkand.[77]

Yakub Beg's proposals came in handy for the British to meddle in Xinjiang's affairs. They lost no time organizing a large mission (led by T.D. Forsyth to Yarkand and Kashgar) to forge direct friendly relations with Yakub Beg and to sign a formal treaty with Kashgaria. Yakub Khan returned to Srinagar on 29 September 1873 on his way back to Yarkand. He reached Leh on 10 October 1873. Forsyth and his mission left Leh for Yarkand on 29 September 1873 and arrived near the Shahidulla border in mid-October 1873, where they were received by Yakub Beg's officials.[78] Yakub Khan joined the Forsyth mission at Shahidulla on 23 October 1873, from where they proceeded together to Yarkand and Kashgar.[79]

In fulfilment of Yakub Beg's proposal, the British Indian government also deputed R.B. Shaw, in autumn 1874, as OSD at Kashgar to represent the British Indian government.[80] Shaw was also entrusted with a letter addressed to Yakub Beg expressing amity and friendship.[81] He was asked to maintain friendly relations with Yakub Beg, to attend to British commercial interests in Kashgaria and to supervise the execution of the treaty.[82] Accordingly, Shaw went to Kashgar, met Yakub Beg on 22 October 1874 and presented the Viceroy's letter to him on a gold-worked silver plate. The letter also contained the ratification of the treaty (accompanied by a Persian translation). But due to the prevarications of Yakub Beg in ratifying the treaty of friendship with the British Indian government, Shaw stayed put in Kashgar without achieving his assigned mission. Yakub Beg was having second thoughts about entering into a formal alliance with the British. It was rumoured that Kashmiri Muslim traders in Yarkand and Kashgar who were apprehensive of the British making inroads into the Kashmir–Leh–Yarkand trade, had planted stories about the larger British design of political penetration into Kashgaria. In fact, Yakub Khan in the course of his meeting with C.U. Aitchison (where T.D. Forsyth was also present) disclosed that 'Kashmiris had sent mischievous letters/messages to Yarkand cautioning the Amir against any alliance with the British'.[83] He mentioned two Kashmiris (Ghafoor Shah and Ghulam Shah) indulging in such mischief.[84]

Yakub Khan used the opportunity of his proximity and friendship with the British Indian authorities to press for the restoration of his ancestral property in Kashmir. The Secretary to the Punjab government took up the matter with Ranbir Singh on 11 February 1875, informing him that the Viceroy would have no objection 'if he should be disposed to accede to the Syed's request for jagir'.[85] Ranbir Singh replied that 'the original villages cannot be restored. But in accordance with the recommendations of the Viceroy, I will not decline to assign a cash allowance of 10,000 rupees and lands yielding 11,000 rupees to the Syed, per annum'. Ranbir Singh was ready to grant the jagir to Yakub Khan, not in recognition of his claims to the ancestral property but only in deference to the wishes of the British Indian government. So, to meet Ranbir Singh's condition, the Viceroy wrote a letter to him on 29 January 1877 on the subject of 're-grant of jagir of 10,000 rupees cash and 11,000 rupees land per year (in Srinagar coins) to Syed Yakub Khan Torah'. The Viceroy assured Ranbir Singh that the 'grant of this jagir to Syed Yakub Khan (who is the envoy of an ally of this government) is much appreciated and will be at all times regarded by the British government as a most friendly act'. Ranbir Singh in his reply informed that he had consented to the valuable grant being made to Yakub Khan only on the recommendations of the British Indian government. Obviously, Ranbir Singh wanted the British to commit on this front, lest he should be accused of hobnobbing with Yakub Khan directly.[86]

With the issue of his land estate in Kashmir settled in his favour, Yakub Khan now expressed his desire to settle in Kashmir along with his family. In a letter dated 15 February 1878 to the Viceroy, Yakub Khan made known this wish.[87] Pointing to the advantages of his stay in Kashmir—due to his being acquainted with the affairs in Kashgar, Balkh, Badakshan, Afghanistan and Turkistan—Yakub Khan requested for the possession of land granted in Kamraj to him.[88] Meanwhile, Yakub Khan's agent in Kashmir, Haji Kurban was entrusted with collecting the yearly allowances due to him from his jagir.[89] That Yakub Khan was at pains to secure a comfortable refuge was known to the British Indian government. The Viceroy found it 'impracticable for the GoI to act as a Banker and collect his rents for him, while he enjoyed in Europe all the convenience of an absentee landlord'.[90] Accordingly, the British Indian government decided to 'pay a stipend of 10,000 rupees per year to Syed Yakub Khan Torah from the British treasury (payable since 1 September 1881)'[91], thus relieving Ranbir Singh of this burden. The Viceroy informed the Maharaja of Kashmir about this decision in his letter of 25 May 1882. However, Kashmir Durbar had paid Yakub Khan ₹21,000 per year (with effect from 12 March 1875 to 31 August 1882).[92]

Yakub Khan had also kept his family and his agent (Haji Kurban) in Kashmir during this period. The British Indian government sanctioned an annual allowance of ₹10,000 to Yakub Khan in 1882, on the understanding that he would forfeit all claims on the Kashmir Durbar and subject to good conduct on his part.

This allowance was accepted by Yakub Khan and enjoyed by him until his death in 1899.[93] On his death, half the amount of his allowance (₹5,000) was continued to his wife and children on the understanding that the allowance of each individual would cease on his or her death.[94] In 1900, the members of Yakub Khan's family living in Constantinople asked for payment of ₹2,500 a year. On this application, the British Indian government paid ₹1,500 a year from 1 July 1900. This was to be paid by the British Embassy at Constantinople through bills drawn on the Accountant General, Bombay.[95] This amount was paid till 31 December 1914, after which the payment was disrupted due to war. With the death of the original beneficiaries Syed Abdul Rahman and Syed Abdullah (in June 1918 and July 1919, respectively), this episode of Yakub Khan's connection with India, including Kashmir, came to an end.

Six

Hunza and Xinjiang

Adjoining the Xinjiang province of China and situated at an elevation of about 8,000 ft, Hunza is strategically important for its possession of Kilik, Mintaka, Khunjerab and Shimshal passes leading to the Pamirs and connecting with the ancient Silk Route. The present-day KKH and CPEC (connecting China and Pakistan) pass through the Khunjerab Pass. The preponderant existence of rock carvings of Buddhist stupas, Kharoshthi inscriptions and the famed Sacred Rock in Hunza provide historical evidence of the sway of Kushan and Hindu/Buddhist Patola Shahi rulers (sixth to eighth centuries AD) over this region in ancient times.

After the advent of Islam, the Ayosho family is believed to have ruled the area since around the sixteenth century. On the subject of Hunza–Xinjiang (China) relations between the eighteenth and early twentieth centuries, we have two available narratives—a European view presented by the German scholar Irmtraud Muller-Stellrecht[1] and a Chinese analysis by Hsiao-ting Lin, which has the distinct advantage of accessing the relevant Chinese records[2]. Four local accounts—Qudratullah Beg's *Tarikh-i-Ahd-i-Aliq-i-Riyasat-i-Hunza* (*History of Hunza*), *Autobiography of Mohammad Nazam Khan* (Mir of Hunza, 1892–1938), S. Shahid Hamid's *Karakoram Hunza: The Land of Just Enough* and Shafqat Hussian's *Deconstructing Discourses of Presentation: Situating Local Agency in Imperial History*—are important for providing the Hunza perspective.

According to Qudratullah Beg, a local historian from Baltit, Hunza, it was the brother of Salim Khan II who had launched a campaign 'to defend Hunza against a Turkish invasion (should be the Kyrgyzs), conquered Raskam, Oprang, Taghdumbash, Dafdar, Erijilga and Wakhijir and levied taxes on the people of these places'.[3] Beg also records the beginning of friendly contacts and diplomatic exchanges between Hunza and Qing authorities in Xinjiang during the reign of Kisro Khan (1750–90).[4] The Mir of Hunza is stated to have sent his second son Salim Khan to Yarkand with a present of gold, receiving in return numerous gifts many times in value. According to Beg, the Mir of Hunza received 12 guns, 8 caparisoned horses, 12 boxes each of black and green tea, 500 green muslins, 500 white muslins and one royal dress of skin.[5] Muller-Stellrecht, in her monograph *Hunza und China (1761–1891),* viewed the tributary relationship between Hunza and China as 'a direct result of the conquest of East Turkestan by the Chinese under Emperor Kien-lung in 1759'.[6] She contended that 'Hunza and other small principalities in the greater Pamir-Karakoram region came under Chinese dominion and as a tributary, it was obliged to pay a nominal tribute regularly'.[7] The first such tribute, of a small bag of gold dust, was sent by the Mir of Hunza through his representative to the Chinese Amban at Yarkand in 1761. However, she has ignored the fact that it was a usual practice of the Qing authorities to foster trade-cum-tributary relations with the Central Asian and outlying principalities to maintain peace and security within their newly acquired territory in Xinjiang.

It had been established that when imperial China was weak at the centre, it sought to bring the outlying Central Asian states and chiefships into the ambit of 'nominal vassalage' system by fostering trade and mutual exchanges. The Silk Route system provided a stable link to facilitate such communication between China and the peripheral areas. The Mings encouraged such tributary relationship with the principalities of Central Asia by offering trade concessions as a bait.[8] On their part, the Central Asian chiefs found it profitable to send such missions bearing gifts for the Chinese authorities, as this facilitated their commercial adventures in Chinese territories. It also fetched them Chinese return gifts, which were several times greater in value.

The Chinese scholar Hsiao-ting Lin (who has accessed the contemporary Chinese official records), affirmed:

> [...] The tribal groups west of the Manchu guard-posts (*kalun*) and in the steppe region beyond the imperial frontiers, such as Tashkent, Bukhara, Badakhshan, Kokand and the Kazakhs were generally regarded as foreign tributaries or 'outer barbarians'(*Waifan*). These outer tributaries sent tribute to the Qing court in Peking and in exchange received official titles from the court, were granted privileges to trade in the markets of Xinjiang.[9]

Quoting from one Chinese record, Lin confirmed that the Mir of Hunza (Kisro Khan) 'sent in 1761 a mission to Kashgar and presented a tael and a half of gold dust to the new Qing Imperial agent'[10], receiving in return goods several times in value. On examination of several Chinese records, Lin concluded that during the Qianlong (1736–96) and Jiaqing (1796–1820) periods, 'the remote Hunza territory was not deemed a Qing internal vassal or inner dependency'. Also, the Qing officials 'never categorized Hunza as one of Qing's Muslim Central Asian "outer tributaries" (*Waifan Chagong*), the rulers of which were asked to send tribute missions to Qings'.[11] Quoting from Wei Yuan's *Shengwu Ji,* Lin wrote, 'Hunza was mentioned as one of many Central Asian petty tribal states that had unimportant commercial connections with the empire, and it was excluded from the group list of the Qing tributary dependencies in Central Asia.'[12]

During the 1880s, the attention of the British was drawn to Hunza's relations with China and its claims over Raskam and Taghdumbash Pamirs. The British became concerned over the then Mir of Hunza Safdar Ali's links with China and his overtures to Russia (despite being a feudatory of Kashmir). The Russian demonstration of interest in Hunza through the dispatch of Captain Grombchevsky to Hunza only stimulated active British interest there. This was particularly so after the occupation of the Bozai Gumbaz by the Russians. The triangular Anglo-Russian and Chinese contest in the Pamirs and proximity to the Kashmir frontiers led the British to consolidate their presence in and around Gilgit. Captain J. Biddulph was appointed in September 1877 as an OSD to monitor the developments in and around the Kashmir frontier. Biddulph's mission was to 'cultivate friendly relations with the tribes beyond the border in order to bringing them gradually under the control and influence of Kashmir'.[13] Biddulph kept a close watch on the Mir of Hunza's friendly communications with the Chinese authorities in Yarkand. When, in April 1878, Fuzl Khan, the vakil of the Mir of Hunza arrived in Gilgit, he informed Biddulph about the Chinese promise of increased subsidy to the Mir of Hunza (Ghazan Khan) for his assistance in the Chinese proceedings against Sarikol.[14] Biddulph told Fuzl Khan that since the Mir of Hunza had already been a dependent of the Maharaja of Kashmir since eight and a half years, he could not be expected to be a dependent of another power (China).[15]

When Yakub Beg had sway over Kashgaria (1867–77), the Mir of Hunza did not maintain any links with the authorities in Yarkand or Kashgar. He also did not send his men to cultivate the lands at Raskam or levy taxes from the Kyrgyzs of Taghdumbash Pamirs. When Yakub Beg was dead and the Chinese had re-established their authority over Xinjiang (including in the Kashgar region), Ghazan Khan wanted to re-establish relations that had existed formerly with the Chinese Amban at Yarkand. Fuzl Khan also informed Biddulph about the Mir of Hunza's intention to resume levying taxes on the Kyrgyzs. Ghazan Khan in his letter, dated 21 April 1878, to Captain Biddulph clarified that 'he is not a dependent and tributary to the Khakan of China, as on the Sarkar (the British Indian government and the Maharaja)'.[16] The Mir of Hunza further informed that 'Mullah Mukeem (Mir's Agent) was present during China's wars with the Khojas and had rendered service to the Chinese, who then increased the fixed *shank* (subsidy) and rewards to the Mir of Hunza. As such Ghazan Khan was sending tokens of friendship to the Amban.'[17] Biddulph, in his prompt response on 24 April 1878, questioned the Mir's action in 'accepting *shank* from the Chinese and sending tokens to the Khakan of China, when he has been receiving the benefits from the Maharaja of Kashmir for the past eight and a half years'.[18] Ghazan Khan in his reply acknowledged his allegiance to the Maharaja of Kashmir while maintaining friendly relations with Wakhan, Badakhshan, Shignan, Chitral, Yasin, etc.

Captain A.H. McMahon—the then Political Agent in Gilgit (August 1897–September 1898)—prepared a detailed report on the issue of Hunza's relations with China and its claims over Raskam and Taghdumbash Pamirs.[19] Taking into view the local Hunza accounts and the prevalent practices, McMahon concluded that the rights of Hunza over Raskam originated from a victory of the Hunza chief Salim Khan over the Kyrgyzs of Taghdumbash Pamirs in 1760. Salim Khan erected a stone cairn at Dafdar and sent a trophy of Kyrgyz heads to the Qing authorities in Xinjiang to announce his victory and the extension of his authority up to Dafdar.[20] The Chinese considered the Kyrgyzs their enemies and expressed their happiness over their defeat by sending gifts to Hunza, which acknowledged the same with a small gift of gold dust.[21] Simultaneously, Hunza received the concessions of cultivation, grazing and taxation rights in Raskam and Taghdumbash Pamirs. Thus began the custom of an annual exchange of presents, which continued late up to the early twentieth century.

McMahon was convinced about the right of Hunza to Taghdumbash, Khunjerab and Raskam, which he found as 'proved beyond doubt'. He described the boundaries of Taghdumbash, Khunjerab and Raskam, as claimed by Hunza and well-known to all the Kanjuts (Hunza people) as:

> The northern boundary of the Taghdumbash Pamir from the Wakhijir pass through the Beyik peak to Iljilga, about

> a mile above Dafdar, thence across the river to the Zankan nullah; thence through Mazar and over the range to Urok, a point on the Yarkand river between Sibjaida and Itakturuk. Thence it runs along the northern watershed of the Raskam valley to the junction of the Bazar Dara River and the Yarkand river. From thence southwards over the mountains to the Mustagh river leaving Aghil Dewan and Aghil pass within Hunza limits.[22]

When in 1885, the Sarikolis of Tashkurghan declined to pay revenue to Hunza on the plea that Tashkurghan was outside Hunza territory, Khan Daotai (the then taotai [commissioner] of Kashgar) visited Tashkurghan and settled the dispute in person in favour of Hunza. He laid down that 'Hunza rights extended over the Taghdumbash and the Khunjerab Pamirs to Dafdar, and an agreement was drawn and signed by him and the Sarikoli headmen'. Copies of the agreement were given to the Hunza Chief and the Sarikolis. In fact, the Taotai in his letter dated 6 December 1897 to Muhammad Nazim Khan (the then Mir of Hunza) regarding Raskam lands reiterated the existence of this document and that he had himself signed that agreement.[23] As per available records, Hunza's annual levies on the Kyrgyz nomads comprised of one sheet, one *numdah* (felt mat), one rope and one pair of felt stockings per yurt or tent.[24]

When, in the autumn of 1889, Captain Francis Younghusband was deputed by the British Indian government on an exploratory mission to the Pamirs, Shahidulla, Raskam and Shimshal, he witnessed 20 Hunza men in physical occupation of a small fort at Darwaz. Younghusband also saw several Hunza men, deputed by the Mir of Hunza, collecting the customary taxes from the Kyrgyzs at Taghdumbash Pamirs.[25] When the Russian Captain Grombchevsky was exploring Raskam, Shimshal and Mustagh in October 1889, he saw a group of Hunza men coming to Pakhpu and collecting yearly taxes.[26] According to Grombchevsky, the Kyrgyzs of Pamirs and the Tajiks of Sarikol paid taxes to the

Kanjutis, with the knowledge of the Chinese authorities.[27]

During the 1820s and in 1845–47, the Qing authorities in Kashgar even sought the support of the Hunza chief to subjugate such rebels to the south of Kashgar and Yarkand, and prevent them from entering his territory. Shahid Hamid stated that the Qing authorities would often encourage the Hunzakuts in their raids on the Kyrgyzs to 'protect their big towns like Yarkand from being occupied by the Hunzakuts'.[28] After the success of the Qing campaign against the Muslim rebels in Kashgaria, 'territory as far as Dafdar near the Murghab river was officially handed over to the Mir of Hunza'.[29] It is worth mentioning that following the defeat of Safdar Ali and the conquest of Hunza by the joint Kashmiri and British forces in December 1891, the British political agent in Gilgit found a trove of official correspondence between the Qing authorities in Kashgar and the Mir of Hunza in the rooms occupied by Safdar Ali.[30] One such letter written in Turki (in the third month of seventh year of Qing Emperor Daoguang [late 1820s]) by the Amban to the Mir of Hunza informed the latter about the defeat of Khoja rebel (Jahangir), who had occupied the four cities of Yarkand, Kashgar, Khotan and Yangi Hissar in 1826.[31] The Qing official asked the Mir of Hunza to capture Jahangir who had fled to Tashkurghan and send him to Kashgar, 'since the district of Tashkurghan belongs to Hunza'.[32] For this task, the Mir of Hunza was promised the title of *wang* (prince) and a reward of 2,000 silver yambus (1 yambu = ₹170).[33] This provides clinching evidence of the dependence of Qing authorities in Xinjiang on the Mir of Hunza for containing anti-Qing rebels in Southern Xinjiang.

The existence of Hunza forts in Azghar and signs of cultivation at other places in this area show that Hunza was in actual possession of Raskam for a considerable period. Hunza's rights in Raskam and Taghdumbash Pamirs were sustained during the period when Chinese authority was weak in Xinjiang. The local Chinese authorities did not wish to run the risk of offending successive chiefs of Hunza. These chiefs often sent foraying missions into Xinjiang to enslave Kyrgyz nomads, plunder their property and loot trading caravans. Besides, the Chinese derived political satisfaction from the receipt of annual presents of gold dust. They deemed this to be a form of tribute from a loyal dependency. For its part, Hunza adhered to the custom of sending an annual present of 15 *miskals* of gold dust worth ₹120. In return, the Hunza chief also received gifts of silk cloth, 200 pieces of cotton clothing, one silver ingot, 10 tea bricks, 8 China cups—all worth ₹1,070—besides other presents for the emissaries sent by the Mir of Hunza.[34]

SAFDAR ALI'S FLIGHT TO KASHGAR AND INSTALLATION OF THE NEW MIR OF HUNZA

Ghazan Khan, the Mir of Hunza had entered into a treaty of allegiance with Ranbir Singh in 1870 after his rebellious forces were quelled by Kashmiri troops. Ghazan Khan not only acknowledged his dependence on the Kashmir Durbar but also admitted that such dependence had existed earlier during the reign of Ranbir Singh's father (Maharaja Gulab Singh [1846–56]). The Mir of Hunza regularly paid tribute to the Kashmir Durbar, and he was granted land estate (jagir) in Kashmir. Thus, Hunza remained under the suzerainty of Kashmir while retaining full autonomy in the management of its internal affairs. But the Mir of Hunza would use every opportunity to challenge the authority of Kashmir. The situation worsened when Safdar Ali usurped the chiefship of Hunza in November 1886, after murdering his father (Ghazan Khan) and three brothers. Conscious of his insecure situation among his people, Safdar Ali lost no time in sending his emissary with a tribute to Kashgar announcing his assumption of power in Hunza and seeking Chinese assistance. While demonstrating his loyalty to the Qing authorities, the new Mir of Hunza requested them to 'bestow upon him a fourth-ranked official title' to enable him to elevate his status and position.[35]

In January 1888, a combined force of 3,000 men from Hunza and Nagar attacked and captured the Kashmir garrisons at Chaprot and Chalt,[36] also threatening Gilgit. Though Safdar Ali had waged war against the frontier outposts of Kashmir, he sent an emissary (Darvesh Ali) to Kashgar requesting Chinese assistance of arms and ammunition against Kashmir's forces.[37] He alleged that Kashmir's forces were harassing him. The Chinese authorities sent a Qing official (Jangdarin) along with Darvesh Ali to verify the situation.[38] It was the first ever visit of a Chinese official to Hunza. Safdar Ali explained to Jangdarin that he feared a counter-attack by Kashmiri forces and sought arms and ammunition. He proposed to send Muhammad Nazim Khan (who later became the Mir of Hunza from 1892–1938) along with Nazar Ali to personally meet the Taotai and the *Chitai* (Military Commander) at Kashgar. This proposal was accepted by Jangdarin.[39] As Muhammad Nazim Khan has recorded in his autobiography, he met the Taotai and presented Hunza's case. The Taotai, who had already been briefed by Jangdarin about the ground situation, asked Nazim Khan to go to Yangi Shahr to meet the Chitai, who was responsible for the military stores.[40] Nazim Khan, accompanied by Jangdarin, met the Chitai who, after verifying the details from Jangdarin, gave two boxes of ammunition and two magazine rifles to Nazim Khan[41] as a token.

Meanwhile, the Taotai of Kashgar reported the matter to the Governor of Xinjiang, stating that the chief of Hunza had repulsed the attack of Kashmiri forces, along with Nagar.[42] The Governor, while referring the matter to Peking, asked for the Tsungli Yamen (the Chinese Foreign Ministry) to ask the British Minister in Peking to take necessary steps to restrain Yin-ti (Kashmir).[43] The Chinese claimed that since Hunza owed allegiance to China, they were concerned over the advance of Kashmiri troops towards Hunza, after the latter had captured Chaprot. So much so, the Tsungli Yamen wrote to John Walsham (the British minister at Peking) on 7 June 1888, asserting China's claims on Hunza and seeking to know the reasons of the disturbance.[44] John Walsham personally explained to Tsungli Yamen (on 16 June 1888) that it was the Hunza chief who, in conjunction with Nagar, had entered Kashmir and attacked its fort at Chaprot. Walsham—in his letter dated 21 June 1888 addressed to Prince Ch'ing and ministers of Tsungli Yamen—notified the Yamen that the Chief of Hunza 'has long been a feudatory of Kashmir, receiving a yearly pension and paying tribute', and that 'it would be impossible, therefore, for the Indian government to allow this petty border chieftain to create disturbances on Indian soil with impunity, and in reliance on his pretension to be a tributary State of the Chinese empire'.[45] That the Tsungli Yamen did not send any rejoinder to Walsham's explanation, signifies Chinese acceptance of the ground situation.

Safdar Ali, the Mir of Hunza, was simultaneously courting the Russians in a bid to play both the Chinese and Russian cards to keep the British at bay. He hosted the Russian officer Captain Grombchevsky, who promised to supply him Russian arms. The Russian Consul at Kashgar, Petrovsky, was keeping a constant watch over the situation in Hunza. He would occasionally meet the Hunza emissaries during their visits to Kashgar. Petrovsky was putting pressure on the Qing authorities in Kashgar to assist Safdar Ali in pushing back the British advance to Hunza. Concerned over Safdar Ali's continued flirtations with the Chinese and the Russian forward movement in the Pamirs, the British re-established the Gilgit Agency in 1889 with Lt Col Algernon Durand as its political agent. Durand arrived in Gilgit in July 1889 and left for Hunza in mid-August 1889, where he held discussions with Safdar Ali. The Mir of Hunza agreed to acknowledge the suzerainty of Kashmir and promised to stop raids on the Leh–Yarkand trading caravans. Durand also asked Safdar Ali to have no contact with the Russians and the Chinese. Safdar Ali contended that as he held a jagir in Yarkand and had rights in Taghdumbash and Raskam, he could not terminate his relations with the Chinese.[46] Around the same time, Captain Younghusband was deputed to explore the passes leading to Hunza from the east and the north. Younghusband travelled to Hunza after returning from Shahidulla through the

Shimshal Pass. He met Safdar Ali and impressed upon the latter the benefits of allegiance to the Kashmir Durbar and the British. After having met the Chinese, Russian and British officials, Safdar Ali suddenly felt important. He assumed that the three mighty empires of Russia, China and British India were courting him for his friendship. He sought to extract higher amount of subsidies and benefits from each of them. Relying on the promise of Russian support (conveyed earlier by Grombchevsky) and expecting Chinese assistance, he remained defiant and even blocked the regular courier service between British India and Kashgar.

In May 1891, the Mirs of Hunza and Nagar launched a joint offensive against the Kashmiri fort at Chalt. Now a joint force of Kashmiri and British troops led by Durand advanced from Gilgit against Hunza, and by December 1891, Hunza and Nagar forces were defeated. After completely subduing Hunza and Nagar, their relations with Kashmir were defined by a *sanad* (official edict), under which the Maharaja of Kashmir appointed the Mirs of Hunza and Nagar. While these mirs were required to pay annual tribute of gold to the Kashmir Durbar, they were granted annual subsidies borne by the Kashmiri and British Indian governments.

Safdar Ali and his wazir Tara Beg fled to Tashkurghan in Southern Xinjiang, along with 100 followers. They were treated as refugees by the Qing authorities in Xinjiang.[47] Jangdarin, the Qing official who visited them and arranged food supplies for the Hunza men, did not approve of Safdar Ali's 'open hostilities against the powerful British'.[48] Jangdarin was right in his estimation of the two wrongs committed by Safdar Ali—first, the murder of his father and second, the fight against the British government.[49] Mindful of the presence of Safdar Ali (who had fled to Xinjiang) and Muhammad Nazim Khan (who was already in Kashgar for some business with the Qing officials), Durand sent a letter to Jangdarin. He informed Jangdarin about the circumstances of war with Safdar Ali, his defeat and flight to Xinjiang. He then asked for the return of Safdar Ali to Hunza.[50] Durand wrote, 'in case he did not wish to return, Muhammad Nazim Khan should be sent back to assume control'.[51] The Qing official duly informed Muhammad Nazim Khan about Durand's letter advising him to return to Hunza and 'do as Colonel Durand wished'.[52] The Chinese who did not want to get embroiled with the British over the issue, put both Safdar Ali and his minister Tara Beg under arrest interning them in a fort in Kashgar.[53] While Safdar Ali's family was sent to his jagir in Yarkand, other Hunza refugees were collected and told that both the Chinese and British governments had decided to install Muhammad Nazim Khan as the new Mir, and hence they 'should return to Hunza'.[54]

China continued to demonstrate its interest in the accession of the new Mir of Hunza, which it wanted settled through direct negotiations between the Chinese officials in Xinjiang and the British Indian government.[55] Tsungli Yamen held discussions with John Walsham on this subject and sought an assurance that 'no re-adjustment of the tributary State should take place except in consultation with China'.[56] The British Foreign Office was disposed to 'allow a Chinese officer to be present at the formal installation of the new ruler, on the understanding that this concession was not to form a precedent for a similar claim on future occasions'.[57] To Salisbury, the British foreign secretary, it was 'a matter of serious importance to have the friendship and goodwill of China and her officers in Kashgar, on the question of North-West frontier of British India'.[58] Accordingly, Marquess of Salisbury, the British foreign secretary, informed Sieh Tajen (the Chinese Minister at London) about the nomination of Muhammad Nazim Khan, a half-brother of Safdar Ali as the new Mir of Hunza.[59] Salisbury also invited a Chinese representative to be present on the occasion of the installation ceremony in Hunza.[60] However, Salisbury made it clear that the '*sanad* (official edict) of investiture to the new ruler of Hunza from the Maharaja of Kashmir would be delivered to him by the British Resident and that the Chinese envoy would not take any active part in this ceremony, but his position would be that of an honoured spectator'.[61]

Since the position of the British representative in Kashgar,

G. Macartney, was not comparable to Petrovsky (the Russian Consul at Kashgar), the British government attached importance to secure consular status and official *locus standi* to Macartney in Xinjiang. This was done so that he could function there at par with the Russian consul. Accordingly, the British followed a policy of appeasement towards the Chinese by allowing the visit of the Chinese delegate to Hunza to be present at the installation ceremony of the new Mir. Though 15 August 1892 was initially fixed as the date of installing the new Mir[62], it was postponed till 15 September 1892 at the request of Chinese Minister at London 'due to time taken by communication between Peking and Urumchi'.[63] On his part, the Chinese Minister at London sought to have the status of the Chinese envoy at Hunza put at par with that of the British government. The Chinese Minister, Sieh Tajen, wrote on 18 July 1892 to Marquess of Salisbury presuming that 'the Chinese envoy shall occupy a place of equal dignity with that of the British Agent, while the envoy from Kashmir would be assigned a place slightly lower'.[64] The two Chinese envoys (Jangdarin and Yangchidarin) arrived in Gilgit,[65] where they stayed for a month, being treated well. From there, they went to Baltit, while being accompanied by Col Robertson, the new British political agent at Gilgit.

The Chinese envoys had brought a present and a document to be given to the new Mir of Hunza. This document was a letter to Muhammad Nazim Khan asking him 'to rule over Hunza kindly and to continue to send the yearly tribute of gold to China'.[66] The British Indian government decided not to allow the Chinese envoy to present this document to the Mir of Hunza or to make any speeches at the installation ceremony.[67] This left the Chinese envoys disappointed and they returned to Kashgar the next day. The ceremony of installation of Muhammad Nazim Khan as the new Mir of Hunza took place as scheduled on 15 September 1892 in the presence of the two Chinese envoys. They were treated as honoured spectators.[68] On their return to Xinjiang, the Chinese envoys presented a false report that 'Chinese and British officials had successfully conducted a "joint installation" in Hunza' and that the 'Emperor's edict was read aloud in front of everyone and handsome gifts were meanwhile bestowed to the new Mir'.[69] In his memorial to the court, the envoys 'proudly claimed that China's reputation was enormously elevated among the Muslim regions in Central Asia, and the emperor's benevolence as well as authority had been extended to the border peoples'.[70]

The Qing rulers, concerned over their waning authority and vanishing prestige both in China and in adjoining regions, tried to use the opportunity of the presence of the Chinese envoys at the installation ceremony, to reinforce their shadowy claims on the suzerainty of Hunza and to propagate the same to bolster their image. The Chinese were particular about the new Mir of Hunza continuing with the practice of sending annual presents to Kashgar. While the Taotai of Kashgar took up the matter with G. Macartney, China's minister at London communicated with the Earl of Rosebury (the British Secretary of State for Foreign Affairs) on this issue. Though the new Mir of Hunza was averse to sending the annual present of gold to Kashgar, 'due to his objection to serve two masters at a time and also due to non-availability of gold'[71] in Hunza, he was persuaded by the British authorities to continue with the tradition. Accordingly, he sent 1.5 ounces of gold from 1894 till the early 1930s, with some exceptions. While doing so, the Mir of Hunza would write to the Taotai requesting him to be allowed to collect taxes from the Taghdumbash Pamir as before. He also wrote for the permission of the Hunza refugees in Yarkand to return to Hunza and to transfer the jagir in Yarkand (in Safdar Ali's possession) to his name.[72] The Taotai of Kashgar in his reply agreed to the Mir's demands.[73] When in early 1896 the people of Taghdumbash petitioned the Taotai against the Mir of Hunza's claims to receive felts, stockings and ropes as taxes; the Taotai in his reply (dated 8 March 1896) ordered them to pay these customary taxes, which had earlier been mutually agreed by the Kanjutis, Sarikolis and the Taotai.[74] The Taotai reprimanded them and asked them to continue to follow the practice as otherwise 'the Kanjutis would come and harm them'.[75] Simulatenously, the Taotai sent a letter to the Mir of Hunza, recognizing his right to collect taxes in kind in Taghdumbash Pamir.[76] As such, the Qing authorities in Xinjiang were scared of the Mir of Hunza causing any trouble in Taghdumbash and Sarikol and sought to buy peace by acceding to his demands of customary taxes.

Seven

The Raskam Issue

When, in the spring of 1897, the Mir of Hunza sent some of his men to resume cultivation of some tracts in the Raskam Valley, the simple affair snowballed into an international issue involving three empires—Britain, China and Russia. It was the action of the Chinese Amban at Yarkand in arresting the two Hunza men, who had stayed back at Raskam to look after their crops, that actually sparked off the crisis. The matter was promptly taken up by the Mir of Hunza with the Taotai of Kashgar (with the knowledge of the British Political Agent at Gilgit), reminding him of the Hunza rights in Raskam and questioning the Yarkand Amban's action.[1] The Mir of Hunza sent his letter to the Taotai through two Hunza men (Nazar Ali and Gul Mohammad) who were witness to the signing of the historical agreement by the Taotai of Kashgar at Tashkurghhan in 1895. As such, they were best suited for the job. The Taotai, after discussing the matter with the *Titai* (Military Commander, Kashgar), gave the Hunza emissaries a letter asking them to go to Yarkand and meet the Amban there. The Amban of Tashkurghan, Huang Wei Sun, was directed to accompany the Hunza men to Yarkand and then to the Raskam Valley.[2]

As the Yarkand Amban was not favourably disposed towards the Hunza case, the Hunza men went again to Kashgar to meet the Taotai. Both the Taotai and Titai of Kashgar were in favour of allowing Hunza to resume their rights at Raskam. Accordingly, the Taotai of Kashgar referred the matter to the Lt Governor of Xinjiang who, in his telegram of 27 December 1897, gave his consent to the cultivation of Raskam Valley by the Kanjutis.[3] The Lt Governor also ordered Brigadier General Chang (one of the Chinese envoys present at the installation of Mir Muhammad Nazim Khan as Mir of Hunza in 1892) to accompany the Hunza men to Yarkand and meet the Amban of Yarkand.[4] As it was too late to visit Raskam, it was decided that in the coming spring, the Amban along with Chang from Kashgar would meet the Kanjutis in Raskam and assign them the land plots for cultivation.[5] The Amban of Yarkand, in his meeting with Nazar Ali (the representative of the Mir of Hunza) on 24 June 1898, agreed to hand over the lands available at Azghar, Kuktash, Ursur, Oprang, Uruklik, Iliksu and Tashmana to the Kanjutis.[6] However, the move was resented by the ever vigilant Petrovsky who warned the Chinese about the possible occupation of Sarikol by the Russians in response to the handing over of Raskam to Kanjutis.[7]

Now, coming to the point of actual Russian involvement in what was a bilateral Hunza–China question concerning small tracts, it may be pointed out that Russia was concerned over the extension of British authority in Hunza in 1891. In fact, Captain Grombchevsky, who was fluent in Turki and Persian, had visited Hunza in 1888. When the Russian officer Grombchevsky and the British officer Younghusband met at the Pamirs in October 1889—both exploring the roof of the world from two opposite directions in pursuit of their respective imperial ambitions—Grombchevsky showed to Younghusband two letters of Safdar Ali Khan, the Mir of Hunza, inviting him to visit Hunza.[8] That Grombchevsky's explorations had the approval of high Russian authorities is evidenced by the Emperor of Russia granting a special audience to him after his Hunza mission.[9] He was also given a gold medal by the Russian Geographical Society for this mission.[10] When Grombchevsky was at Shahidulla, he sought permission from the British Resident in Kashmir to visit Ladakh. This further alarmed the British in India, which decided not to allow him to come down to Ladakh.[11] Reports about Safdar Ali's friendly communications with the Russian authorities in Turkestan were already causing discomfiture to the British. In fact, Captain A. Durand found several letters written in 1888 by Grombchevsky and Petrovsky to Safdar Ali in the fort of Hunza, after its capture by the British and Kashmir forces.[12] Durand reported in February 1892, after the flight of Safdar Ali to Yarkand, about the former mir having received a letter from the Russian Governor General of Turkestan in the autumn of 1891.[13] The Russian Governor was reported to have advised Safdar Ali 'to remain quiet till the spring and be on good terms with the British and that in the spring the Russians would come and build forts at Aktash, Soma and Bozai'.[14]

Safdar Ali, while in exile in Xinjiang, continued to be in touch with Petrovsky, the Russian consul at Kashgar, who was taking active interest in Hunza's affairs. Petrovsky even wrote a letter at the behest of Safdar Ali to the Taotai of Kashgar, seeking Chinese assistance against the British advance to Hunza.[15] That the Xinjiang authorities reported the matter to Tsungli Yamen, was confirmed when John Walsham (the British ambassador at Peking) met the Tsungli Yamen on 10 March 1892.[16] Walsham was shown the original letter written by Petrovsky to the Taotai of Kashgar. Seeing that the Chinese Taotai at Kashgar had favourably disposed of the Hunza representation, allowing the Kanjutis to cultivate some plots in Raskam Valley, Petrovsky sent a letter to the next higher authority, the Lt Governor (*Futai*) of Xinjiang, advising him not to allow Kanjutis to settle down at that place as it lay on the frontier.[17] But the Futai too was in favour of granting this right to Hunza, though he sought to allay the Russian fears by proposing to levy an annual grain tax on such cultivators so that there remained no distinction between an ordinary Chinese subject and a Hunza cultivator at Raskam.[18] So, when the actual possession of seven plots at Raskam was being handed over to the people of Hunza in early 1899 by the local Chinese authorities[19], Russia started pressurizing China against such a course of action. The Russian representatives stationed at Peking and Kashgar warned the Chinese government about the possible Russian occupation of Taghrama (in Sarikol) as a quid pro quo to grant Raskam's lands to Hunza.[20] Consequently, the Tsungli Yamen stalled action on the promises made to the Hunza chief and also took further steps to evict the recent Kanjuti cultivators from Raskam, in a bid to save itself from possible Russian inroads into the frontier district of Sarikol.[21]

On receipt of fresh directives from Peking, the local authorities in Xinjiang hastened to inform Mohammad Nazim Khan of Hunza about the revised Chinese decision to not allow any Kanjutis to settle in Raskam, in view of the Russian objections.[22] The Amban at Yarkand also offered to compensate Hunza for the loss of grain that would result from the abandonment of Raskam lands by Kanjutis.[23] In order to placate his hurt sentiments, the Amban even sent two Begs of Sarikol to meet the Chief of Hunza personally and to explain the row between Russia and China over this issue.[24] Seeing that China had, under Russian pressure, gone back on its agreement of giving seven tracts in Raskam to Hunza, the British government decided to resist the action. Accordingly, the British Ambassadors at Peking and St Petersburgh took up the matter with the Tsungli Yamen and the Russian Foreign Minister, respectively. If the Russian Foreign Minister Mouraviev's assurance, given on 17 May 1899 to C. Scott (the British Ambassador at St Petersburgh), is any indication then Russia was not inclined to use the grant of Raskam lands as a 'pretext for acts of aggression on Kashgar'.[25] But the Russian War Minister Kuropatkin's views coupled with the Russian Consul at Kashgar Petrovsky's pleadings from Kashgar against allowing any further extension of the British influence in Sarikol hardened the Russian stand. This is evident from their action in seeking details about the extent and position of lands at Raskam from the British government[26], and from the objections raised by Giers, the Russian ambassador at Peking before the Tsungli Yamen in Peking.[27]

Russian concern over the reported construction of a carriage road from the Indian frontier towards Sarikol was not only conveyed through the usual diplomatic channels in London[28] but also by General Kuropatkin in the course of his private conversation with a visiting British Military Officer Col Mac Swiney.[29] On both occasions, the report was denied strongly.

The Russian War Minister's casual remarks made before Mac Swiney on 9 June 1899 that 'if your Kanjutis go into Raskam, we shall be forced to take over Kashgar, Tashkurghan etc.'[30], point to the seriousness attached by Russia to the Raskam affair. In such an atmosphere of mutual distrust and acrimony between the two imperial powers, China got encouraged to resist British pressures by playing upon Russian objections. When approached by the British representative at Peking, the Tsungli Yamen openly disclaimed the existence of any arrangement between the Taotai of Kashgar and the Chief of Hunza over Raskam lands.[31]

Both the Secretary of State George Hamilton and the British Indian government agreed that the 'attempt of Chinese to ignore the well-established rights of cultivation possessed by the subjects of the Mir of Hunza should be resisted'. So, at the behest of India Office, London, the British Foreign Office asked the British Ambassador at Peking to urge upon the Tsungli Yamen to issue orders for adhering to the existing arrangement between Hunza and Xinjiang over Raskam lands.[32] Meanwhile, Claude MacDonald, the British ambassador at Peking, addressed a letter to the Tsungli Yamen on 14 March 1899 advocating an understanding about the frontier between Xinjiang, Hunza and Kashmir. Recalling the 'Hunza claims on extensive tract of land in the Taghdumbash Pamir, extending as far north as Tashkurghan and on the district of Raskam to the south of Sarikol'[33], MacDonald drew attention to the letter from the Taotai of Kashgar (to the Mir of Hunza) sent in February 1896, which acknowledged these rights of the Mir of Hunza.MacDonald proposed that in order to come to a clear understanding of the frontier between China and India, and to avoid any dispute or uncertainty in the future, China should 'relinquish her shadowy claim to suzerainty over Hunza, and India will on behalf of Hunza relinquish her claims to most of the Taghdumbash and Raskam districts'.[34] When, in mid-1899, the Chinese authorities in Kashgar informed the Hunza chief that the decision to disallow the use of Raskam lands by Kanjutis had been arrived at Peking, after mutual discussions between the Tsungli Yamen and the British representative[35], they only made a half-hearted attempt to solve the issue on the basis of the British offer of 14 March 1899. China did not, however, make any official commitment in response to these package proposals, which involved the actual delimitation of the India–China border in this sector, thus precluding any agreed solution.

While Britain and Russia were engaged in resolving the issue both in Peking and London, Scott was labouring hard in St Petersburgh to allay Russian apprehensions. It was only after receiving a written assurance that Britain sought only cultivation (rather than territorial) rights for Hunza in Raskam lands[36] and not along the Taghdumbash Pamir (as suspected by Kuropatkin), that the Russian government agreed to drop its objections to its lease to Hunza. When Giers wrote to the Tsungli Yamen in Peking, informing him about his government's withdrawal of the objections raised earlier, the former gave the green signal to the local authorities in Xinjiang to carry out the lease of five Raskam lands to the people of Hunza.[37] Simultaneously, the Amban of Yarkand wrote separately to the Mir of Hunza informing him that the Tsungli Yamen, in consultation with the British and Russian Ambassadors at Peking, had decided that Hunza did not have any proprietary rights to Taghdumbash and Raskam.[38] It was decided to allot five lands situated on the western side of the Raskam River to Hunza for cultivation, as insufficient grain was produced in the region.[39]

The British Indian authorities counselled the Mir of Hunza to accept the new offer of five land plots, on the conditions set by the Chinese.[40] But Petrovsky was not going to let this happen. He continued to apply pressure on the Taotai of Kashgar by demanding the lease of Sarikol to the Russians. Accordingly, the Tsungli Yamen sent a telegram to the Governor of Xinjiang on 24 December 1899, asking him 'to defer the lease of land to Hunza pending further consultation, in view of Petrovsky's demand of equal (*quid pro quo*) treatment'.[41] Both Giers (Russian foreign minister 1882–95) and Mouraviev (Russian foreign minister

1897–1900) denied before the British ambassadors at Peking and St Petersburgh, respectively, having instructed Petrovsky to stake a counterclaim for compensation in Sarikol.[42] But they did not reprimand their representative at Kashgar for reopening the issue nor assuage China's fear of fresh Russian demands in Sarikol as hinted at by Petrovsky. Instead, Petrovsky's views were openly appreciated as 'reasonable'[43] by Giers in the course of his conversation with MacDonald at Peking.

When MacDonald took up the matter with the Tsungli Yamen on 1 March 1900, urging China to adhere to its earlier agreement on lease of the Raskam lands to Hunza, he was told that 'Russia had not given any assurance as to not making counter-claims'.[44] China feared that any concession to Hunza would be made the basis of territorial claims on China. Finding another chance to defer the lease of the Raskam lands to Hunza cultivators, the Chinese authorities now began to strengthen their position in and around Sarikol. They not only encouraged the settlement of Kyrgyz and other Chinese subjects in Raskam but also terminated any remaining traces of Hunza's foothold in that Valley by expelling the Kanjuti cultivators. When the British Indian government, acting on Curzon's complaint, lodged a protest note to China on 29 May 1901 against this action, demanding the removal of Chinese settlers and the reinstatement of Kanjutis in Raskam[45], it received vague, unsatisfactory and evasive replies from the Tsungli Yamen. Seeing renewed British pressure being applied on China, Russia 'took steps to keep the Raskam pot mildly simmering'[46], thus forestalling any possible settlement of the issue in favour of Hunza. The Russian Ambassador at London Baron Graevenitz addressed a note on 14 January 1903[47] to Lansdowne, protesting against the terms claimed by Satow in his notes from May and November 1901 to the Chinese. Lansdowne's assurance that the proprietary rights claimed by Hunza in Raskam (and supported by Britain) were not political or territorial in character[48], appeared to have answered the Russian purpose more so because the British did not pursue the matter any further.

The roots of Russian reaction to this whole affair lay in their apprehensions about the prospective British penetration into this area in order to outflank the Russian position in the Pamirs.[49] Petrovsky was also worried about the growing British influence over the frontier area of Taghdumbash due to the presence of a British informer, Munshi Sher Mohammad at Tashkurghan. In response, in 1900, the Russians got Mirza Suleiman stationed as their agent at Tashkurghan, with the approval of the Taotai of Kashgar. Soon after, in early 1901, a Russian officer, accompanied by four Cossacks, arrived at Tashkurghan to remain there permanently, ostensibly 'for the supervision of Russian postal service between Kashgar and the Russian Pamirs'.[50] Lord Curzon, the viceroy of India (1899–1905), reacted strongly saying that 'this is the first step to ultimate Russian claim over entire Taghdumbash and Sarikol'[51], and suggested that a remonstrance should be sent to the Russian government. He proposed to post a British officer at Tashkurghan or nearby 'to supervise our postal arrangements'.[52] But both George Hamilton and Lord Lansdowne were not disposed to agree with Curzon, as they believed that Tashkurghan was 'so far removed from our frontier'.[53] Dissatisfied at the home government's passivity about the matter, Curzon sent a dispatch on behalf of the Governor General of India in Council to George Hamilton on 9 May 1901 reiterating the earlier demand that the British government should protest against Russian activity in Taghdumbash and Sarikol.[54] It warned that 'Kashgar and New Dominion (Xinjiang) will sooner or later fall into the hands of Russia, leading to the disappearance of British influence and trade in these regions'.[55] Curzon argued that while the British Indian government 'did not advocate the policy of an advanced British frontier beyond the Hindu Kush', it 'did not wish to sacrifice the undisputed possession of Chinese in Taghdumbash, recognized claim of Kanjutis to share in its revenues, and admitted and as yet unsurrendered rights of Hunza on the Raskam lands', which were 'all pawns in the diplomatic game and may be of use in securing better terms upon this border for ourselves and our allies when the inevitable advance of Russia takes place'.[56] The Secretary of State still did not agree with Curzon that the establishment of a Russian post at Tashkurghan with Chinese consent afforded sufficient ground for remonstrance with Russia.[57]

By June 1904, the strength of Russian troops in Tashkurghan increased to 22.[58] The Anglo-Russian rivalry on the roof of the world took an ugly turn with recurrent sparring and abuses between the British native agent and the Russians over trivial issues. So much so, the local news writer at Sarikol (Munshi Sher Muhammad) was provided by the British with one Webley revolver and 50 cartridges for his safety.[59] However, the Russian post at Tashkurghan wielded considerable influence over the local officials and Begs in Sarikol, thereby weakening the position of the British news writer to a great degree. Since the activities and influence of the British news writer at Sarikol were no match to the enormous increase in the Russian influence, the British Consul at Kashgar withdrew the news writer in 1910 and replaced him with a menial to look after the local postal arrangements.[60] Instead of gratifying the Russians about the 'no forward policy' of the British on this remote frontier, the withdrawal of the news writer actually dealt a blow to British prestige there. Now the British GoI sent a dispatch to Marquis of Crewe, the secretary of state, London, on 7 March 1912 recommending that a representation be made to the Russian government bringing to their notice the proceedings of Russian agents at Sarikol and Kashgar. India Office, London, while agreeing with Hardinge's proposal, wrote to the then British Foreign Secretary E. Grey to ask the British Ambassador at St Petersburgh to intimate the Russian government that 'the British government continue to support the long standing claims of the Mir of Hunza to cultivation rights in Raskam, as well as his claims to a share of the revenues of the Taghdumbash Pamir'.[61]

The Chinese recognition of Hunza claims over Raskam and Taghdumbash Pamirs was important for the British because it could be utilized to their advantage, in the event of any future Russian advance towards Kashgaria. Their fears assumed serious proportions in early 1901 when Russia secured Chinese permission to station a military post at Tashkurghan to checkmate any future British forward move in this area. Such a clash of imperial interests in the Pamirs from two opposite directions was behind the whole Raskam issue, which remained undecided even after the Tsarist and British rules were terminated in Russia and India, respectively. The issue would have been decided in Hunza's favour in 1898 itself but for the Russian pressure for not allowing the lease of Raskam lands to Hunza men until, in 1903, the British disclaimed any political or territorial (in other words sovereign) right for Hunza there—confining the same to cultivation and other proprietary rights.

After 1903, the settlement of the outstanding Raskam issue got relegated to a secondary position because the British attached primary importance to the conclusion of the Anglo-Chinese Convention on Tibet and to securing of a consular status for Macartney so as to bring him at par with his Russian counterpart in Kashgar. Despite their desire to sever all connections of Hunza with China,[62] the British did not abandon the Hunza claim in Raskam and Taghdumbash Pamir. The Politcal Agent at Gilgit Captain B.E.M. Gurdon, who was in favour of severing the relations of the Mir of Hunza with China, proposed in his letter of 19 May 1904 to the Resident in Kashmir E.G. Colvin that the Mir of Hunza be paid an annual compensation of ₹3,000 which was much more than the value of return gifts of about ₹1,000 received by him from China, besides the loss of revenue collected by the Mir at Taghdumbash Pamir.[63] Gurdon also proposed to arrange the settlement of some Hunza families at Gilgit, besides encouraging the poor classes to get employment in Gilgit.[64]

The Kashmir Durbar offered to establish a colony of Hunza people at Matan Das in Gilgit, which was accepted by the Mir of Hunza.[65] Earlier, the British GoI had recommended the severing of the connection between Hunza and China in its dispatch of 24 March 1904 to John Brodrick (the secretary of state, London). The British Indian government endorsed the proposed boundary by Claude MacDonald on 24 March 1899, and stated that since 'the

Chinese have not shown any disagreement with the proposal, we shall henceforth assume Chinese concurrence'.[66] The Secretary of State while agreeing with the view that 'it is desirable to terminate the relations existing between Hunza and China and to secure the line of frontier laid down by MacDonald note'[67], wanted the Indian government to exercise effective control upto the frontier claimed. The British GoI, after getting a report of the ground situation from the Political Agent at Gilgit (Captain Gurdon) and the Resident in Kashmir (E.G. Colvin), sent a detailed dispatch on 26 January 1905 to the Secretary of State, London, stating that the Mir of Hunza maintained for many years a regular post of four men at Darwaz without any objection of the Chinese.[68] The British Indian government proposed the inclusion of Ghorzerab Valley, which lay about 8 miles below the junction of the Shingshal stream with the Mustagh River, as it was important for Shingshalis whose flocks depended for their grazing in the valley between Shingshal (Shimshal) Pass and Darwaz (on the British side of the boundary line).[69] The British Indian government wanted to have a simultaneous settlement of various issues with China: Hunza's relations with China, definition of a frontier line to be formally recognized by China and Macartney's position at Kashgar. In specific terms, the British Indian government proposed that China should sever all connections with Hunza, recognize the appointment of Macartney as British Consul at Kashgar and agree to the inclusion within the British frontier, the small projection (Ghorzerab Valley) in the vicinity of Shingshal Pass and Darwaz, in return for abandoning of all Hunza claims to Raskam and Taghdumbash.[70] The British government, while recognizing the importance of early settlement with China, decided to keep the matter pending till the Anglo-Chinese negotiations on the Tibet Convention were concluded.[71]

On his part, the Mir of Hunza continued to levy annual grain taxes from the Kyrgyzs of Tagdumbash Pamir, with the concurrence of the British Indian government.[72] News reports from Sarikol confirmed that the Mir of Hunza had sent his men in July 1908, August 1913 and August 1914 to collect taxes at Taghdumbash.[73] In 1913, the agent of the Mir of Hunza collected grazing taxes even from three Russian subjects at Taghdumbash, that had been outstanding for few years. This had been facilitated by Captain Babushkin, the Russian officer posted at Tashkurghan.[74] However, in order to regulate the collection of taxes by the Mir of Hunza and to prevent Kara Beg (Mir's agent) from collecting taxes unscrupulously, Babushkin sought details of the quantum of such taxes from Macartney.[75]

The British Political Agent at Gilgit informed Macartney that for the past 30 years the Mir of Hunza was levying tax on all persons grazing their flocks on Taghdumbash Pamir at the rate of one numdah and two *gulach* (four yards long) from each *kirgah* (tent). In case of poor families, a small piece of numdah, a rope or a pair of felt stockings (*paipakh*) was collected.[76] From 1914 onwards, when the Russian influence in Kashgaria was on the decline, Hunza adhered strictly to the practice of deputing its men to cultivate the lands at Raskam and collecting taxes from the Kyrgyzs at Taghdumbash Pamir. The Mir of Hunza sent his men to Raskam in 1914 and also in 1915 to cultivate the fields there. Three maunds of wheat and five and a half maunds of barley (roughly two and a half quintals of grain) were sown in 1915, which was in excess of the area brought under cultivation in 1914.[77] Mir of Hunza's agent (Faizi) collected grazing taxes at Taghdumbash (60 maunds, 30 ropes and 6 *kirpas* [cotton cloth pieces]) in August 1922, which was almost recovered in 1921.[78] In August 1923, 80 maunds, 40 ropes, 10 kirpas and 10 *chogas* (gowns) were collected by the Mir of Hunza as annual grazing tax in Taghdumbash, which was in excess of the taxes collected earlier.[79] Similarly, 12 maunds of grain (more than in 1915) were sown at the Raskam lands in 1923, which yielded 40 maunds of wheat and 8 maunds of barley.[80]

Four men were usually kept by the Mir of Hunza at Raskam permanently to look after the cultivated lands on the west side of the Yarkand River. Twenty more men were sent in spring to assist in the cultivation. The average annual produce of grain was about 50 maunds.[81] However, in September 1923, the Taotai of Kashgar wrote a letter to the Mir of Hunza, asking him to remove his men from Raskam, which he claimed as Chinese territory.[82] The Mir of Hunza in his reply, dated 21 February 1925, reiterated that his men have been cultivating the lands at Raskam 'within Hunza limits'. Referring to the annals of his ancestors, the Mir of Hunza clarified that 'Raskam extending from Bazardarah upwards is included in Hunza territory. And the frontiers of Hunza and China being contiguous there has not been exact delimitation.'[83] Recalling the historical documents, he specified 'the places of Kuktash, Arjai, Bash Andijan, Ui Bulang, Tuqaz Bulaq, Oprang and Uruksu, having been in possession of Hunza at Raskam'.[84] The Mir of Hunza clarified that 'in deference to the wishes of the Chinese, who were being pressurized by the Russians to cede Taghrama, Hunza had suspended cultivation at Raskam for few years. But for the past 10 to 12 years (i.e. from around 1912), Raskam lands were brought under cultivation' with the knowledge of local Chinese officials.[85] Notwithstanding the Chinese objections, the Mir of Hunza's men harvested about 12 maunds of grain at Raskam in 1924, which was considerably lower than in the previous years, due to inclement weather.[86] Both the British Consul General at Kashgar and the Political Agent at Gilgit in their periodical reports sent in 1925, 1926 and 1927 reported the Mir of Hunza's agents collecting annual grazing taxes in Taghdumbash and Dafdar, and also cultivating the Raskam lands, with the consent of the Chinese authorities.[87] They also informed about the Mir of Hunza's representative coming to Kashgar to hand over the customary gift of gold dust to the Taotai and receiving in return the Chinese presents of tea, China ware, country cloth, satin and one silver ingot.[88]

In early 1930s when the Chinese regime in Xinjiang was displaced by the Tungan rebels, leading to chaos and collapse of Chinese authority, the Mir of Hunza toyed with the idea of taking possession of Taghdumbash Pamir and Raskam Valley. The Mir of Hunza sought the opinion of the British Political Agent in

Gilgit, who strongly advised him against this idea.[89] However, he wanted the Mir of Hunza 'to continue to maintain his established rights of grazing and levying taxes in the Taghdumbash and of cultivation in Raskam'.[90] The Mir of Hunza was also advised to send a strong party to do the Raskam sowings, send animals to graze on the Taghdumbash and to send a friendly letter with a small present to the Tungan Governor in Tashkurghan.[91] However, the Mir of Hunza was asked not to send the annual present to Kashgar this time.[92] A piquant situation arose when the Begs of Sarikol petitioned the Mir of Hunza to intervene and assist them against the Kyrgyz heads of the new regime.[93] The Begs pleaded with the Mir of Hunza to send 100 of his men for their protection against Kyrgyz atrocities. The Mir of Hunza was advised not to get involved in Sarikol politics. At the same time, he received a friendly letter from Timur (the new chief of Xinjiang) 'announcing his victory and hoping to continue and strengthen friendship and alliance with the Mir of Hunza'.[94] The Mir of Hunza sent his present of gold dust to Kashgar, as late as in 1935 (that is during the Chinese warlord regime in Xinjiang) which in turn ordered the release of the Mir of Hunza's sheep that had been confiscated during grazing at Sarikol the previous year.[95] All through this period, the British GoI policy remained to encourage the Mir of Hunza to assert his claims on Raskam and take possession of his lands for cultivation[96], till a final settlement of the border between Hunza and China was reached.

The Soviet success in dominating the greater part of Xinjiang and its potential threat to the Indian frontier in and around Gilgit, became a source of anxiety for the British. Olaf K. Caroe, the foreign secretary of India, while contemplating the possible course of action by India, considered the alternatives of:

> [...] (i) demand for frontier delimitation either along the presumptive frontier or upto the limits claimed by the Mir of Hunza, or (ii) to at once challenge Kashgar claim by refusing to permit Mir of Hunza to pay an annual tribute

> or quit rent to Chinese authorities for his grazing and cultivation rights across the presumptive frontier.[97]

Caroe also wanted the Assistant Political Agent at Chilas to be stationed at Baltit either throughout the year or for summer months.[98] The Resident in his reply of 30 July 1935, explained:

> Mir's annual present of gold dust to the Chinese representative at Kashgar is not a tribute appertaining to suzerainty but (i) merely the continuance of an old custom which included the interchange of presents between Hunza and the Chinese, or (ii) a quid pro quo for the right of Mir of Hunza to graze his flocks in the Taghdumbash Pamir and to cultivate in the Raskam valley.[99]

Subsequently Col Lang, the Resident in Kashmir, went to Baltit in August 1935 and discussed the matter with the Mir of Hunza to secure his consent to the British Indian government's proposal to end his relations with China.[100] The British Indian government decided that 'Mir of Hunza should refrain from sending annual present to China in future and abandon all his rights beyond the presumptive border, such as the right to cultivate lands in the Raskam valley and to graze cattle and to collect grazing dues in the Taghdumbash Pamir'.[101] It was also decided to grant the Mir of Hunza 'a jagir, free of assessment, consisting of 312 acres of land in Bagrote nullah in Gilgit Sub-Division, besides increase of 3,000 rupees in his subsidy'.[102] The Mir of Hunza conveyed his agreement to abide by the arrangements sanctioned by the British Indian government.[103] In view of the increased activity of Chinese and Russian troops near the Hunza borders, a post of 50 Gilgit Scouts was established at Darwaz with the approval of the Secretary of State, London.[104] Earlier, a wireless station had been established at Kashgar in November 1934 to facilitate communication with India.[105] In late 1940, a wireless station was also installed at Gilgit.

NEW ALIGNMENTS

The British fully understood the strategic importance of using Hunza's rights over Raskam and Taghdumbash Pamir to their advantage, in the event of any future Russian incursions into Xinjiang. But due to their preoccupation with other issues that were more relevant to their broader imperial interests, they refrained from pressuring China into solving this issue. The British did not pursue the matter of definition of Hunza's border with Xinjiang, as their priority remained to secure consular status for their representative at Kashgar (apart from the ongoing Anglo-Chinese negotiations on Tibet). As a result, the India–China border in Hunza and Ladakh sectors skirting Xinjiang was not demarcated. Finally, the British reached the conclusion that the Mir of Hunza should sever his relations with China, in return for China renouncing its claim over Hunza. The British policy remained to appease China, even if it meant abandoning Kashmir's claims over Shahidulla and keeping the Hunza claims over Raskam and Taghdumbash on the back burner. The British encouraged the Chinese to occupy the 'no man's land' in the Taghdumbash Pamir to forestall the Russians from occupying it.

The early twentieth century witnessed the conclusion of Anglo-Russian Convention relating to Persia, Afghanistan and Tibet in 1907; the fall of Qings in 1911; outbreak of the Chinese revolution; strengthening of Russian/Soviet presence in Xinjiang; and the establishment of regular British Consulate in Kashgar with George Macartney as its first consul. Even during the warlord regimes in Xinjiang, when the warlords would act independently of Peking, Hunza exercised its cultivation rights in Raskam and collected taxes from Taghdumbash Pamir. After the Chinese warlord Sheng Shih-ts'ai broke his alliance with the Soviets and ousted the Soviet military and technical personnel from Xinjiang in 1942, Xinjiang felt the presence of Chiang Kai-Shek's nationalist government. It was in the summer of 1947, when the British were about to leave the Indian subcontinent that

Mohammad Jamal Khan (the Mir of Hunza, 1945–74) dispatched a two-man mission to Kashgar, seeking to restore the traditional relationship with Xinjiang.[106] This activated the interest of the ruling nationalist government, which was unfamiliar with the intricacies of Hunza–Xinjiang linkages, in the restoration of previous connections between China and Hunza. Accordingly, negotiations with the Hunza envoys were initiated in Kashgar. In early 1948, the Hunza envoys and General Zhao Xiguang (nationalist deputy commander-in-chief of the Xinjiang Garrison Force in Southern Xinjiang) signed an agreement to restore the old connections between Hunza and Xinjiang.[107] But due to the ongoing armed conflict between India and Pakistan in Kashmir and occupation of Gilgit (including Hunza) by Pakistan, the events took a different turn, as now all the external relations of Hunza were conducted by Pakistan. With this, the Chinese dream of luring Hunza into China's fold was dashed. Yet, the Chinese General Zhao Xiguang sent his officials secretly to Baltit (capital of Hunza) in February and June 1948 to 'persuade the Mir to join the Chinese Republic'.[108] While the Mir of Hunza was reported to be willing to 'restore ties with China, he rejected the idea of political submission of Hunza to China'.[109] Besides, 'the Mir reiterated his desire for the immediate return of "lost privileges" in the Hunza-Xinjiang border region, including the pastoral and grazing rights'.[110] With the collapse of nationalist rule in China and with General Zhao Xiguang and his Nationalist forces (stationed in Southern Xinjiang) shifting their allegiance to and joining the Chinese communist regime in 1949, and Hunza being occupied by independent Pakistan (which was now responsible for its external relations), this chapter of Hunza–Xinjiang linkages came to a close.

SINO-PAK BOUNDARY AGREEMENT

Post-1949 China continued to evince interest in Hunza, showing parts of its territory within China in its maps.[111] In 1951, a Chinese delegation reportedly visited Hunza and held talks with the Mir of

Hunza and his associates regarding material assistance to improve the local economy.[112] In 1952, Chinese goods including silk, green tea, cloth, transistors and cameras were reportedly sold in Hunza and Nagar at 'throwaway prices'.[113] In August 1957, a team of Chinese officials was sent by Po Yi-Po, chairman of the Chinese Economic Commission, to Pakistan (including Hunza and Gilgit) to find out the economic requirements of the area.[114] In late 1950s, reports came in about Chinese troops entering Hunza border and taking away cattle from there.[115] Concerned over Chinese maps showing the territory of Hunza in China, Pakistan's President Ayub Khan declared in December 1959 that Pakistan would approach China for boundary negotiations. He also ordered the Gilgit Scouts to move along the Hunza–Xinjiang border, which was sealed.[116] Pakistan's Foreign Minister Manzur Qadir disclosed on 15 January 1961 that China had agreed to demarcate its boundary with Pakistan and that negotiations had begun.[117] After Pakistan supported China's admission to the United Nations and declared its support to One China policy, China withdrew its earlier disputed maps in January 1962.[118] On 3 May 1962, both China and Pakistan announced the conclusion of a provisional agreement to conduct negotiations to reach an agreement on the location and alignment of the boundary. After the negotiations, which began on 13 October 1962, Chinese Foreign Minister Chen Yi and Pakistan's Foreign Minister Z.A. Bhutto signed the Sino-Pak Boundary Agreement on 2 March 1963 in Beijing. Both the governments released the new maps of the frontier. While Pakistan recognized Chinese sovereignty over thousands of square kilometers in the Trans-Karakoram areas of Raskam, Shaksgam and Taghdumbash Pamir, it claimed to have gained about 750 sq. miles of territory including the salt mines of Oprang.[119]

The preamble of the Sino-Pak Boundary Agreement states that both China and Pakistan have agreed to formally delimit and demarcate the boundary between 'China's Xinjiang and the contiguous areas, the defence of which is under actual control of Pakistan'. Though Xinjiang's border abutting the Pak-occupied

Hunza, Shigar and Ghanchi districts of Gilgit–Baltistan (west of the Karakoram Pass) is 438 km (272 miles), the rest of the boundary is between the Indian union territory (UT) of Ladakh and China's Xinjiang. Pakistan described itself as the gainer by entering into this agreement, which eliminated the potential source of conflict between the two countries. It laid the foundation of the all-weather friendship and strategic alliance between China and Pakistan, with India being their main target.

According to some Pakistani scholars:

> Pakistan recognized the Chinese sovereignty over hundreds of square kilometers of land in Northern Kashmir and Ladakh. The agreement was a win-win situation for both countries. Pakistan got a large area and China too consolidated its position in Ladakh. By giving the Ladakh area under the Chinese authority, Pakistan withdrew from its previous claim and gave an upper hand to China over India.[120]

Naturally, India lodged a strong protest against the Sino-Pak Boundary Agreement, declaring it as illegal and invalid, as it violated the sovereignty of the Indian State of Jammu and Kashmir. Indian Prime Minister (PM) Jawaharlal Nehru made a statement in the Parliament of India, stating that if one went by these maps, Pakistan had obviously surrendered over 13,000 square miles (34,000 square kilometers) to China. Even though Article 6 of the agreement includes a provision for its renegotiation after the final settlement of the Kashmir dispute between India and Pakistan, it altered the balance of forces in the region in favour of China. That China refused to discuss during the Sino-Indian border talks held in 1960; the alienation of the Ladakh–Xinjiang border west of the Karakoram Pass[121]; and it being under the occupation of Pakistan, points to the pre-meditated design of China on this issue. This was followed by concrete steps in forging the Sino-Pak strategic alliance through the building of the KKH and now the CPEC, which passes through the Pak-occupied territories of Gilgit and Baltistan. Reports have also come in about China having built 'feeder road eastward through the Shaksgam, Raskam and Shimshal Valleys linking Gilgit with Khotan, which is an important military base situated at the cross-section of the Tibet–Xinjiang Highway and Hotan–Golmud Highway'.[122] As such, China shrewdly utilized the historical legacy of Xinjiang–Hunza linkages to its great strategic advantage vis-à-vis India.

Eight

The 'Great Game' and Its Impact

The 'Great Game' was a political and diplomatic contest between the British and Russian empires over Central and South Asia during the nineteenth and early twentieth centuries. While Russia was concerned over the British commercial and political inroads into Central Asia, Britain was fearful of Russian overland advance through Central Asia and the Pamirs up to India. The 'Great Game', a phrase popularized by the British novelist Rudyard Kipling in his novel *Kim*, is about how the two powers played it.

By 1820, both Britain and Russia had emerged as the most powerful states in Eurasia. Exercising control over vast territorial empires in Asia, both these powers were separated from each other by weak and unstable Khanates of Central Asia. So, during the first half of nineteenth century Britain was busy exploring the means to prevent the absorption of the intervening Central Asian Khanates into Russia. It also sought to extend commercial activities in the area. Both these powers viewed Central Asia as a huge market for their manufactured goods and a point of supply for raw materials like cotton, silk and wool. The activities of British officers—like Moorcroft, Burnes, Connolly, Abbott and Shakespeare in Bukhara, Khiva and Kokand—during the first half of the nineteenth century, instead of meeting the desired objective of creating a permanent influence in these Muslim Khanates, only helped in activating the Russian-forward policy towards Central Asia.

Even after the incorporation of the Central Asian Khanates in the Russian empire, the British continued to send experienced officers on reconnaissance and diplomatic missions to this area. In doing so, their modus operandi was not dissimilar to that adopted by Tsarist Russia. Thus, Valiknanov of Russia and Robert Shaw of Britain went as traders to East Turkestan to test its commercial and political climate. Ignatyev and Kuropatkin (of Russia) and Forsyth and Younghusband (of Britain) went on official diplomatic missions. Grombchevsky of Russia met his British counterpart in Younghusband in Hunza. Once Russia had gained total control over West Turkestan, Britain geared up its machinery to carve out a friendly buffer in East Turkestan (Xinjiang).

THE BRITISH EMPIRE'S DESIGN ON CENTRAL ASIA

To put India–Xinjiang trade on a firm footing was the watchword of British policy. Since this trade passed through Kashmir and Ladakh, Kashmir's ruler was coaxed to concede the right to station a British officer in the frontier town of Leh, ostensibly to look after the interests of Central Asian traders but in actuality to monitor the developments across the borders.

Britain's fear of a possible Russian expansion towards Kashgaria led it to follow a policy of appeasement towards the Chinese authorities in Xinjiang. The reports about the overtures made by certain Indian chiefs to Russia, and the psychological impact created by Russian successes in Asia among Indians at large were additional factors determining the British attitude towards Kashmir. The 1873 agreement, by which Britain secured Russian assurance to treat Afghanistan as outside its sphere of influence, could not keep the two-power rivalry in check. Only the centre of rivalry shifted from the Hindu Kush to the Pamirs. Even the Pamir Boundary Agreement of 1895, by which the Pamirs were demarcated and the coterminous spaces between the two empires was eliminated forever, could not end the bitterness between them. The colonial rivalry found expression in the frequent exchange of verbal duals between Petrovsky and Macartney (the representatives of Russia and Britain in Kashgar) on various issues such as the petty property disputes of Ladakhi,

Andijani and Kashgari traders, nationality cases of these traders, Hunza claim on Raskam lands, etc.

The Anglo-Russian contest then shifted to the borders of Kashmir (skirting Xinjiang) and its effect was felt in the remote but strategically located Tashkurghan and Raskam lands. It is this two-power conflict of political and commercial interests in the vast expanse of Central Asia that had a direct bearing on Kashmir. In such a competition on the international chess-board of Central Asia, Britain used Kashmir not only as a listening post to monitor Russian activities (beyond the Hindu Kush and Karakoram ranges) but also as a base to secure control right up to the south of Hindu Kush. This implied a greater degree of control over the state of Jammu and Kashmir by the British. This objective was achieved in 1885 by appointing a full-fledged Resident in Kashmir.

It was Moorcroft who sowed the seeds of a future British policy towards Central Asia. During his mission to Bukhara (1819–25), Moorcroft threw open the internal political and economic conditions prevailing in the Central Asian Khanates to the British Indian authorities. He indulged in such political activities such as the reconnaissance of the territories then unknown to the British; establishment of friendly ties with the chiefs of Ladakh and Bukhara; and communication of up-to-date intelligence concerning the territories traversed by him in the context of the apprehended Russian advance towards Central Asia and Kashmir. When Moorcroft reached Lahore in May 1820, he entered into friendly negotiations with Maharaja Ranjit Singh and secured his permission to go to Ladakh through Mandi and Kullu.[1] He also obtained the freedom to travel through Kashmir in case he could not proceed to Bukhara via the Leh–Yarkand route.

Soon after his arrival at Leh in September 1820, Moorcroft tried in vain to obtain the permission of Yarkand authorities to pass through that city en route Kokand and Bukhara.[2] He had to extend his stay at Leh for two years. He made full use of his presence in Ladakh to negotiate with the Ladakhi authorities an agreement to secure for the British 'liberty to trade with Ladakh and through it to other countries, moderate duties and a permanent factory at Leh'.[3] He succeeded in concluding a treaty with Ladakh that, in his own words, was 'calculated to throw open to the enterprise of the British merchants and through them to the manufactures of Great Britain the whole of Central Asia from China to the Caspian Sea'.[4] Alarmed by the dispatch of a Russian mission to Ladakh under Agha Mehdi, Moorcroft became alive to the need of extending British influence over Ladakh, which would prove a 'strong outwork'[5] against the Russian expansion on the north, besides being the centre of trade between Central Asia and India.

The year 1830 marked the beginning of the British-forward policy in Central Asia. Though the British did not anticipate any direct invasion of India by Russia, yet the Russian presence in Central Asia was thought to provoke unrest in India and also compelled Britain to adopt expensive military postures to preserve security and provide defence. This alleged Russian threat to India was also viewed to operate as a check upon the free course of British policy in Europe. To prevent any such possibility, the British government began to think in terms of extending its political influence over Central Asian Khanates by means of commerce. To this end, the possession of direct control over the Indus and Punjab was a must.

Burnes travelled to Sind and Punjab in 1830s to probe the navigational possibilities of the river Indus and also study its possible role in the future commercial intercourse with Central Asia. The importance of Indus as an easy route for transporting British goods into Central Asia (via Kabul) came into sharp focus. The British wanted to send their materials (and not men) to Central Asia in the first instance.

This policy was clearly spelt out by the Secret Committee of the Court of Directors in its dispatch dated 12 January 1830 addressed to Lord Bentinck. The secret committee stressed the need for obtaining 'every possible information regarding countries situated between Caspian Sea and the Indus'.[6] The committee was not worried so much by the actual Russian invasion of India as by the moral effect likely to be produced among the British subjects in India and 'the financial embarrassments due to necessity of military preparations'.[7] Bentinck was, thus, prompted to dispatch Burnes and Connolly to Sind, Punjab and Central Asia with the double object of gathering all possible information about these unknown tracts and to explore the possibility of opening the Indus for navigation.

By underlining the advantages of Indus for promoting trade between India and Central Asia, both Burnes and Connolly prepared the ground for future British policy towards Sind and Punjab. The signing of a commercial treaty with Ranjit Singh, and a convention with the Amirs of Sind to open the river Indus to British commerce were preliminary steps towards future British activity in Central Asia.

The need to safeguard British interests in Kashmir, Ladakh and adjoining territories was highlighted both by Moorcroft and Burnes. While Moorcroft wanted Ladakh to be placed directly under the British, Burnes desired his government to forestall the Russians by helping the divided Uzbeks to form 'one grand confederacy which would be an effectual barrier to the progress of Russian and Persian ambitions'[8] in Central Asia. In the development of commercial intercourse between Russia and Kokand Khanate, Burnes saw the possibility of extension of Russian commerce and political influence to Xinjiang and from there to Kashmir and Ladakh.[9] By pointing out the easy means of communication available between Kokand and Russia on the one hand, and Kashgar, Yarkand and Ladakh on the other, Burnes only hinted at the possible direction of Russian threat.[10]

During the second quarter of the nineteenth century, the main thrust of British policy was to carve a useful influence in the Central Asian Khanates to thwart the Russians present there. Despite the geographical barriers, the British went ahead with dispatching experienced officers to the Muslim Khanates to forge friendly ties with them. During 1840, several officers like Abbott, Shakespeare and Connolly operated in Khiva. From there

Connolly extended his operations to Kokand, from where he went to the court of Amir Nasrullah at Bukhara (in a bid to persuade him to rise against Russia). But the despotic ruler of Bukhara made both Stoddart and Connolly suffer inhuman torture. The British debacles in Afghanistan also acted as a factor in influencing Nasrullah's decision to execute these British officers. Thus, British efforts to establish friendly rapport with the Central Asian rulers, and the dream of creating a confederacy of Central Asian Khanates as a buffer against Russian expansion, met a crushing blow. Not only that, the fate of Stoddart and Connolly proved to be a big deterrent to the dispatch of British officers to Central Asia for a long time to come.

The British policy towards the Muslim Khanates in Central Asia was put to a critical test when the rulers of Kokand and Bukhara sought British assistance in repelling the forward thrust of Russia. In the eyes of Central Asian rulers, the British authorities in India were powerful enough to thwart the Russian designs on their Khanates. So, fearful of the Russian advance and desirous of securing their realms, these rulers made several attempts to establish cordial relations with the British in India. Kokand was the first Khanate to make such overtures, soon after it lost Ak Musjid to Russia. It was in 1854 that the Khan of Kokand dispatched an envoy to Punjab to meet the British authorities to seek the services of some European officers who could drill troops in that Khanate, thus making them capable of withstanding any future Russian aggression.[11]

Since the tragic fate of Connolly and Stoddart still loomed large over the British official mind, H.B. Edwardes (superintendent and commissioner of the Peshawar Division) thought it would be advisable to lend native drill instructors drawn from the cavalry of the Sind Corps and Gorkha Infantry regiments rather than any British military officers to Kokand.[12] John Lawrence, the chief commissioner of Punjab, took a more cautious view and proposed to dismiss the Kokand envoy with just a 'friendly letter for the King of Kokand' and 'a moderate sum' besides allowing him to 'enlist a given number of native officers,' who would volunteer themselves for their own safety.[13] But Lord Dalhousie, the then governor general of India, attached great importance to this event, as it provided reliable intelligence about the Russian activity in Central Asia.[14] He instructed the Punjab government to assist the Kokand envoy in obtaining the services of native officers who would like to volunteer for service in Kokand.[15] Since the British rulers of India were not prepared to allow themselves to be militarily involved in Central Asian affairs, the Kokand mission to India failed in its object. It could neither secure the services of British officers[16], nor did any of the native officers from Punjab volunteer to go to such a distant place. The British Indian government limited its role only to provide utmost hospitality to the Kokand envoy and gifted arms for use of the Kokand army, against any possible Russian aggression.[17]

The year 1866 saw the arrival of an envoy from the Amir of Bukhara in India, Khoja Mahomed Parsa, who was the Chief Mufti in Bukhara. Apart from bringing along with him friendly letters and presents (both for the Queen of England and the Viceroy of India)[18], the Bukharan envoy sought British support against Russia which had placed a Bukharan agent in captivity. Though this mission was well received, the Viceroy while regretting Russian proceedings against Bukhara expressed his inability to render 'any effective aid either by advice or in any other form'.[19] A few years later, in 1872 when the ruler of Bukhara expressed his desire to have an accredited British agent resident there, the British Indian government spurned the offer considering the 'interests of British subjects at Bukhara not of sufficient importance' as to warrant representation through an accredited agent.[20]

Obviously, the British did not want to incur any trouble for themselves by getting involved in any military conflict between the Central Asian Khanates and Tsarist Russia. They did their best to stall the Russian advance towards Central Asia, employing all the means at their disposal, short of a direct military involvement, in any conflict between the Central Asian Khanates and Tsarist

Russia. Sensing the danger to the lives of English officers in the Khanates ruled by barbaric despots, the British put into service the native Indian agents. They feigned friendliness with these Central Asian rulers, but when asked to render military aid in times of distress did not even lend the services of military officers. In doing so, their gestures were quite similar to the Russian response to overtures of friendship from certain Indian princes. The circumstances of Russian advance in Central Asia were fully utilized for consolidating British control over Kashmir and its frontier tributaries and for extending it up to the Hindu Kush. Unsuccessful in extending their influence beyond the Hindu Kush watershed, the British directed their energies to Xinjiang across the Karakoram and Kuen Lun ranges.

POSTING OF BRITISH OFFICERS IN KASHMIR AND LADAKH

Soon after handing over Kashmir to Gulab Singh in 1846, the British started meddling in the state administration. Despite Gulab Singh's protests, a British OSD was installed in Kashmir during the summer seasons to supervise the conduct of European visitors to the Valley.[21] From 1852 onwards, the practice of deputing a British officer to reside in Srinagar during the summer season continued uninterrupted. Later, soon after the death of Ranbir Singh, he was replaced by a full-fledged British Resident in the state. Since the activities of the OSD were confined to Kashmir only (and that too for six months), he had no apparent role to play in the internal administration of the state. But officers like Girdlestone, Wynne and Henvey—who were astute observers—used to file important reports on the political and economic situation in Kashmir to their government. In view of the stubborn resistance put up by Ranbir Singh, at attempts to erode his authority within his jurisdiction, the British government resorted to a process of gradual but cautious interference in Kashmir. In view of the changing imperial priorities vis-à-vis the Russian advance in Central Asia, the British sought to impose their effective control over the internal and external affairs of the state by appointing experienced officers in the frontier outposts of Ladakh, Gilgit, Chitral, etc., to monitor the developments in Central Asia.

It was William Moorcroft who had, as early as in 1820s, advocated the British takeover of Ladakh to exercise a dominating influence over the commerce and politics of East Turkestan and other Central Asian Khanates. But the British preoccupation with the affairs in Sind, Afghanistan and Punjab had practically put Moorcroft's proposals into cold storage. The importance of Kashmir for the extension of the British Indian influence over Central Asia came to the fore in 1847, when the British officers sent to demarcate the boundaries between the territories of Jammu and Kashmir and Xinjiang witnessed the multinational trading operations in Ladakh. The British policy towards Kashmir was first directed at breaking the monopoly of this state over the import of shawl wool from Tibet and Xinjiang, so as to let the British Indian territory in Koonawar and Blusher benefit from this position of being an established emporium of trade between India and Central Asia. Then, the political pressure on Gulab Singh began to be built up to reduce customs duties levied on this trade. Certain Yarkandi merchants who travelled from Leh to Shimla in 1848 to place before the Superintendent of Hill States their complaints of undue exactions by Basti Ram (Gulab Singh's officer in Ladakh) turned out to be the wilful instrument of the British in browbeating Kashmir's ruler. A perusal of the papers relating to the arrival of these Yarkandi traders in Shimla reveals that they were encouraged by Strachey at Leh to petition the British Indian government, seeking protection through the appointment of a British officer in Ladakh. On the basis of these complaints, Edwardes made a strong plea for the posting of a British officer at Ladakh to 'protect our commercial interests'.[22] The Punjab government, which was directed to take up the matter with the Kashmir ruler 'in courteous but very decided language'[23], accordingly sought the dismissal of Basti Ram from state services.[24]

The developments in this affair—which involved the summoning of Basti Ram to Lahore in early 1850 for cross-examination, followed by a personal visit to Ladakh by Henry M. Lawrence (president, Board of Administration, Punjab) to examine the extent of trading operations there and also the stand taken by Dalhousie—point to the way the British humiliated Gulab Singh's administration just to appease the Central Asian traders, with a view to bolstering their image across the Karakoram mountains. Dalhousie did not agree with Lawrence who, during his on-the-spot enquiry, had come to the conclusion that the cause for diminishing Indo-Central Asian trade lay in 'the difficulties of the route and competition from the Russian market more than the imposts on the road'.[25] The Russian advance towards Kokand, the details of which were personally conveyed by an envoy from that Khanate to the British Indian authorities in 1854, gave another dimension to the British attitude towards Kashmir. While Dalhousie was convinced that any invasion of India from that side was next to impossible, at the same time, he thought that the extension of Russian influence into the Central Asian Khanates would be 'infinite evil to the British Power in the east'.[26]

The enthusiasm of British officers like Davies and T.D. Forsyth proved to be of vital importance in the formulation of an active policy towards Jammu and Kashmir. By stressing its importance for the development of Indian trade with Central Asia, both these officers urged their government to build-up pressure on Kashmir's ruler to get customs duties on foreign trade reduced. The first important breakthrough in this direction was achieved in 1864 when Robert Montgomery, lieutenant governor of Punjab, acting on the basis of Davies' proposals, made Ranbir Singh agree to limit transit duties on goods bound for Central Asia to 5 per cent ad valorem. Forsyth described this reduction of duties as 'little more than a sham' and pleaded for the posting of a British Agent at Leh 'to protect the interests of British merchants'.[27]

Finally, in early 1867 a unilateral decision to appoint Dr Cayley as the British officer at Ladakh was taken in utter disregard of the wishes of Ranbir Singh. The duties assigned to this officer in 1864 were ostensibly to maintain the tariff fixed by the Maharaja of Kashmir, but it was actually to enquire 'into the state of trade between India and Central Asia' and to 'collect and sift political information regarding the progress of events in Chinese Turkestan'.[28] While conveying its sanction to the deputation of a British officer to Ladakh every season, the Secretary of State made it clear to the British GoI that the said officer would 'abstain from any pre-emptory acts and dictatorial language calculated to give offence to the Maharaja'.[29] Both the then Governor General of India and the home government were of the opinion that there should be no undue interference in the internal affairs of the Maharaja. Naturally, such an arrangement was bound to be irksome and inconvenient to the Maharaja, since the arrival of a British officer at Ladakh and his direct dealings (with Indian and Central Asian traders) meant a sharp erosion of the authority and prestige wielded by him—both inside the Ladakh territory and in the neighbouring Xinjiang and Central Asian Khanates. The Maharaja now came up with a reasonable proposal to remove all duties hitherto levied on merchandise conveyed by traders to and from British India (via Ladakh), and also allowed the British OSD in Kashmir to visit Ladakh for a month to see if the traders had any grounds for complaint.[30] In return for these concessions, Ranbir Singh requested the British Indian government that the appointment of the British officer to Ladakh should not be renewed next year.[31] Though the Governor General was inclined to accept Ranbir Singh's proposal, his hand was forced by the Punjab government, which pressed to continue this arrangement. Lawrence wrote to the home government that the arrangement should be reviewed periodically.[32] At Leh, Cayley proved himself quite indispensable to the British government by making startling disclosures about the frequent exchange of envoys between the Kashmir Durbar and Yakub Beg. His reports about the commercial intercourse with Central Asia (via Ladakh) were extensive and authentic. His presence in Leh proved to be extremely useful for monitoring the developments in Central Asia, particularly the state of affairs in Kokand, Kashgaria and the diplomatic exchanges between Russia and Yakub Beg.

The importance of Ladakh as a frontier listening outpost to track Russian movements in the adjacent regions of Khanates of Kokand and East Turkestan was fully realized by Lord Mayo. What was originally intended by Lawrence to be a seasonal and temporary measure was thus turned into a permanent Leh Agency by his successor. By virtue of a treaty concluded with Ranbir Singh in April 1870, the British government bound Kashmir's ruler to treat the suitable trade route as a 'free highway in perpetuity and at all times for all travelers and traders', and to the appointment of two joint commissioners (one each for supervising the trade route and settling disputes).[33] Thus came into existence British Agency in Ladakh represented by the British Joint Commissioner at Leh. The opposite stance taken by Lawrence and his successor Mayo with respect to the British policy towards Kashmir vis-à-vis Central Asia, leads us to believe that Lawrence sought to maintain the friendly alliance with Kashmir's ruler by giving him the least cause for offence. He did not want to run the risk of political complications for the sake of cumbersome trade relations with Central Asia. On the other hand, Mayo set upon himself the task of promoting even such a modest connection to gain political influence over Xinjiang in a bid to outwit Russia. The reported hostilities between the Russians and Yakub Beg's men at the Russo-Kashgar frontier on the Naryn River[34] further alerted Mayo to the possibility of a Russian threat to Kashgaria. His main concern remained extending the British influence in Xinjiang, which was easily accessible from Ladakh.

However, so far as the immediate results of British Agency at

Leh are concerned, it did help in promoting the development of Indo-Central Asian trade. This resulted in the overall prosperity of both the Kashmiri and Punjabi traders. But the agency played a vital role in eroding the influence of Kashmir's ruler, not only over the Central Asian trading and official class but even over his subjects in Ladakh. Henceforth, the frequent bilateral exchanges between the rulers of Kashgaria and Kashmir could not be kept secret from the ever-vigilant British Officer. By directing the Kashgarian missions to Punjab, the British Officer helped in the establishment of direct political intercourse between the British Indian government and Yakub Beg. He played a vital role in monitoring the developments across the Karakoram mountains.

PERMANENT BRITISH RESIDENCY IN KASHMIR

Even though their officers had started functioning out of Srinagar and Leh from 1852 and 1867, respectively, the British were anxious to widen the limited spheres of activity of these officers. Every action of Mayo and his successors was directed at further tightening the British control over Kashmir. Their policy towards this northernmost area had ceased to be 'one of avowed conciliation and scrupulous forbearance'[35], as it had been under Lawrence. The very idea of a British officer staying in Kashmir for the summer months only, and that too functioning under a local government in Punjab, was ill-suited to the ambitious British policy in Central Asia. The first step towards improving the position of the British OSD in Kashmir was taken in 1871, when the Punjab government's control over this appointment was withdrawn and vested directly in the foreign department. This time, neither the Maharaja was taken into confidence nor was an official communication made to him announcing such a significant change. The revised copy of rules, governing the visit of Europeans to Kashmir, that was sent routinely to the Kashmir Durbar in 1872 did not get noticed there until after Robert Shaw was found to be staying in Srinagar during the winter of 1875–

76.[36] When Kashmir's ruler brought the matter to the notice of the imperial government, he was simply informed about the revised arrangements made in 1872.

The reports about Russian overtures to Kashmir's ruler, as communicated by the Maharaja himself, came in handy to the British for forcing a permanent British Resident upon Kashmir. This was despite their opinion that the 'reported correspondence of Kashmir with Russia is prima facie improbable'.[37] Even in anticipation of the required approval from the home government, Northbrook (governor general of India, 1872–76) decided to have a permanent British Resident in Kashmir. In a bid to implement his scheme, he informed the Punjab government that H.L. Wynee (then OSD at Kashmir) and R. Shaw (then Joint Commissioner at Leh) should remain at their respective posts for the whole year[38], instead of the usual six months. However, the said British Officer in Kashmir was to continue the political relations of the British GoI with the Kashmir ruler through the Punjab administration.[39] It was only due to the serious differences of opinion in the India Office, London, which refused to approve Northbrook's proposals, that the question of appointing a permanent British Resident in Kashmir was deferred.[40] On closer examination of Northbrook's stand on this issue, it becomes apparent that despite the Secretary of State's clear-cut directive that London did not want to 'interfere with any temporary arrangements already communicated to Maharaja'[41], the Lt Governor of Punjab, R.H. Davies, was allowed to go ahead with the plans to persuade the Maharaja to accept the new arrangements.[42] The stiff stand taken by the British Indian authorities forced the Maharaja to offer an alternative, which provided for the stay of the British joint commissioner at Leh for the full year and the OSD in Kashmir for eight months.[43] He was, however, firm in his opposition to the appointment of a British Resident in Kashmir and to the proposed alteration of his system of communication with the Punjab government through his agent (Moutemad).[44] These concessions were sufficient for the present for Northbrook, who had already received London's disapproval to any alteration in the existing arrangements.

However, the British could not establish total paramountcy over the state as long as Ranbir Singh was there on the scene. During his lifetime, Ranbir Singh treated the OSD simply as a police magistrate to keep order among the European visitors in Kashmir. But Ranbir Singh's protracted illness came in handy for the British to revive the move to replace the OSD by a full-fledged Resident with powers to supervise the state government. This time, Oliver St John[45] happened to be in charge. Lord Ripon (viceroy of India, 1880–84) was also in favour of taking a more decisive course of action, to bring the state at par with other feudatories of the British in India. But he wished to postpone his operations till a suitable moment after Ranbir Singh's death with which 'certain obligations and unwritten bonds would pass away'.[46]

London now felt that circumstances had greatly changed since 1873 when a similar request from Northbrook had been turned down.[47] Considering this measure 'not only desirable but necessary'[48], the home government in 1884 authorized Ripon to have a Resident appointed in the state at any time after the death of Ranbir Singh. After his death on 12 September 1885, while the state was still in mourning, the British Indian government appointed St John as the first Resident in Kashmir. St John's successor Plowden used his authority to the extreme, getting certain British officers appointed to vital posts in the state. Plowden's successor Nisbet saw to it that full powers of the state government were vested in a council, which was to work under the umbrella of the Resident. This was an important step towards implementing active British policy along the northern frontier, which included the re-establishment of the Gilgit Agency. Now such projects as the construction of Jhelum Valley cart road, Jammu–Sialkot railway and military road connecting Gilgit with Srinagar were taken up expeditiously (under direct instructions from the British Resident in Kashmir). Similarly, by placing the state army under seasoned English officers, the efficacy of the newly created Imperial Service Corps and the Gilgit Force for defending the turbulent frontiers was much improved.

Nine

Extending British Control

The Anglo-Russian agreement of 1873, whereby the British and Russian spheres of influence over Central Asia and Afghanistan were mutually agreed upon, instead of ushering in a new era of cordial relations between the two rival powers, added new dimensions to the Great Game. While this agreement in effect gave the two sides freedom and a sort of legitimacy to their advance within their respective zones[1], it also brought to surface the new problem of the actual delimitation of Afghan, Chinese and Russian frontiers in the upper Oxus region of the Pamirs. British attention to the complexity of this question was drawn by officers like Gordon, Trotter and Biddulph who explored the Wakhan and Pamirs in 1874. They discovered that the Afghan territory in the eastern extremity lay on both sides of the river Oxus, which, under the 1873 agreement, was declared to be the dividing line between Afghanistan and Russia. This discovery disputed the very foundation of this accord. On examination of the Hindu Kush passes, the British explorers found them easy to cross. This made India vulnerable to attack from across the Hindu Kush. Both these discoveries were important from a strategic point of view, and the British modified their frontier policy accordingly.

THE BRITISH STRATEGY AGAINST THE RUSSIANS

It was Lord Mayo (governor general of India, 1869–72) who initiated a process of enforcing British influence over all the external diplomatic proceedings of the Kashmir ruler. In 1874–75, the British Indian government received valuable survey reports on Wakhan, Pamirs and Sarikol from Col Gordon, Biddulph and Trotter who had been purposefully sent to Kashgar in the company of Forsyth's second mission of 1873. Gordon's disclosures about the existence of a practicable road from the Russian military post of Osh, across the Alai to Sarikol brought into sharp focus the strategic importance of this area. When Gordon pointed to the vulnerability of India from the direction of Wakhan (via Ishkoman and Baroghil Passes), the need to strengthen the British position in the tribal territories of Gilgit, Yasin and Chitral assumed importance. The discoveries made by Biddulph during his exploration in the Wakhan area during 1874 and at the passes lying south of the Hindu Kush during 1876 only reinforced Gordon's viewpoint. By 1876, the British Indian government appeared to be convinced about the necessity of extending Kashmir's control over Chitral and Yasin, right up to the south of Ishkoman and Baroghil passes. The incorporation of Kokand into Russian territory, which pushed the Russian frontier beyond Osh, only helped in catalysing British counter moves in Dardistan and Kashmir. The deputation of Biddulph in 1876 to survey the Hindu Kush, followed by the establishment of a British Agency in Gilgit under the same officer in 1877, reflected the new British strategy to meet the challenge posed by the Russian approach to the Pamirs.

C.M. Mac Gregor, the quarter master general of Indian army, (1880–85) also contributed a lot to mould British policy in the cast of Russophobia. In his book *Defence of India,* which was published in 1884, Mac Gregor openly aired his anti-Russian sentiments and recommended several measures to achieve the fragmentation of the Russian empire. He apprehended a Russian attack on India from the direction of Kabul, Herat, Chitral and Gilgit. Mac Gregor wanted the British government to: play the game of diplomacy with Russia; destroy Russian trade; form a coalition with Austria, Germany and Turkey; dispatch commissions for demarcation of northern and north-western frontiers of Afghanistan; transfer Herat province to the British; transfer to the British the regions of

Wakhan, Chitral and Yasin; attract Persia to the British side; come closer to China; improve the means of acquiring information about Russian movements; dispatch emissaries for instigating disorder in the Khanates of Central Asia and among the Turkmens; and to fragment the Russian empire.[2] When his book, though a classified publication, fell into the hands of the Russian Military Attaché at the Russian Embassy in London a serious view was taken of the British plans to fragment the Russian empire.[3] Mac Gregor's proposals aroused Russian suspicions about British intentions and became a subject of diplomatic exchanges between the Russian and British governments.[4]

In 1885–86, Ney Elias was deputed by the British Indian government to reconnoitre the frontier areas of Xinjiang, Wakhan, Badakhshan and the Oxus headwaters. On his return, Elias came up with startling information. He pointed out that the two extreme ends of the Afghan and the Chinese frontier in the Pamirs could be stretched and joined together to form a neutral buffer, thus preventing any direct contact between India and Russia in the Hindu Kush and Dardistan regions. Elias's discovery later became 'a cardinal feature of British policy towards the Pamirs'.[5] It also led the British to induce China to extend its control over Pamirs and the Trans-Karakoram area including Shahidulla against the wishes and interests of the Kashmir government. The Wakhan corridor stands there even today as a testimony to Elias's stratagem. The British forward policy in the area lying south of the Hindu Kush was also activated due to reports of direct dealings between Safdar Ali and the Russian Officer, Grombchevsky.

F.E. Younghusband was deputed in June 1890 to the Pamirs to see as to 'where the Afghan and Chinese boundaries should be made to meet'.[6] Younghusband did succeed in persuading the Chinese authorities in Xinjiang to send a force to occupy Somatash, but he found himself outmanoeuvred by the Russians. They had already occupied Somatash, thanks to the ground work done by the Russian Consul in Kashghar with the Chinese Taotai there. A timely hint from the Taotai had enabled Petrovsky to forewarn Grombchevsky, the Russian frontier officer at Marghilan, about British ambitions. In fact, Younghusband's mission to Xinjiang activated the Tsarist government, which had followed a policy of 'wait and see' towards the Pamirs until then. This mission resulted in the visit of the Governor General of Turkestan A. Vrevsky, to the Alai Pamirs.[7] When Younghusband was making a return journey to India (via the Pamirs) in August 1891, he was forcibly expelled by a party of Russian Cossacks (led by Colonel Ivanov) near Bozai Gumbaz (which was declared to be within Russian territory). This fresh development sparked off a crisis in the Anglo-Russian relations and conflict was averted with the Russians adopting a low profile. But this incident made the British occupation of the Dardic territory below the Hindu Kush an urgent necessity.

By now the strategic importance of the Pamirs had become clear to both the British and the Russians. Pamirs was the meeting point of Kashmir's frontiers in Gilgit, Hunza and Chitral; the Afghan provinces of Badakhshan and Wakhan; the Russian territory of Kokand; and the Sarikol area of Xinjiang. It was a potential gateway to India. The British strategy was geared towards the task of creating a barrier between Russian and British empires on the Pamirs, simultaneously extending their effective control over the frontier areas in Gilgit, Hunza, Chitral and Yasin through the Maharaja of Kashmir. Several factors contributed to the shifting of British interest to Kashmir's frontiers, which, from late 1870s, became the focal point of the Great Game. First, by occupying Kokand, Russia had acquired a legitimate claim over the Pamirs, which were the summer pastures of Kyrgyz subjects (of the erstwhile Khanate of Kokand). Second, Xinjiang now came within the effective range of Russia from their newly acquired territory in Kokand. As the Chinese authority in Xinjiang was weak at that time, the British feared that the Russians would occupy Xinjiang. This could prove to be an important supply base in the event of any further Russian attack on India via the Kashgar–Karakoram–Ladakh route. Third, the reports of Gordon,

Trotter and Biddulph had underlined the strategic importance of the Hindu Kush passes, which were now considered to be easily accessible. This made India vulnerable to any outside attack from across the Hindu Kush and the Pamirs. Fourth, neither the Chinese nor Afghans possessed any effective control over the Pamirs, leaving the area open for Russian penetration. Last, reports of Russian officers having explored the Pamirs and the Hindu Kush region further strengthened British apprehensions.

THE BRITISH TAKE DIRECT ACTION

Confronted with strategic considerations, the British encouraged the Maharaja of Kashmir to bring the warlike and recalcitrant Dardic tribal chiefs (inhabiting the obscure mountainous valleys of the Hindu Kush and Karakoram) under his effective control. The Maharaja was given the freedom to choose any means from conciliation to military expeditions, or both and was provided the necessary arms and ammunition too. However, soon it was found that the Maharaja could not check Dardistan from drifting into a state of turmoil and instability. This fluid situation was the result of frequent internecine wars between the tribal chiefs and also due to their occasional attacks on Kashmir's troops. This often resulted in the lapse of Kashmir's control over these frontier dependencies. The wavering loyalty of the Muslim frontier chiefs towards the Hindu ruler of Kashmir (and through him, towards British India); the exalted image of Tsarist Russia in this region; the display of active Russian interest in this frontier belt; and the open defiance of British power by Safdar Ali, who claimed both Russian and Chinese support, forced the British to resort to direct action. The idea behind several military expeditions carried out jointly by Kashmir's forces and the British officers against Hunza, Nagar, Chitral and Yasin was to put the defence of north and north-western frontiers on a firm footing. By 1891, both Hunza and Nagar were brought under the effective control of Kashmir using military force.

Punial, which was administered by the Gilgit Wazarat of Kashmir's government, came under the control of the Gilgit Agency in 1893, though it continued to be under the suzerainty of Kashmir. Chilas was made into a sub-division of the Gilgit Agency and was placed under the control of the assistant political agent. The agent's control extended to the neighbouring territories of Darel and Tangir as well. Thor Valley was incorporated in Chilas in 1893. In 1905, Ghizar was incorporated with Kuh and Yasin. In 1911, Yasin, Kuh–Ghizar and Ishkoman were placed under separate governors, and their salaries were paid by the Kashmir Durbar. There was an advanced military post in Kuh–Ghizar, which was the corridor leading up to Chitral and onwards to Afghanistan and Central Asia. Once these unruly tribes were coerced into subjugation to Kashmir, a strong military garrison was established at Gilgit. This made Gilgit the nucleus of the whole defence arrangements. Then, the construction of the Jhelum Valley cart road, the Jammu–Sialkot railway and the road connecting Gilgit with Srinagar was expedited under the direct instructions of the British Resident in Kashmir.

The Jammu and Kashmir State Forces were reorganized into a newly created Kashmir Imperial Service Corps and Gilgit Scouts, who were raised from among the local tribes and placed under the command of British officers. In doing so, firstly, the British channelled the loyalty and energies of the warlike and turbulent Dardic tribals to suit British interests, and they became an inalienable part of the defence of the north-western frontier. Secondly, this reduced the actual expenditure of the British Indian government, which had already been spending lakhs of rupees for maintaining a garrison at Gilgit. However, this meant the erosion of the authority of Kashmir's Maharaja over his frontier dependencies.

British diplomacy achieved the objective of creating a buffer between the British and Russian empires in the Pamirs by concluding the Pamirs Boundary Agreement in 1895. Although the Great Game appeared to be over now, the focus of the two-power rivalry shifted to Sarikol and Taghdumbash Pamirs, where Chinese possessions in Xinjiang and the British Indian territory of Hunza converged. Russian interest in this area emanated from their fears about the possibility of the British extending their control over the Taghdumbash Pamirs, where Chinese authority was nominal. The British and Russian official representatives kept themselves engaged in a war of nerves, each trying to outwit the other to have closer access to the Chinese authorities in Xinjiang. The British support for certain Hunza claims on Raskam lands and Taghdumbash Pamirs attracted a strong Russian reaction. On their part, the British considered the establishment of a Russian post in Tashkurghan, with the consent of the Chinese, as a new move to threaten Hunza and Gilgit (and from there to threaten Kashmir and India).

STATIONING A BRITISH AGENT IN GILGIT IN 1877

The importance of Gilgit as a convenient base for extending British influence over the territories lying south of the Hindu Kush, had now been fully realized. According to G.J. Alder, Gilgit was a 'natural choice' being situated at the 'hub of routes leading off to all parts of Dardistan'.[8] Though Xinjiang continued to be regarded as a rich supply base to support any Russian force coming from its western flanks, the defence of the Hindu Kush watershed was of immediate concern to the British. Following the advice of his predecessor, Lord Northbrook, Lord Lytton formulated his proposals about the future course of action to be taken in this frontier belt. He finally conveyed this to Ranbir Singh personally at Madhopore on 17 and 18 November 1876. Lytton impressed upon Kashmir's ruler the need to strengthen Indian frontiers by assuming control over the territory that lay between the Hindu Kush and Kashmir's frontiers. This had to be done in order to secure command over such passes that were thought to be practicable for the passage of Russian forces.[9] To the British, it was of vital importance that the states like Chitral and Yasin 'should come under the control of a friend and ally, like the Maharaja of Kashmir, 'rather than be absorbed by powers inimical to Kashmir'.[10] While encouraging Ranbir Singh to obtain 'an effective but peaceful control over the countries lying between those passes and Kashmir frontier namely Chitral, Mastuj, Yasin and their dependencies',[11] the British also secured the right to station an Agent at Gilgit 'to collect information regarding the frontier and the progress of events beyond it'.[12] Kashmir's ruler relented to this measure only after obtaining written assurance from Lytton that the Gilgit Agency would in no case interfere with his internal administration. The Maharaja also volunteered to connect Gilgit, Srinagar and Jammu with the British Indian telegraph system.

After having obtained Kashmir's concurrence, the formal announcement about the appointment of Captain J. Biddulph as an OSD in Gilgit was made on 22 September 1877. The tasks assigned to him were not limited to mere collection of information about the topography and resources of the territory beyond the Kashmir frontier but also included the extension of British influence among the tribal people by cultivating a friendship with them.[13] Soon after Biddulph was joined by a medical officer who was to help in popularizing the British image among the locals through the healing touch of a doctor. Though Biddulph was quite successful in keeping a watchful eye on Russian movements in Badakhshan, Afghan Turkestan and Kokand, he could not win over the support of Kashmir's officials. One cannot dismiss his accusations against the state officials of plundering his baggage and driving a wedge between the tribal chiefs and the British government as unfounded. Biddulph's suspicions were strengthened by the experience of Shah Khushwakt, a native agent sent by him in May 1878 to Hunza, Kabul, Bukhara and Kokand on a spying mission.[14] He suffered imprisonment at Hunza during his return journey for being a British emissary. He believed that no person other than Babu Nilambar, one of the Kashmir ministers, had disclosed to Ghazan Khan (through his vakil) the nature of Khushwakt's activities.[15]

To Biddulph's surprise, the 5,000 rifles gifted by the British GoI to Kashmir's ruler for strengthening his frontier defence had not been sent to Gilgit.[16] When Henvey raised this issue with the Kashmir Durbar, he was curtly told that no conditions had been attached to these arms being gifted.[17] Obviously, Kashmir disparaged the foisting of a British agent on its territorial jurisdiction. By getting Kashmir's governor at Gilgit removed, Biddulph only added to his difficulties. The end result was that the British did not achieve the desired objective of creating direct influence over the tribal chiefs. They also could not enforce their authority over Kashmir, which continued to resist such interference.[18]

The Gilgit Agent persisted alone in this remote end of the Indian northern frontier till 1880. The matter came to a head when the successful assault by Hunza and Yasin on Gakuch and Sher Kila on 28 October 1880 exposed the military weakness of Kashmir to hold this territory. The precarious situation at Gilgit's frontiers even put the personal safety of the British Agent at Gilgit in danger. The inaccessibility of Gilgit, barely connected with Srinagar by a rough track running over high mountains for 230 miles and open to traffic for six months only, encouraged the frontier chiefs of Dardistan to be insolent. The frontier uprising of late 1880 proved to be the proverbial last straw for the Gilgit Agent. To Ripon, who already considered the Gilgit appointment 'a mistake'[19], the advantages accruing from its continuation were disproportionate to the embarrassment and anxiety suffered by the British. Finally, it was decided, in July 1881, to withdraw the Gilgit Agent, which, however, did not mean British non-involvement in this area. In fact, the Agency was only kept in abeyance till 1888. The British reserved their right to re-appoint the Agent at Gilgit when necessary. The Secretary of State, while consenting to this measure, gave vent to his reservations over the issue by underlining the point that the withdrawal of the Agent might practically close a valuable channel of information to the course of unfolding events in the countries between Kashmir and Russian Turkestan.[20]

THE RE-ESTABLISHMENT OF GILGIT AGENCY IN 1889

The British policy of withdrawing the Gilgit Agency in 1881 was bound to change in the face of intricate problems involved in the defence of the northern frontiers. Their desire to have firm control over the territories up to the Hindu Kush could not be met by being out of the spot. The Afghan pressures on Chitral, which had already been drawn close to the British Indian empire through its allegiance to Kashmir in late 1876, assumed seriousness in 1882 when Kabul claimed this territory 'as one of its protected states'.[21] Though the British Government in India was quick in rebutting such claims[22], the reported Russian intrigues in and around Chitral caused additional concern. The newly established Resident in Kashmir could hardly exert effective control of the Kashmir Durbar or even the British Indian government over the turbulent chief ships of Hunza and Nagar. The Panjdeh[23] crisis of 1885 also helped in focussing British military opinion on the need to make elaborate arrangements for the defence of the north-west frontier. So, it was not a mere coincidence that 1885 was marked by the dispatch of two exploratory missions: one under Col Lockhart, the deputy quarter master general of India, to survey the lands south of Hindu Kush (via Gilgit and Chitral); and the other under Ney Elias to Xinjiang and the Pamirs.

Meanwhile, the Defence Committee's recommendation for extending the Srinagar–Rawalpindi cart-road to Gilgit and Chitral,[24] was approved by Dufferin. The new Commander-in-Chief F. Roberts even suggested that 'we should have political control over the country around Chitral and Gilgit in order to secure the approaches to the former by the Dora pass and to the latter through Wakhan'.[25] The purpose of Col Lockhart's mission was to establish friendly relations with Chitral and Kafiristan and also to obtain accurate information about the routes, passes and resources of the country lying below the Hindu Kush.[26] During 1885–86, he not only surveyed about 1,200 sq. miles of territory of

Gilgit, Chitral, Hunza, Taghdumbash Pamirs and all the important passes across the Hindu Kush[27] but also secured the Chitral ruler Aman-ul-Mulk's promise to allow the passage of British troops through his territory (in the event of a Russian attack from that side).[28]

Lockhart's recommendations, though not accepted at the time, did provide a basis for future British policy towards this frontier belt. He wanted the British government to acquire Gilgit from the Kashmir Durbar and establish a garrison of locally-raised troops under a British commandant to carry out both political and civil functions.[29] The importance of Gilgit 'as the defensive nucleus of Dardistan'[30] was once again underlined by Lockhart in the following words: 'The acquisition of Gilgit would secure us the continued loyalty of Chitral, carrying with it our right of way through the Mehtar's dominions, and his active cooperation in time of need. In my opinion it would ensure the safety of Hindu Kush.'[31]

By May 1887, H.M. Durand too had reached almost the same conclusions.[32] It was in October 1887 that more clear directives reached the Resident in Kashmir, regarding the revised policy of the British Indian government about the frontier defence. He was informed:

> Time has come for establishing on the north-west frontier of Kashmir an effective political control, which will enable us to watch the passes of the Hindu Kush and the country beyond, and a military organization sufficient both to control the Chiefships over the border and also to check, in the event of war with Russia, any demonstration towards the passes not backed by a respectable force.[33]

Since the British wanted to execute their scheme with the cooperation of the Kashmir Durbar, Plowden was asked to use his influence there to run the process smoothly.[34] In fact, Plowden was authorized to promise a military rank to the Maharaja's younger brother for making the Gilgit scheme palatable to the Kashmir Durbar.[35] But H.M. Durand's guidelines to the Resident left little room for doubting the British intention to secure political control over the frontier territory in Gilgit (till the Hindu Kush), though the Maharaja's governor and his troops stationed in Gilgit were to be nominally left under the Kashmir Durbar.[36]

The need to strengthen Kashmir's hold over its frontier territories assumed urgency in view of a joint attack by Hunza and Nagar on Kashmir's posts (at Chaprot and Chalt) in early 1888. Besides, the British Indian government had in mind Ghazan Khan's refusal to permit Col Lockhart through his territories in April 1886 and the Chinese links with Hunza. It was against this backdrop that Dufferin decided to depute Captain A.G.A. Durand (younger brother of Foreign Secretary H.M. Durand) on a mission to Gilgit. He was required to:

> [...] report on the military position at Gilgit with reference to the recent tribal disturbances and to future possible complications with Russia, and to work out a scheme for rendering Gilgit secure without the aid of British troops and for dominating from Gilgit, through the Kashmir forces, the country upto the Hindu Kush; thus rendering Kashmir territory thoroughly secure against attack and guarding against the possibility of a Russian force penetrating to Chitral and threatening our lines of communication between Kabul and Peshawar through the Kunar Valley.[37]

On his return in late 1888, Captain A.G.A. Durand (while reporting about the visit of a Russian officer [Grombchevsky] to Hunza in the autumn of that year) underlined the need to close the gap between the Chinese frontier post at Aktash and the Afghan frontier at Lake Victoria, which could otherwise give Russians access to Hunza.[38] Taking full note of the possible lines of Russian advance to Chitral and Hunza, Captain A.G.A. Durand sought to seal them by proposing the re-establishment of a political agency at Gilgit and the stationing of about 2,000

Kashmiri troops there to function under four British officers.[39] He also recommended the improvement of the Kashmir–Gilgit–Chitral road and the early completion of the telegraph line to Gilgit.[40] The local chiefs of Chitral, Punyal, Hunza and Nagar were to be encouraged to become an inseparable part of the British Indian empire, through the grant of increased subsidies to them.[41] Owing to Dufferin's departure from India, the task of implementing his active policy towards Gilgit fell upon his successor Lansdowne, who readily accepted Captain A.G.A. Durand's scheme. Lansdowne's task was rendered easier by the political changes in Kashmir in April 1889, when the state administration was brought under the direct control of the British Indian government through the Resident. Accordingly, Captain A.G.A. Durand, along with two British officers, Dr Robertson and Lt Manners-Smith, arrived in Kashmir in April 1889 to make preparations for their journey to Gilgit.[42] In fact, Captain A.G.A. Durand left Srinagar for Gilgit in the middle of June 1889[43], a few days before the home government's approval for the re-establishment of Gilgit Agency had reached Lansdowne.[44]

The Anglo-Russian Convention of 1907, which had a relaxed aura could not totally eliminate the deep-rooted mistrust between the two erstwhile rivals. However, the First World War brought the two countries together to meet the common threat from Germany. As a result, even the imperial agents posted in remote pickets like Tashkurghan and Kashgar (both in Xinjiang) used to work in unison on several matters of common interest, quite contrary to their constant mutual strife. But this brief period of mutual cooperation came to an end on the eve of the October Revolution in Russia. After that, the British geared their imperial machinery to prevent the entry of Bolshevism into India by plugging the overland trade and transit from Xinjiang to Kashmir and then to the rest of India.

Ten

The Shahidulla Affair

Situated about 79 miles across the Karakoram Pass and near the southern foot of the Kuen Lun mountains, Shahidulla used to be the camping ground for caravans travelling between India and Xinjiang via the Leh–Yarkand route. Its importance lay in the fact that caravans could find plenty of grass and fuel after they had travelled about 170 miles of mountainous and barren terrain (from the Ladakh side). That three routes branched off from Shahidulla to Yarkand (by the Kilik, Kilian and Sanju passes), provided it a vantage point to keep a vigil on the movement of traffic along these routes. Another route from Shahidulla went along the Karakash River, through the Aksai Chin plains and then to Ladakh. Since the Chinese had established their frontier posts on the north side of Kilian and Sanju passes, and at Kokyar while leaving Shahidulla outside their jurisdiction, the Kashmir authorities in Ladakh did not encounter any problem in extending their influence up to Shahidulla.

The fact that Dogra rulers of Kashmir (Gulab Singh and Ranbir Singh) exercised their influence across the Karakoram range is testified by several contemporary accounts. A Georgian merchant, Rafail Danibegov—who made his return journey from India to Russia by the overland Ladakh–Yarkand route in 1796–97—stated in his travelogue that the Chinese frontier in the southern part of East Turkestan was at Kokyar.[1] Even as late as 1860s, the presence of a Chinese frontier post at Kokyar—where a frontier guard of Chinese soldiers used to check the entry of unauthorized travellers into East Turkestan from Ladakh—has been recorded.[2] All the travellers who passed through the area during the nineteenth century have noted the existence of a small stone fort at Shahidulla, erected by Kashmir's authorities.[3] This fort was reported to have been held by a small Dogra detachment for some years. Mehta Sher Singh—who was deputed by the Kashmir Durbar on a fact-finding mission to Afghanistan, Central Asia and East Turkestan in 1866–67—explicitly stated in his tour report that 'Shahidulla was and continues to be under the control of the Maharaja of Kashmir'.[4] He saw a serai on the banks of the river Karakash at Shahidulla, that had been built by the Kashmir officials.[5] Mehta Sher Singh also noticed a grave of Sadulla Khan, an ex-employee of the Kashmir government, at Shahidulla.[6] This explains why Shahidulla has also been referred to as Shahidulla Mazar in Mehta Sher Singh's report, or as Shahidulla Khoja in several other accounts.

Kashmir's officials in Ladakh provided all the official assistance and requisite supplies from Leh up to Shahidulla for Forsyth, Trotter and other British dignitaries during their missions to East Turkestan. This was subsequently furnished as part of evidence by the Kashmir Durbar to support its claim of Shahidulla being the state frontier in Ladakh. T.D. Forsyth—who led the second Yarkand mission, making a journey of 240 miles from Leh to Yarkand in 1873—has made specific mention about Shahidulla Khoja being the frontier outpost of Jammu and Kashmir.[7] In fact, the Maharaja of Kashmir Pratap Singh in his memorandum dated March 16 1892, addressed to the British Resident in Kashmir, recalled the dispatch of a Kashmiri military detachment to Shahidulla at the behest of the Resident to stop the Russian officer Grombchevsky from coming into Ladakh territory in 1889.[8] The Maharaja provided unimpeachable evidence of Kashmir's jurisdiction over Shahidulla and the construction of a fort there by Mehta Mangal, the late wazir wazarat of Ladakh around 1865.[9] The Maharaja also recalled that Kashmir's authorities had made arrangements for the supply of provisions up to Shahidulla for T.D. Forsyth during his mission to Yarkand.[10] In fact, Mehta Sher Singh had accompanied this mission to supervise the provision of supplies en route and to see Forsyth off at Shahidulla.[11] But the British Resident in Kashmir responded by disallowing the reoccupation of Shahidulla by the Kashmir Durbar.[12]

NO MAN'S LAND

The occupation of Shahidulla by Kashmir's forces for more than 20 years, after they had taken over Ladakh in 1842, is attested to by Ney Elias and F.E. Younghusband in their separate confidential memoranda written later to the British GoI on this subject.[13] However, they pointed out that after occupying Yarkand in 1865, Yakub Beg advanced his frontier close to Shahidulla and his forces remained there till 1876–77 when the Chinese reoccupied Kashgaria. But Elias conceded that the Chinese did not move up to Shahidulla during their 'present term of rule in Chinese Turkestan' and it remained a sort of 'no man's land'. On its part, the Kashmir Durbar was feeling concerned about the security of Ladakh's frontiers following the lapse of its authority in Shahidulla. And the Maharaja of Kashmir sought to use this occasion to send 200–300 of his regular troops to Leh and Nobra to prevent any Kyrgyz incursion from the direction of Shahidulla.[14] When the Maharaja of Kashmir raised the question of the uncertain state of political affairs in Xinjiang, and the consequent need to strengthen Ladakh's defences in an informal meeting with the British OSD (F. Henvey) in November 1878, the matter attracted the attention of the British authorities in India.[15] It was at this point that Ney Elias was asked by Henvey to examine the issue and make suitable recommendations. In his report, Elias saw no advantage in the Maharaja reoccupying Shahidulla either as a defensive post or as a demarcation of the border between Ladakh and Xinjiang. Being situated much farther from the last inhabited portion in Ladakh than from some towns in Chinese territory, Elias found Shahidulla more accessible to the Chinese than to the Kashmiris.[16] Regarding the determination of the boundary, Elias proposed:

> Beginning in the west, the crest of the Mustag (Muztagh) or Baltoro pass might be demarcated as the first point. The summit of the glacier at the head of the Nobra valley as the second point. The summit of the glacier at the head of the Shyok valley as the third point. The crest of the Karakoram Pass where the main road to Yarkand crosses as the fourth. The crests of the two Chunglung passes at the crossing point of the alternative routes via Changchenmo as fifth and sixth, and finally some point on the present Chinese-Tibetan boundary to be afterwards decided.[17]

While Henvey approved of Elias's proposal as a fair solution for determining the Ladakh frontier, he dismissed the Maharaja's plans to reoccupy Shahidulla as extravagance.[18]

The Shahidulla affair came to fore again in 1885, when the Wazir Wazarat of Ladakh Pandit Radha Krishan—attracted by the discovery of a lapis-lazuli mine near Shahidulla—began preparations to send Kashmir's troops to reoccupy that place. Ney Elias was not disposed to allow this adventure, as it could, in his opinion, mean an offence to China and thus give rise to an unnecessary frontier problem. Elias pointed out that Shahidulla was cut off in winter and lay too far from the base from Ladakh (about 240 miles from Leh and 170 miles from farthest outlying village in Ladakh) to be held effectively, whereas it was only 65 miles from the Chinese outpost on the other side.[19] In view of these geographical factors, Elias strongly advised the British Indian government to restrain the Kashmir Durbar from taking any step towards occupying Shahidulla (or any part of the Karakash Valley).[20] Consequently, Kashmir's authorities, succumbing to the pressure of British Indian government, dropped the idea of reoccupying Shahidulla.[21]

Sometime later, Captain Henry Ramsay, who succeeded Elias as the British joint commissioner in Ladakh, apprehended the Russian advance into Kashgaria and, therefore, pressed for an early demarcation of the Ladakh frontier at Shahidulla.[22]

However, he clarified that the 79 miles of mountainous territory from Karakoram Pass to Shahidulla could be kept without roads, which would 'in itself act as a barrier against Russian aggression via Karakoram and also place in our keeping the entrances from the Yarkand side to the several Changchenmo routes towards India'.[23] But the British Indian government informed the Resident in Kashmir that it was not interested in raking up a boundary case with China.[24] This did not deter Ramsay from pursuing the case of settling the frontier between Ladakh and Chinese Turkestan. Elias maintained his earlier stand that it was of no use to hold the no-man's land between Karakoram and Shahidulla. The then Viceroy of India, Lord Lansdowne while agreeing with Elias, was in favour of encouraging the Chinese to take possession of the territory between Karakoram and Kuen Lun rather than leaving the no-man's land. He wished to make China stronger in the whole of Kashgar–Yarkand region, hoping that it could act as an 'obstacle to Russian advance along this line'.[25] However, Lansdowne wanted to take the requisite steps in this regard only after he received the results of Younghusband's explorations in that area.

KANJUTI (OF HUNZA) RAIDS

It was in the summer of 1889 that a group of Kyrgyz inhabitants of Shahidulla visited Ladakh and sought the Kashmir Durbar's protection against the raids of Kanjutis (of Hunza). They asked for financial aid and the help of Kashmir's forces to reoccupy the old fort at Shahidulla.[26] Musa Kyrgyz (the representative of Turdi Kol, the headman of the Kyrgyzs living in and around Shahidulla) and 20 other Kyrgyzs arrived at Leh in May 1889. The government records for Kashmir during 1890–91 confirm that Kyrgyzs sought 'Kashmir Durbar's protection against the raids of Kanjutis and with that view prayed for pecuniary aid and a military force, to restore and occupy the old fort of Khoja Shahidulla'.[27] Musa met Captain H. Ramsay on 25 May 1889 and sought assistance against the Kanjuti (Hunza) raids upon the

Kyrgyzs near Shahidulla in 1888.[28] Musa informed that when Turdi Kol, the headman of the Kyrgyzs, had met the Chinese Amban of Yarkand to seek help against the Kanjuti raids, the Amban had categorically refused any assistance on the plea that 'the Chinese frontier extended only to the Kilian and Sanju passes, and that if we come to live within this border, he would protect us, but that he could do nothing as long as we remained in Shahidulla'.[29] The Amban was reported to have advised Musa and Turdi Kol to seek assistance from the authorities in Ladakh.[30]

Musa sought funds from Ramsay to rebuild the fort at Shahidulla and about 20–30 sepoys to hold the fort, so that the Leh–Yarkand trade could be protected from the Hunza raids.[31] Ramsay promptly reported the matter to the British Resident in Kashmir, R.P. Nisbet, and proposed to 'encourage the Shahidulla Kyrgyzs by giving them a few hundred rupees for the repair of Shahidulla fort and take the Kyrgyzs under our protection'.[32] Ramsay took up the matter again with the British Resident in Kashmir on 16 June 1889, stating that 'Chinese regard Kilian and Sanju as their frontier'.[33] He recommended sending Kashmir's troops to escort the caravans till Shahidulla to keep the Leh–Yarkand trade route open.[34]

The British authorities used the occasion to have the Muztagh range of the northern frontiers of Kashmir and the territory between Karakoram and Kuen Lun explored by F.E. Younghusband, utilizing the services of Kyrgyz guides who were handy at Leh at that time. Younghusband reached Leh on 31 July 1889 and met the Kyrgyzs there.[35] Taking an escort of 17 Kashmiri troops, Younghusband left for Shahidulla to inquire into the case.[36] Turdi Kol was provided money for repairing the old fort at Shahidulla and to make further defences against the Kanjuti raiders.[37] Besides, an escort of Kashmiri troops was left at Shahidulla for their protection. It was around this time that Grombchevsky was also busy exploring the area around Hunza and Shahidulla. Grombchevsky was aware of Kanjuti raids on the Kyrgyzs of Shahidulla, and also about the Younghusband mission to meet the demands of the Kyrgyzs.[38] According to Grombchevsky, the Kashmir garrison posted at Shahidulla was forced to abandon the fort in the autumn of 1889 after the Chinese authorities banned the export of grains to Shahidulla.[39] This paved the way for its occupation by the Chinese, who after arresting Turdi Kol (for his dealings with Kashmir), entrusted the job to another local Kyrgyz.

The British Indian government deputed F.E. Younghusband on a special mission to Xinjiang for one year (from 1 June 1890). He was accompanied by G. Macartney, a Chinese language interpreter and an assistant. Younghusband was instructed to proceed to the Pamirs and 'examine thoroughly the exact limits of Chinese authority'.[40] He was specifically 'directed to impress upon the Chinese officials the need to strengthen and assert their occupation on the extreme limits of the country, over which their dominion claims to extend, so that no unclaimed strip intervenes between Afghan and Chinese territories'.[41] Younghusband, on reaching Yarkand, discussed the issue with the Chinese authorities there. In his letter, dated 20 August 1890, sent from Shahidulla to the British GoI, Younghusband gave information about the erection of a new fort by the Chinese at Suget, about 8 miles south of Shahidulla.[42] Younghusband was not only satisfied to see this 'tract of no-man's land' being claimed by a 'friendly power'[43] but he even pleaded for further 'inducing or mildly provoking' the Chinese to act in a similar way westward in the Pamirs, so that Russia could be prevented from making any advances in that direction.[44] Younghusband was only reiterating what Elias had advocated earlier and had been accepted as a policy by the British authorities. The extension of Chinese control up to the limits of Afghan territory could be helpful in Russia not filling the vacuum. The merits or demerits of Kashmir's claims across the Karakoram, or the pleadings of Captain Ramsay to stop the Chinese from occupying Shahidulla were of no consequence for the British authorities in India. They were more concerned about the Russian factor.

Though Lansdowne had already made up his mind on this issue, Younghusband's conclusions only strengthened his resolve to push the matter with China through the home government and the British Legation in Peking. Accordingly, Lansdowne briefed the India Office, London, and also the British Minister at Peking John Walsham about the Shahidulla affair and his government's policy on this issue. Walsham was informed about the British Indian government's willingness 'to acquiesce' in the Chinese occupation of Shahidulla.[45] He was also requested to 'encourage the Chinese to assert their authority over the tract in question and upto the limits of Afghan territory', so that there was no gap left to attract Russian exploring parties.[46] The GoI stressed the need to secure the right to station a British officer in Xinjiang, to monitor developments there and extend British influence and promote British interests in that direction.[47]

THE CHINESE TAKE CONTROL OF SHAHIDULLA

Clearly, Kashmir's authorities had established a frontier post at Shahidulla even though it was beyond their capacity to maintain the force there (however small in number). Kashmir had a vested interest in the free flow of trade that passed through the Leh–Yarkand route, particularly because the bulk quantities of fine shawl wool imported from Turfan, Yarkand and Lhasa sustained the lucrative shawl industry in the Valley. It was, therefore, desirable to provide protection to traders passing through Ladakh onwards to Yarkand against the Kanjuti (of Hunza) and Kyrgyz robber attacks. Besides, Dogra rulers were conscious of the need to insulate the northern frontiers of Kashmir from any possible alien incursions, following the political strife and instability in Xinjiang. Thus, Shahidulla was sought to be used by the Kashmir Durbar as a forward outpost in the fringe of Central Asia to monitor developments in that quarter.

The strength of Kashmir's claim over Shahidulla was also based on the fact that the Chinese, even after their reoccupation of

Kashgaria in 1877, did not claim the territory beyond the Kokyar, Kilian and Sanju passes on the Kuen Lun range.[48] In fact, the Chinese authorities in Xinjiang continued to deem Shahidulla outside their jurisdiction, as late as 1888. Though Kashmir's authorities were anxious to reoccupy Shahidulla (which they had abandoned around 1867), they were dissuaded from doing so by the British representatives in Kashmir and Ladakh. The British Indian government viewed the whole issue in the context of possible Russian threat from across the Pamirs. The weak Chinese authority in Xinjiang, the high degree of political influence exercised by the Russian Consul in Kashgar and Grombchevsky's explorations in Hunza and the Pamirs, only added to British fears. It was believed that the area lay open for Russian penetration, as neither the Afghans nor the Chinese exercised any effective control over the Pamirs.

The British priority was to join the two ends of the Afghan and Chinese frontiers at the Pamirs, in a bid to create a wedge to separate the British and Russian empires in Asia. The reluctant Chinese authorities were induced to extend their control beyond the Kuen Lun till the Karakoram. The British also wished to use this concession to China for securing the latter's consent to station a representative in Xinjiang. They were desperately looking for such an opportunity to monitor developments in that area, to come at par with the Russians who already had a consulate in Kashgar. So, while Younghusband was practically inducing the Chinese authorities in Yarkand to control the area up to Karakoram effectively, his interpreter and assistant Macartney was directed to station himself there for the time being. Initially designated as special assistant to the Resident in Kashmir, Macartney's position as the British consul in Kashgar was recognized by the Chinese government after years of consistent persuasion by the British foreign office.

Soon after this 'inducement', the Chinese became active on this part of the frontier. They pulled down the fort at Shahidulla and built a new one 8 miles further south near the summit of the

Suget Pass. Later, in September 1892, they erected a boundary pillar 64 miles to the south of the new fort and a notice was set up at the Karakoram Pass, asserting it to be the boundary. The matter was promptly reported by the Wazir Wazarat of Ladakh to the British Joint Commissioner of Leh and to Kashmir's authorities. In his letter dated 27 October 1892 to the Kashmir Durbar, the Wazir Wazarat sought approval to the 'dispatch of one or two military guards in the coming spring to Shahidulla, where they would remain in the State fort in accordance with the old practice and watch the borders too'.[49] Raja Amar Singh, vice-president of Jammu and Kashmir State Council, brought the matter to the notice of the Resident in Kashmir on 2 November 1892 and asked the 'Government of India to repel the unlawful aggression of the *Khitais* (Chinese) and to restore the original boundary'.[50] But the Kashmir Durbar's protestations to the British Indian authorities, against the Chinese encroachments, were brushed aside. The British Indian government, while agreeing that 'the boundary marks have no international value unless they were erected with the concurrence of both sides', decided to acquiesce in the Chinese unilateral action. It informed the Kashmir Durbar:

> In principle the Government of India favour the idea of getting the 'no man's land' in this locality filled up by the Chinese, subject to future delimitation of boundaries. It does not seem desirable that the responsibilities of the Kashmir State, already heavy, should be increased by the assumption of control over the country beyond the Karakoram.[51]

The British Indian government in its letter dated 18 January 1893 to the Secretary of State, London, stated: 'It would be matter for congratulations if the Chinese were to assert effectively their claims to Shahidulla and the tract between Kuen Lun and Karakoram ranges.'[52] The British did not protest against Peking and also felt relieved to see the 'Chinese asserting their claims to Shahidulla and the tract between Kuen Lun and Karakoram ranges'.[53] The Secretary of State followed it up by asking the British Minister at Peking N.R. O'Conor to communicate the views of the British government on this matter to the Chinese government. Accordingly, O'Conor met the Minister of Tsungli Yamen on 12 June 1893, who acted promptly and seeked the views of the Xinjiang government.[54] On hearing from Xinjiang, Tsungli Yamen wrote to O'Conor on 31 March 1894 informing, 'Karakoram is the south limit of Yarkand territory[...] The Taotai of Kashgar was ordered to erect a boundary round Karakoram for making clearly the frontier. This mountain range is the watershed between rivers flowing north and south and is the natural boundary.'[55] On hearing about the Chinese action, the British government decided to 'acquiesce in the matter and agree to the stand taken by China, as it suited the views and interests of British government'.[56] When the Earl of Dunmore travelled through the area, he lamented that Shahidulla was no longer the border between China and Ladakh, as the Chinese had claimed 'the watershed of the Karakoram' and the British Indian government had allowed the claim.[57] Shahidulla ceased to attract any further attention particularly after the Pamirs Boundary Agreement of 1895, which delimited the frontiers of British and Russian possessions in a manner that their borders were not coterminous.

The Shahidulla affair provides concrete historical evidence of the Chinese jurisdiction in Xinjiang never extending to the south of the Kuen Lun range. It has been corroborated in a contemporary Chinese source titled *Hsin-Chiang Tu-Chih* (*Geographical Records of Xinjiang*), compiled and edited by the Governor of Xinjiang in 1911, which described the southern boundary of Xinjiang as 'turning in an east-west direction beyond Kanjut (Hunza)'.[58] At another place in the book, the Governor of Xinjiang described Shahidulla as part of Kashmir, thus indicating that as late as 1911, Chinese authority had not even been extended as far as the Kuen Lun range.[59] The Chinese did not exercise their administrative jurisdiction over Shahidulla until 1928. This was admitted by the Chinese official delegation in 1960 during their talks with India. They produced a copy of the petition from Yan Tsung-hsin (Governor of Xinjiang) who, in 1927, had proposed that Shahidulla be made a *Sheh-Chih-Chu* (bureau of administration) 'due to its history, alien affairs, geography and administration of that place'.[60] It was in 1928 that the Chinese government approved the proposal to set up an administrative post at Shahidulla.[61] Subsequently, we do not hear anything about Shahidulla, because it was not a factor in the Sino-Indian border dispute. Due to its strategic importance, Shahidulla has been developed as a town in Pishan County in south-western Xinjiang, with the PLA barrack named Sanshili Yingfang located nearby.

Eleven

The Kashgar Consulate

Kashgar was important in terms of its central location on the Silk Route, connecting mainland China with western Turkestan (Central Asia) and with India through Yarkand, Ladakh and Kashmir. Kashgar was enclosed by lofty mountain ranges—Tien Shan to the north, Pamirs to the west and Kuen Lun–Karakoram ranges forming the border with India to the south. While all trade of western Turkestan (later Russian Central Asia) entered Kashgar, that of British India and Kashmir came through Ladakh and Yarkand. Being nearer to Kokand in Russian Turkestan, and Tashkurghan in the Pamirs, Kashgar offered a vantage position to monitor Russian movements in the Pamirs, restrict the eastward extension of Russia in Xinjiang and have first-hand experience of the actual state of Chinese affairs in Xinjiang. During the Khoja Muslim rule (and also that of Yakub Beg), Kashgar was the seat of government in Kashgaria. Most of the British Indian traders from Punjab, Hoshiarpur and Kashmir lived and traded in Yarkand and Kashgar, thus representing Indian commercial interests, however small, in the region.

At the behest of Yakub Beg, the British Indian government had deputed R.B. Shaw as OSD to represent the British government in Kashgar in 1874. While Shaw could not accomplish anything during his year-long stay in Kashgar, the Chinese forces reoccupied Kashgaria in 1877. With Yakub Beg's death, the British hopes of offsetting the Russian presence in Xinjiang were dashed. The region posed further challenges to the British, after Russia signed the Treaty of St Petersburg with China on 12 February 1881, which provided for establishment of Russian consulates in Xinjiang and accorded privileges to Russian trade in the region. Soon after, in

1882, Russia posted its Consul General M. Petrovsky at Kashgar. The ever vigilant and assertive Petrovsky busied himself with pushing Russian economic and political interests in Xinjiang, and, more importantly, staking Russian claims on the Pamirs—where the three empires of Russia, China and Britain met. This gave sufficient cause of concern to the British.

Ney Elias made several exploratory travels to Yarkand and Kashgar. Elias was convinced about the need for a permanent British representative in Kashgar, 'which was a far better post for keeping an eye on Russian intrigues and approaches in the direction of Pamirs and Badakshan, than behind the passes of Kashmir and Gilgit'.[1] In his confidential memorandum to Henry Rawlinson on 16 May 1884, Ney Elias pointed to the privileged position of Russia in Xinjiang due to favourable terms of the Treaty of St Petersburg. It provided Russia the right to station consuls in Kashgar and chief towns of Xinjiang and also allowed duty-free trade (both import and export)[2], among other things. As opposed to this, British Indian political and commercial interests were 'entirely unprotected' in Xinjiang.[3] Elias stressed the importance of the Ladakh–Yarkand road being 'the only one between India and Central Asia at all times safe and peaceful and open as a channel for news from the countries north and east of the Oxus'.[4] As such Xinjiang was 'the most convenient and safest position' for stationing of British Agent to 'watch, report and possibly influence events in the eastern regions of Central Asia'.[5]

Soon after, Elias sent a summary of his proposals for 'establishing an Agency in Chinese Turkestan' to Lord Dufferin, the then viceroy of India.[6] Elias pointed out that India being unrepresented in Chinese Turkestan had 'no means of counteracting or even watching Russian proceedings'.[7] Indian trade with Xinjiang amounted to about ₹2 million annually and about 1,000 British subjects resided there, but the whole trade was unrecognized due to a lack of a treaty with China.[8] Alluding to his interaction with the Chinese Legation, Elias reported that 'the Peking government are in favour of English mission or Resident

Agent in Chinese Turkestan, as a counterpoise to the exclusive Russian influence'.[9] Elias underscored:

> An Agent at Kashgar or Yarkand would be in a position to furnish trustworthy information of events taking place over a large section of Central Asia, as he would be in a constant stream of traders, pilgrims and others, from all parts. He would also be in a position to prevent false or distorted accounts of India or of British relations with China, Russia, Afghanistan & C. from obtaining currency.[10]

Concurring with Elias, the then Viceroy of India telegraphed on 10 March 1885 to the Secretary of State, London, expressing the need for expediency of an Agent at Kashgar and having information of events in Central Asia. The Viceroy also sought approval for Ney Elias's mission to Xinjiang and the neighbouring regions, which was instantly granted on 18 March 1885. Indian Foreign Secretary, H.M. Durand informed Ney Elias on 26 May 1885 about his mission to Chinese Turkestan and the neighbouring regions. The objects of his mission were: improving the political relations of GoI with Chinese provincial government in Turkestan, to remove restrictions placed upon Indian trade in that country, to watch movements of Russians in the region and to explore the Afghan districts on Upper Oxus.

Safdar Ali's close dealings with Chinese authorities in Xinjiang and his flirtations with Russians, catalysed British activity in this frontier region. The British felt the urgent need to cultivate friendly relations with the Chinese after their reoccupation of Xinjiang (to keep Russians at bay). Then, the British Indian government urged the Secretary of State, London, to negotiate a convention with China to regulate Indian trade with Xinjiang and also to establish a consulate at Kashgar.[11] Both Lord Kimberly (secretary of state for India) and Earl of Rosebury (secretary of state for foreign affairs) concurred with this view and accordingly asked John Walsham (British minister at Peking) to secure the said convention.[12] Seeing that China was not inclined to agree, the GoI dropped its proposal of negotiating a convention with China. It was now unambiguous in its demand for appointment of a British Consul in Kashgar or Yarkand 'for general political purposes irrespective of the question of trade between these places and India'.[13] The GoI viewed the development and regulation of trade between Xinjiang and British India as an object of secondary importance.[14] So, it asked Secretary of State to take steps for 'securing the right of appointing a Consul in Chinese Turkestan, the officer to be appointed by the GoI and not by the British Minister in China'.[15] Both the home and foreign offices at London concurred with the revised proposal and the British Minister at Peking was asked to pursue the matter with China. John Walsham visited the Tsungli Yamen in Peking on 12 September 1990 (followed by another visit on 30 April 1891) and personally took up the matter of appointment of a British Agent at Kashgar, with the Chinese Minister Prince Ch'ing.[16] On both occasions, the Chinese pointed out that the treaties had no such provision.[17] However, they agreed to do so in return for stationing a Chinese Consul in Hong Kong.[18]

The exigency of increased Russian activity in the Pamirs, Safdar Ali's open hostility and Ney Elias's recommendation to join the Afghan and Chinese frontiers in the Pamirs (so that there was no coterminous border between the British and the Russian territories in the region), led the British Indian government to depute F.E. Younghusband in June 1890 to survey the limits of Chinese claims on the Pamirs. As mentioned earlier, he was to persuade them to extend and assert their claims up to the Afghan frontier. Younghusband was directed to 'impress upon the Chinese officials the need to strengthen and assert their occupation on the extreme limits of the country, so that no unclaimed strip intervenes between Afghan and Chinese territories'.[19] George Macartney, who had command over Chinese language 'due to his mixed parentage (a Scottish father and Chinese mother) and his upbringing for first ten years of his life in Nanking',[20] was deputed to assist Younghusband, besides being his Chinese interpreter (as mentioned earlier).[21] Both Younghusband and Macartney reached Kashgar on 1 November 1890, and the Taotai allotted them a house and garden called Chini Bagh (Chinese Garden), which remained the Indian Consulate till 1949–50.

Younghusband, before leaving Kashgar for India on 22 July 1891, proposed that Macartney should stay behind on special duty in Kashgar. The GoI then decided to station Macartney on special duty in Xinjiang until further orders.[22] He was also provided with a Chinese Munshi. The British Indian government asked the India Office, London, to 'obtain from the Chinese government a recognition of Macartney's employment as a British Agent, or failing that obtain a passport from Peking for Macartney'.[23] The India Office also attached importance to continued presence of Macartney at Kashgar due to the advantages of obtaining accurate information of events on the Pamirs and in Kashgaria. Since China was not disposed to recognize the appointment of a British Agent at Kashgar, the British foreign office had to be content with securing from the Chinese Minister at London, a passport and a recommendation to the Taotai of Kashgar for Macartney.[24] In the meantime, in 1893, the British Indian government with the approval of the Secretary of State for India made Macartney's appointment official with the title of 'special assistant to the Resident in Kashmir for Chinese affairs'.[25] But he continued to be unrecognized by the Chinese as a British representative, and the Russian Consul at Kashgar left no stone unturned to make things difficult for Macartney.

With the conclusion of the Pamirs Boundary Agreement in 1895, tensions over strategic frontiers on the Roof of the World eased. However, British policy continued to support Chinese position in Xinjiang and to thwart any Russian advances in or threats to the region. Despite the handicaps of living in isolation, without any official recognition and facing Russian hostility, Macartney demonstrated his tact, caution and clarity about the objects of his mission in Kashgar.

Macartney was content with having 'gained the friendship

of the local Chinese authorities', even without possessing an officially recognized position.[26] The Chinese were cooperating in the release of Kashmiri slaves in Xinjiang. They abolished all duties on Indian goods and also opened the Sanju and Kugiar routes.[27] At the same time, Macartney was candid about the impossibility of obtaining political information about Russian Turkestan, despite the movement of thousands of Andijanis and Kashgaris, because of the fear inspired by the Russian Consul at Kashgar (nobody dared to visit Chini Bagh or to give any information).[28] Macartney also admitted that Russian trade was 'free from the hindrances of physical obstacles, the caravans passing practically all the year round, backward and forward, between Kashgar on the one side and Osh and Naryn on the other'.[29]

In 1895, the British Indian government in a reversal of its earlier stance, proposed to London to resume negotiation of trade convention between India and China, and to accord Macartney the consular status.[30] Both the Secretary of State for India (G. Hamilton) and Foreign Secretary (Marquis of Salisbury) agreed to this proposal.[31] But when the British Minister at Peking took up the matter with the Chinese, they once again declined to agree to the demand for the appointment of a British Consul in Xinjiang.[32] However, the circumstances changed due to the easing of tensions between Russia and Britain, departure of Petrovsky from Kashgar in 1903 and more importantly the continuous residence of Macartney in Kashgar for 12 years, without any encumbrance from the local Chinese authorities. When Ernest Satow, the British minister in Peking, visited India he suggested to the then Viceroy of India (Lord Curzon) that Macartney should be appointed as the consul 'without asking the consent of the Chinese government in advance'. Accordingly the Governor General in Council of India wrote to the Secretary of State for India (Hamilton) on 13 August 1903 stating that circumstances had 'now greatly changed'.[33] Agreeing with E. Satow's suggestion, the British GoI pressed London for Macartney's recognition as Consul in Kashgar.[34] Accordingly, Lord Lansdowne, the then British foreign secretary, notified Macartney on 1 February 1904 about his appointment as the British Consul at Kashgar.[35] Macartney was empowered to deal with all cases, in which British interests were involved, that might arise within the limits of Xinjiang.[36] E. Satow informed the Chinese government on 30 April 1904 about Macartney's 'promotion as Consul' and requested it to inform the Taotai at Kashgar.[37] China responded by refusing to assent to the appointment of a British consul at Kashgar.[38] However, the unrelenting Prince Ch'ing was courteous and assured that the 'Taotai at Kashgar would be instructed to act in accordance with procedure of past years'.[39] When Macartney was granted leave for 16 months in September 1908 to go to his home in London, Captain A.R.B. Shuttleworth was deputed from Gilgit as acting British consul at Kashgar during the period Macartney remained on leave.[40] The then British Minister in Peking J.N. Jordan again took up the matter of Macartney's recognition as British consul with the Chinese government. This was an opportune moment, as, after the signing of the Anglo-Russian Convention of 1907, Russia did not pursue with its opposition and Peking also came on-board. Now the Chinese conceded the British demand and issued a passport to Macartney, styling him as a consul,[41] and also instructed the Governor of Xinjiang to recognize him as a consul. The Taotai of Kashgar called on Shuttleworth on 25 August 1908 and congratulated him on the recognition as British consul.[42] The Acting Russian Consul at Kashgar Bobrovnikov also called on Shuttleworth on 6 September 1908 to offer his congratulations.[43]

The long-outstanding issue of Chinese recognition of British Consul at Kashgar was resolved. Macartney returned to Kashgar on 1 November 1908 and registered about 200 British subjects at Yarkand, 50 at Karghalik (mostly Afghan couriers from Wakhan), 40 at Goma and 70 at Khotan.[44] He also got a few hundred British Indian slaves freed. In 1910, Macartney was elevated as consul general. This brought him at par with the Russian representative in Kashgar.

The British Consulate at Chini Bagh was first rented by Macartney in 1891. Measuring about 8.3 acres, it was acquired in 1911 at a cost of about ₹10,257 and a further ₹2,000 were spent for the construction of boundary wall and entrance gate.[45] Consulate buildings were built at the total cost of about ₹73,000.[46] Macartney spent 28 years in solitude due to long distance and difficulty in communicating with his superiors, and being without any soldier guard (unlike his Russian counterpart). When Macartney left Kashgar on 11 August 1918, he was given a warm send off with 'the British subjects, the whole Russian colony, the Swedes and the Chinese turning out en masse to see him leave'.[47] His capability, modesty and courage had made him incredibly popular.

Macartney was succeeded by P.T. Etherton, who had travelled overland from India to Trans-Siberian Railway in 1909–10, and had authored several books on Inner Asia. Etherton was also chosen due to his knowledge of Russian language and his anti-Bolshevik sentiments. This was the time when the Soviets were pushing forward in Central Asia. Etherton was provided a vice consul, a wireless receiver and funds for expanding his intelligence network.[48] He developed a network of British Indian elders (*aksakals)* in the towns of Xinjiang, cultivated Kyrgyz tribal leaders in the Pamirs (Samad Shah, cousin of Agha Khan and several Tajik Ismaili followers of Agha Khan), White Russian (anti-Bolshevik) officers in Ili and Urumqi for getting first-hand information about the Bolshevik activities in the Pamirs, Central Asia and Xinjiang. However, with the conclusion of the Anglo-Soviet Accord in March 1921, anti-Bolshevik activities of the Kasghar Consulate stopped. Etherton remained consul general in Kashgar from 1918–22. His tenure was not extended because he was found to have misappropriated the consulate funds.[49]

Etherton was followed by C.P. Skrine (1922–24), R.A. Lyall (1924–25), G.N.B. Gillan (1925–27), J.W. Thomson Glover, M.C. Gillet and Eric Shipton. R.D. Sathe was the last Indian consul general in Kashgar. After the establishment of the Soviet power in Central Asia, expanding Soviet influence in Xinjiang and local disturbances/rebellions, the British Consulate had its hands full. However, with communist China assuming full control over Xinjiang in 1949, the province was declared as a closed territory. Its external trade with British India also ceased to operate and the remaining Indian traders returned to India.

The British Indian Consulate at Kashgar was closed and India handed over the building and other properties belonging to the British Indian government in Chini Bagh premises to China on 25 September 1953. The Chinese government issued a statement that 'according to the provisions of Chinese law, all land of the Chini Bagh compound including the base of the building, belong de jure to the People's Republic of China and by the act of handing over the buildings in Chini Bagh, the GoI have returned the land thereof to the PRC'.[50]

One wonders why India agreed to abandon its Kashgar Consulate, given the strenuous efforts made over decades in its establishment and its invaluable first-hand feedback on developments in that remote frontier. India could have bargained for the continuation of Indian Consulate at Kashgar while agreeing to the Chinese position on Tibet and the Panchsheel Agreement of April 1954. On its part, China demonstrated its astute diplomacy and resolve by closing India's only window in that region, while focussing on the occupation of Aksai Chin, construction of the highway through Aksai Chin to connect Tibet with Xinjiang. This was followed by the Sino-Pak boundary agreement of 1963 and construction of the strategic KKH (linking Kashgar to Pakistan through Pakistan-occupied territory of Kashmir). Clearly, Chinese moves were premeditated and part of a bigger plan to shift geopolitical balance of power to its advantage vis-à-vis India.

Twelve

Soviets in Central Asia and Xinjiang

THE BOLSHEVIK REVOLUTION AND BRITISH INTERVENTION IN CENTRAL ASIA, 1917–20

Soon after the October 1917 revolution in Russia, the new Soviet government made significant announcements regarding the decree on peace, withdrawal from war, release of Austrian and German prisoners of war and repudiation of secret treaties. All such foreign policy moves and launching of the propaganda crusade against British colonialism in the East posed a serious challenge to British colonial interests, particularly in Persia, Afghanistan and India—where nationalist movements were gaining momentum. The British reaction to Soviet moves was strong and spontaneous. Their immediate fear was that the success of the Bolshevik Revolution in Central Asia would stir up 'political disorder and ideological conflagration' in Persia, Afghanistan and India.[1]

The collapse of Russian authority in Trans-Caspia and Central Asia encouraged the British to 'exploit the anti-Bolshevik and pro-autonomous sentiments' among the Muslims there.[2] They planned to create and buttress 'tiny independent states in the Caucasus, Transcaspia, Central Asia, Persia and Afghanistan, near the borders of India hostile to Bolshevik Russia and under the tutelage of Britain.'[3] The British Indian government dispatched several military-cum-political expeditions to Caucasia, Trans-Caspia and Central Asia with an avowed object of forestalling any possible Turko-German advance towards the Indian frontier. However, it was implicitly done to stall the establishment of Soviet power in

Central Asia.[4] The allied intervention did not deter Soviet Russia from continuing with its propaganda offensive against the British. A centre was established in Tashkent to train young Asians to stir up revolutionary activity in India and neighbouring countries.[5] The emigration of a number of Indian Muslims to Soviet Central Asia (via Kabul, Chitral and Kashgar) came as a rude shock to the British who began to see the Bolshevik hand behind every advance of the national liberation struggle.[6] Insulating India from any Bolshevik influence became the cornerstone of the new British policy.

Lenin's declaration to grant the right of self-determination and the Soviet appeals to the toiling masses of Russia and the East (including the Persians, Turks, Arabs and Indians) exhorting them to 'rise and free themselves from yoke of alien capitalists'[7], was regarded by Britain as the Soviet ideological challenge to British power in Asia. A series of anti-Bolshevik measures were initiated both in and outside India. In India, the entry of Bolshevik literature was not only censored but a section of the Indian press was also used to circulate anti-communist propaganda to develop hostility among the Indian masses towards the Soviet Union. Outside India, the British embassies in Peking, Tokyo, Washington and even Batavia (Dutch East Indies) were used to prevent the publication of the Soviet proclamation within their host countries[8], so that the possibility of its transmission to India from those countries was averted.

The British War Cabinet put the responsibility for undertaking various anti-Bolshevik measures in Meshed, Trans-Caspia, Turkestan and Kashgar upon the British GoI, thereby putting a heavy burden on India in terms of men and materials. On the Central Asian front, the British Consul General at Meshed, Major General W. Malleson, opened a front in 1918 in Trans-Caspia fighting desperately alongside the anti-revolutionary forces[9] to stop Bolsheviks from taking control of the whole of Central Asia. The British dispatched another mission, under the leadership of F.M. Bailey, from India, to organize and operate the anti-

Bolshevik forces there. As in the past, Kashmir came in handy as a base for organizing this expedition. Bailey left Srinagar on 22 April 1918[10], taking the shorter route via the Gilgit–Mintaka Pass–Tashkurghan–Yangi Hissar route to reach Kashgar on 7 June 1918.[11] Kashmiri coolies (numbering about 160[12]) were used to carry the loads of the English sahibs over the snowy peaks up to the Chinese frontier. Bailey was also authorized to draw an advance of ₹29,500 at Shimla, Lahore or Srinagar treasuries[13] and the British Resident in Kashmir was to provide all the necessary assistance in this regard.

Though Bailey reached Tashkent on 14 August 1918 quite safely, his arrival at the capital of Soviet Turkestan synchronized with the attack by a British force upon the Bolsheviks in Ashkabad (Trans-Caspia)[14], creating unfavorable conditions for his proposed operations. He not only found it difficult to move freely within Tashkent but also had trouble communicating with either Malleson (at Meshed) or Etherton (at Kashgar). The carrier pigeons brought over by him from Srinagar to meet such an eventuality had already fallen prey to the falcons of the Hunza Valley and the Pamirs.[15] Notwithstanding his wit and resources, including the fruitful cooperation received from Tredwell (the American Consul at Tashkent) and other anti-Bolshevik elements, Bailey could do nothing more than fritter away his energies in seeking safe hideouts till he found a chance to escape to India (via Bukhara and Meshed).[16] Both Malleson and Bailey failed in destabilizing Soviet power in Turkestan, Trans-Caspia, Bukhara and Khiva. But Bailey's experiences in Soviet Central Asia brought him glory at home, and he was appointed as the political officer in Sikkim, with the rank of second-class Resident. In 1932, Bailey was posted as the British resident in Kashmir[17], which was then considered a prestigious job among the second-class residencies in India.

BRITISH CURBS ON MOVEMENT OF PEOPLE, LITERATURE AND TRADE BETWEEN KASHMIR AND XINJIANG

The British sealed off the north and north-western borders of India to prevent any possible entry of Bolshevik agents, literature and Russian roubles overland into India. Weekly and monthly reports about the activities of Indian revolutionaries in India or abroad, and also about their contacts with the Bolsheviks, were now regularly circulated among the British officers posted at the frontier stations in Kashmir, Gilgit, Chitral, Kashgar and the North-West Frontier Province (NWFP). They were especially alerted to check the possible infiltration of Bolshevik emissaries and Indian revolutionaries from Soviet Central Asia into India. Meanwhile, the Resident in Kashmir apprised the state government of the policy of the British Indian government to combat Bolshevik propaganda. The British Resident asked the Kashmir Durbar to cooperate with the British authorities by taking all such measures within the state.[18] He advised the state government to depute special officers for making enquiries if any Bolshevik agents had already entered the state. The Kashmir Durbar was also asked to proscribe all types of Bolshevik literature, if found in circulation within the state.[19] In order to prevent any possible influx of Bolshevik agents into India via the Kashgar–Gilgit–Srinagar or Yarkand–Leh–Srinagar routes, the British agents posted at Gilgit and Leh were empowered to turn back all those travellers coming from Xinjiang, who did not possess credentials bearing the signatures of the British consul general at Kashgar.[20]

Special care was taken to prevent the entry of Bolshevik literature and agents into India from Soviet Central Asia (via Wakhan and the frontiers of Kashmir). The Political Agent in Gilgit acted as a watchdog throughout this frontier belt.[21] Similarly, the state government took steps to watch and search all strangers coming to Kashmir from the direction of Central Asia. For this purpose, additional police force was created to be deployed at Ganderbal, Bandipora and Uttarmachipura—the gateways to Kashmir from Ladakh and Gilgit.[22] As if this was not enough, the Resident in Kashmir asked the state administration to plug the gap at Skardu as well. This was done so that any Bolshevik agents entering Kashmir (via Mustagh Pass) could be interrupted.[23] Following this fresh directive the Wazir Wazarat, Ladakh was instructed to keep a strict watch over any such suspected arrivals at Skardu. The Kashmir ruler, Maharaja Pratap Singh, was even prepared to raise the Wazarat of Ladakh to governorship with headquarters at Skardu, so that such an emergency could be handled adequately.[24]

The British imposed curbs on the overland trade and traffic between India and Central Asia that passed through Kashmir and Xinjiang. Since the import of Russian roubles into India formed an important item in the traditional Xinjiang–Ladakh–Kashmir trade, it was feared that these roubles would be used to further the revolutionary activity in India. So, the British Indian authorities issued two ordinances (in December 1919 and June 1920) prohibiting the circulation of this currency into India and also providing for its confiscation from any possessor.[25] Trade in Russian roubles was rendered profitless in India, and their value also depreciated in the outside markets. Since Kashmir occupied a key position in facilitating the import of Russian roubles and entry of Bolshevik emissaries and literature via the Leh–Yarkand–Kashgar–Ferghana or Srinagar–Gilgit–Pamirs routes into India, special care was taken to empower the British agents stationed in Kashmir and Gilgit to meet such an eventuality. Kashmir was painted as a sensitive spot in the intelligence reports of the British Indian government, which underscored the smuggling of Bolshevik propaganda material directed against British rule in India from Soviet Central Asia (via Afghanistan, Pamirs or Kashgar). The circulation of communist literature was, therefore, banned. It was the Resident in Kashmir who, acting under the directions of the imperial government, prevailed upon the Kashmir Durbar to issue the ordinance prohibiting the possession of rouble notes by any person within the Jammu and Kashmir State.[26] As a result of this measure, about 3 million Russian rouble notes were voluntarily deposited at the Leh and Srinagar treasuries by various traders and individuals during a short period of three months (January–March 1920).[27] Besides, about 1,000 rouble notes were forcibly confiscated from a Khotani trader at Leh under the state ordinance 3 of Samwat 1976.[28]

When trade between India and Central Asia was largely diverted to the Leh–Yarkand route as a natural sequel to the disturbed conditions in Soviet Central Asia, the British Indian government took steps to stop the export of dyes, dye-stuff, leather, cotton, woollen and silken goods from India[29], contrary to their earlier policy of developing Indo-Central Asian trade. Such a commercial blockade was designed to prevent essential commodities like cloth, leather, etc., from reaching the Bolsheviks in Soviet Central Asia.

In 1919, the British Indian government was perturbed at the reported departure of two Kashgarians, namely Yusuf Akhoon and his brother Ibrahim, for Leh (from Xinjiang). They carried along with them huge quantities of Russian roubles, gold and silver, with the alleged objective of promoting Bolshevik activity in India.[30] The British Consul General stationed at Kashgar, who shadowed their movements up to Yarkand, promptly informed the Resident in Kashmir, advising him to keep a strict watch over the two Kashgarians soon after they entered the territories of Jammu and Kashmir.[31] The British Consul in Kashgar alleged that these Kashgarians were in touch with the Bolsheviks and had left for India ostensibly for trade but actually to forge a contact with the Indian revolutionary party.[32] However, the two Kashgarians arrived in Kashmir and left Srinagar for Rawalpindi by car on 20 August 1919.[33] They were detained by the Punjab police at Rawalpindi, and about 8 lakh rouble notes lying in their possession were confiscated from them.[34] They also had with them 240 tolas of gold and 20,996 tolas of silver.[35] The British Consul General at Kashgar pursued the matter and wired the British GoI on 1 September 1919, informing them about Yusuf's connection with the local Bolshevik organization at Tashkent, and his visit to that place in the spring of 1919.[36] With this background in view, the Consul General advised the British GoI to refuse permission to those travellers who came overland from Xinjiang to India via the Leh–Srinagar route if not provided with credentials of the British Consulate at Kashgar.[37] While endorsing this proposal, the Resident in Kashmir advised the Foreign Department to turn back all those travellers coming from the direction of Xinjiang (within the jurisdiction of the Gilgit Agency and Kashmir State) who did not possess any credentials from the British Consul General at Kashgar.[38] The British GoI not only approved this proposal but even went a step ahead by asking the Resident in Kashmir to appoint a special officer to deal with the problems arising out of the influx of Bolshevik emissaries into India.[39]

Soviet support to the national liberation movements of the East had already proved a strong attraction to thousands of Indian Muslim emigrees (*muhajirs*) who were disillusioned with the British due to the overthrow of the Caliphate. These muhajirs travelled long and hazardous distances over the Hindu Kush and Karakoram mountain ranges on foot to reach Soviet Central Asia. There, they were kindly received and trained in Bolshevik ideology, and given military training. The fact that the Srinagar–Leh–Kashgar–Ferghana route was also taken by some muhajirs becomes clear from a report sent by the Comintern's Turkestan Branch in Andijan (to Tashkent) on 18 May 1921. It stated that 36 Indians who had left India for Russia (via Yarkand and Kashgar) had been detained in April 1921 and escorted back to India by the British Consul General in Kashgar.[40]

When, in 1922, a party of Indian revolutionaries arrived at Chitral via Osh, Marghilan, Kharog and the Pamirs route, they were soon arrested and later convicted on the charge of conspiracy against the British crown.[41] A young and educated Kashmiri, Mir Abdul Majid, who was residing in Lahore was one of them. He was going to India to do some revolutionary work and was subsequently arrested and sentenced to rigorous imprisonment.[42] The British intelligence network in the NWFP, Chitral, Gilgit, Ladakh and Kashmir was so alert that almost all the visiting Indians from Central Asia were easily exposed and trapped, rendering it difficult for Indian revolutionaries to gain a foothold in India.

Thus, Kashmir and its frontier dependencies, which commanded overland routes from Central Asia to India, once again came into the sharp focus of the new British strategy towards Soviet Central Asia. The strong British reaction to the success of the Soviet revolutionary movement had its roots in the British colonial policy in India. Their hold over India was already getting weak and the Soviet stance on the right of nations to self-rule was seen in the context of the Indian liberation movement. When, in July 1920, intelligence regarding the overland journey of Raja Mahendra Pratap (through Tashkurghan) reached the British authorities in India, a special detachment of Gilgit Scouts comprising a subedar major, one havaldar, two naiks and 13 sepoys was deputed by the Political Agent in Gilgit to the Kilik Pass for the purpose of intercepting the Raja during his wanderings in the Pamirs.[43] There, in Kashgar, the British Consul General launched combing operations in the frontier areas of Sarikol, Raskam, Yarkand and Khotan to apprehend Mahendra Pratap and his party. But the Raja escaped all these traps and retreated to Afghanistan, finding that the Chinese authorities in Xinjiang were hindering his forward movement from Tashkurghan.[44]

The problem of Soviet propaganda[45] against British colonialism in the East proved to be an important factor during Anglo-Soviet negotiations, which stretched for about a year from May 1920–March 1921, when the trade agreement was finally signed. While the Soviet side was skilful in using anti-British propaganda in the East as a diplomatic weapon for combating British pressures, the British PM Lloyd George employed all his diplomatic prowess to keep the revolutionary essence of Soviet Russia confined within its boundaries. Britain agreed to lift the commercial blockade against Soviet Russia in 1921, only after the latter had agreed to refrain from hostile propaganda against British interests in Asia (especially in India and Afghanistan).[46] This agreement accorded the Soviet Union 'de facto recognition' and also brought to an end the Allied intervention against the Bolsheviks, and British moves to destabilize the Soviet power in Central Asia.

SOVIET INROADS INTO XINJIANG

With the termination of Qing rule in China (1911) and the establishment of Soviet power in Central Asia (1917–20), Soviet influence in Xinjiang registered a sharp increase. As the Chinese warlords ruling over Xinjiang chose to follow semi-independent policies, taking full advantage of the communication gap with the central authority at Peking, they developed direct and close economic, political and military linkages with the Soviet authorities. During the regime of Yang Tseng-hsin (1911–28), the first Republican provincial governor of Xinjiang, close links were established with the Soviet Union. On 6 October 1924, Yang Tseng-hsin signed an agreement (without the approval of the Chinese central government) providing for the establishment of consulates general between Tashkent and Urumqi, and also for the establishment of Soviet consulates in Xinjiang at Chuguchak, Kulja, Sherasume and Kashgar.[47] In return, Xinjiang was allowed to establish consulates in Soviet Central Asia at Semipalatinsk, Alma Ata, Andijan and Zaisan.[48] In this way, the Soviet influence increased not only in northern Xinjiang but also in Kashgar (in Southern Xinjiang) much to the chagrin of the British. During the Tsarist Russian period, the existence of both the Russian and British consulates at Kashgar had already unleashed a bitter contest between the two rival empires (as discussed previously).

With the revival of the Soviet consulate at Kashgar, the British were alarmed at the increased Soviet foothold in Southern Xinjiang, which was viewed as a serious challenge to the British political and commercial influence over the region. In 1926, the Soviets started constructing a new railway line linking Frunze (now Bishkek) in Kyrgyzstan with Semipalatinsk, running parallel to the frontier of Xinjiang for about 400 miles. The railway known as Turksib, which was completed in 1930, increased the Soviet economic presence in Xinjiang. Subsequently, China's share of Xinjiang market dropped to 12.5 per cent and the value of Soviet trade with Xinjiang rose to over 32 million roubles in 1930.[49] The Turksib also enhanced Soviet political influence over Xinjiang which then became easily accessible from Soviet Central Asia. By 1933, Xinjiang—which was a rich source of raw wool, cotton, hides and livestock etc.—exported about 82.5 per cent of its goods to the Soviet Union, leaving only 5 per cent of trade opportunity with India and the remaining with China.[50]

Following the assassination of Yang Tseng-hsin in July 1928, Chin Shu-jen succeeded him as the provincial governor of Xinjiang (1928–33). Faced with a Tungan rebellion led by Ma Chung-ying, Governor Chin sought Soviet help. He signed a secret agreement (without reference to the Chinese central government) on 1 October 1931, which gave the Soviet Union several privileges, such as the right to open eight Soviet trading agencies in Xinjiang at Urumqi, Chuguchak, Kulja, Kashgar, Aksu, Kucha, Yarkand and Khotan; reduction of customs duties on goods of Soviet origin; and opening of direct telegraphic and wireless communication between Xinjiang and the Soviet Union.[51] In return, the Soviet Union provided substantial economic and military assistance to Xinjiang besides sending Soviet experts in electricity, telecommunications, animal husbandry, etc., to Xinjiang.[52] Soviet fears of Japanese expansion to Manchuria in 1931; the potential threat to Outer Mongolia and Xinjiang; and Nanking's inability to counter the Japanese advance led the Soviet Union to have such a forward policy in Xinjiang. The Soviets were also concerned with the active British interest in Southern Xinjiang, particularly in the Kashgar region.

Chin Shu-jen's successor Sheng Shih-ts'ai (1933–44) was even more inclined towards the Soviet Union, which was increasingly concerned over the fluid situation and Japanese activities in Xinjiang. The Soviets were also worried about the British economic and political influence in the Kashgar region and the potential British support to Uyghur Muslims and the Turkish Islamic Republic of Eastern Turkistan (TIRET). Pravda openly accused Britain of supporting the pan-Islamic rebels of TIRET in Southern Xinjiang.[53] The Soviets feared that the success of TIRET in Xinjiang would fuel Muslim unrest and anti-Soviet activities in Soviet Central Asia, abutting the borders of Xinjiang. When, in late 1933, Sheng Shih-ts'ai appealed to the Soviet Union for assistance to quell the Tungan rebels (led by Ma Chung-ying) and the Uyghur forces of TIRET, the Soviet Union readily intervened in Xinjiang's affairs. In early 1934, Red Army troops (about 7,000) supported by tanks, planes and artillery moved across the border into Xinjiang and repulsed the Tungan rebels.[54] By September 1934, TIRET was also defeated.

With Sheng Shih-ts'ai assuming full control of the provincial government of Xinjiang, close relations were developed with the Soviet Union. In January 1936, Sheng concluded a secret agreement with the Soviet Union which reportedly provided for Soviet political, economic and military assistance to Xinjiang in case of any external attack upon the province.[55] Back then Russian was taught as a foreign language in schools, particularly in northern Xinjiang. Hundreds of Muslim youth, including girls of Xinjiang, were sent for studies to Soviet Central Asia. When Sheng Shih-ts'ai visited Moscow in 1938, he became a member of the Communist Party of the Soviet Union (CPSU).[56] Stalin viewed Xinjiang to be within the Soviet sphere of influence. Under Stalin's pressure, Sheng Shih-ts'ai signed the Tin Mines Agreement with the Soviet Union on 26 November 1940, which was valid for 50 years and granted the Soviets 'exclusive rights for the prospection, investigation and exploitation of tin and its ancillary minerals' within Xinjiang.[57]

The secret Soviet–Xinjiang Treaty of Mutual Assistance of

1 January 1936; the 5 million rouble loan on 16 May 1935; Tin Mines Agreement of 26 November 1940; stationing of Red Army units with tanks, artillery and planes; and the presence of a large number of Soviet advisers and technicians in Xinjiang, amply demonstrate the extent of Soviet economic, political and military influence in Xinjiang. Soviet Consul General Garegin Apresoff was more powerful in Xinjiang. Sheng Shih-ts'ai followed a strong pro-Soviet policy during the years 1934–42. Sheng firmly believed that 'before India's independence, Great Britain hoped to make southern Xinjiang a sphere of influence, which would safeguard India against Russia or Japanese penetration'.[58] In the words of Sheng himself, 'British imperialists incited the Uighurs to launch the "Eastern Turkistan Republic" movement with Khodja Niaz as President and Sarpiti as Premier. Their hope was to make southern Sinkiang a sphere of exclusive British influence, profitable for extension of trade from India.'[59] Sheng confirmed that he briefed Stalin during his meeting with the Soviet leader at Moscow in 1938 about 'Ma Chung-ying's abortive efforts to create a Muslim state in Sinkiang and the collapse of the so-called "Turkistan Republic" in the south, a movement backed by Britain operating from India'.[60] Sheng claimed to have assured Stalin that 'at the present, there is no major conspiracy active except for some scattered groups in southern Sinkiang who occasionally are lured into becoming British agents'.[61]

The Soviet military intervention, which led to the defeat of Tungan and Turkic Muslim rebellion between 1934 and 1937, enabled Sheng Shih-ts'ai to consolidate his position in Xinjiang. After extending his control over Southern Xinjiang by September 1937, Sheng took steps to diminish British influence and prestige over the Kashgar region. Though British policy was in favour of Chinese control over the whole of Xinjiang, particularly after the death of Yakub Beg in 1877, both the Russians and Sheng harboured deep suspicions about British intentions and activities in the Kashgar region. Sheng introduced anti-British trade embargo and also interfered with consular mails between Kashgar and India.[62] British Indian nationals long residing in Yarkand and Khotan were expelled and forced to return to India, across the Karakoram Himalayas in deep winter.[63] In June 1938, K.C. Pickernman, the British consul general at Kashgar, summed up the situation in his report to Delhi:

> Soviet Russia has at last regained in full the influence Russia used to exercise in Imperial days, and which was temporarily lost, as a result of the Russian revolution, during the period 1917-31. Russian merchants, Russian ideas and Russian trade predominate throughout the province; most of the important posts in the province are filled by Russophile officials and both provincial and local authorities frequently seek the advice and assistance of the Russian Consular establishment in the province.[64]

Sheng Shih-ts'ai shifted his loyalty to the nationalist government of Chang Kai-Shek in 1942. He asked the Soviets to withdraw all their technicians, army personnel, etc., from Xinjiang. Sheng was subsequently transferred by the Kuomintang to Chungking in September 1944. Withdrawal of Soviet advisers, technicians and Red Army's 8th Regiment, Soviet military equipment, etc., from Xinjiang began in 1942. The establishment of central Chinese control over Xinjiang, first by the nationalist government in 1944 and later in 1949 by the communists, marked the end of the Soviet influence over Xinjiang.

THE BRITISH TAKEOVER OF GILGIT

After Xinjiang, the British were scared of the Soviet extending their political clout over Kashmir and its frontier territories of Gilgit, Hunza, Nagar, etc. To prevent any such possibilities, the British sought to consolidate its authority in Kashmir. Undermining the authority of the Maharaja of Kashmir, the British policy was to woo the tribal chiefs of the frontier dependencies into their fold by paying them enhanced subsidies and dealing with them directly through the British Agent at Gilgit. As mentioned previously, this resulted in the erosion of the Kashmir Durbar's authority over its frontier territories.

This system of dual authority was proving too irksome to the Maharaja of Kashmir and his officials in Gilgit. With the accession to the throne of Maharaja Hari Singh in 1925, the new Maharaja began to assert his authority over this frontier. He objected to the flying of the Union Jack and insisted that only the state flag would fly in his frontier territories. A long correspondence with the British Indian authorities ensued to resolve the anomalous situation of dual authority in the frontier. The British Resident in Kashmir sent a memo to the Kashmir Durbar, admitting therein the fact that 'the interests of the British Government and the Kashmir State on the Gilgit frontier are common interests'. He then put forth a new proposal to the British GoI by which 'the appointment of Political Agent, Gilgit, should be abolished and in his place a Political Officer should be lent to the Kashmir State to hold the appointment of Governor of Gilgit and to conduct political relations on behalf of the Government of India and the Kashmir Government with the Political Districts'.[65] The main features of the proposal were:

1. abolition of the political agency;
2. bringing of the unsettled districts under the full administrative control of the state;
3. cementing relations between the Maharaja and the frontier chiefs and nobles;
4. maintaining the prestige of the British GoI on the frontier without any detrimental effect on the prestige and the rightful authority of the state;
5. transfer of the Indus Kohistan and Kandia to NWFP;
6. the Union Jack continuing to fly alongside the state flag on the Chilas and Gupis forts.

But before these proposals could be given a practical shape, there broke out internal disorders in the state. The matter was discussed by the Political Committee, India Office, London, in its meeting on 18 November 1931. Soon after, the Secretary of State for India sent a telegram to the British GoI on 26 November 1931 giving explicit instructions for asking the Resident in Kashmir to suspend any further action in pursuance of his proposals, as the recent events in Kashmir give us an opportunity and make it desirable to reconsider proposals for future of the Gilgit Agency which were put forward informally as basis for discussion. Eventually, the proposal was withdrawn by the Resident at the instance of the British government. This was mainly because British fears had increased after the success of the Bolsheviks in Central Asia and particularly when the Soviet authorities became too close to Chinese warlords' regimes in Xinjiang.

The British swiftly moved to take over the strategic base in Gilgit to thwart any possible Soviet adventure through Xinjiang into Kashmir frontiers. Thus, the British used the circumstances of domestic political pressures caused by the Muslim upheaval and riots in Kashmir, to coax Maharaja Hari Singh to accept the new proposal of leasing the Gilgit Agency to the British for 60 years. The lease agreement, which was signed by the Maharaja and Col L.E. Lang (the British Resident in Kashmir), on 26 March 1935, authorized the Viceroy and Governor General of India to assume the civil and military administration of the Gilgit Agency, subject to the condition that the territory would continue to be included within the dominion of the Maharaja. Additionally, the rights pertaining to mining would also be reserved with the Government of Kashmir. On 1 October 1935, the British Political Agent in Gilgit Major G. Kirkbride assumed full control of the Gilgit Agency.

Before the Government of Kashmir handed over the administrative control of the Gilgit Agency to the British Indian government in 1935, under the terms of a 60 year lease, the area of the Gilgit frontier was divided into three categories of administration—the Gilgit wazarat, political districts and unadministered area,[66] as detailed below:

1. Gilgit wazarat comprised of the tehsil of Gilgit (including Bunji) and the Niabat of Astor. This area remained under the direct control of the Kashmir Durbar and was administered by a Wazir-i-Wazarat.
2. Political districts comprised of Hunza, Nagar, Punial, Yaṣin, Ishkoman, Kuh–Ghizar and Chilas.
3. Unadministered area comprised of Darel, Tangir, Kandia, Jalkot, Sazin, Shatial and Harban.

When the political status of the unadministered area was enquired about, the Chief Commissioner, NWFP, clarified to the Survey of India that 'Tangir, Darel and Jalkot are all under the political control of the Resident in Kashmir through the Political Agent, Gilgit and are not part of the NWFP'.[67] New schemes for the defence of the Indian northern frontier in and around Gilgit were initiated. These included the construction of air-landing facilities, installation of wireless sets and strengthening of the British force in these strategic pickets. What proved to be catastrophic for independent India was the takeover of complete political and administrative control of the Gilgit Agency from the Maharaja of Kashmir on lease in 1935 by which time the Maharaja's grip over this frontier area had loosened for all practical purposes.

Thirteen

Operation Datta Khel in Gilgit

In Xinjiang, armed rebellion erupted in November 1944 in Ili against the Chiang Kai-shek government of the Republic of China. The rebellion, which soon spread to Chuguchak and Altai in northern Xinjiang, was reported to be backed by the Soviet Union which had a strong foothold in that region. By late 1947, the Ili rebels had taken control of Ili, Chuguchak and Altai. Earlier, in late 1945, the Sarikol rebellion had taken place in Southern Xinjiang, with the rebels having captured Karghalik and also cutting off the route from Kashgar (across the Karakoram Pass) to Kashmir. The consular services between Kashgar and Gilgit were also stopped.[1] The British Consul General in Kashgar, Michael Gillet regularly reported to the British government about the situation getting murkier in Xinjiang. This, thereby, posed a challenge to the security of Gilgit and Ladakh, which commanded the overland passes to Xinjiang. In this context, holding on to the strategic point of Gilgit—where the three empires of Russia, Britain and China met—became the priority in the British plans while transferring power to the dominions of India and Pakistan.

Lord Mountbatten advancing the deadline for the transfer of power to 15 August 1947, from the earlier target date of 30 June 1948; George Cunningham's appointment as the governor of the NWFP for the third time from 15 August 1947; and the shifting of Major William Brown as commandant of the Gilgit Scouts, all point to British moves to execute their master plan of secession of the strategic Gilgit region from Kashmir and its subsequent merger with Pakistan. The secret plan, code named Operation Datta Khel, aimed at organizing the rebellion of the frontier tribes led by Gilgit Scouts against the Maharaja of Kashmir. It also included the incorporation of the strategic Gilgit region into Pakistan, which was executed perfectly by Major Brown with the assistance of Captain Jock Mathieson as his assistant commandant.

In early 1943, Captain William Brown, a Pashto speaking army officer, was posted to the Gilgit Agency as adjutant of Gilgit Scouts and as assistant political agent in Chilas for two years.[2] During his tenure in this frontier, Brown travelled widely in Hunza, Nagar, Yasin, Ishkoman, Punial and Kuh-Ghizar gaining sufficient experience, proficiency and knowledge in the local language. He developed close friendships with the chiefs of Hunza, Nagar, Yasin and Punial with the objective of swinging their loyalty away from the Maharaja of Kashmir. In November 1946, Brown was transferred to Waziristan in the NWFP, where he briefly served as an officer in the Tochi Scouts.[3] There, Brown met Jock Mathieson whom he later chose to serve as his assistant in Gilgit Scouts. In June 1947, Brown was posted as the acting commandant of Chitral Scouts.[4] Around the same time in early 1947, Col Roger Bacon was appointed as the new political agent in the Gilgit Agency, on the recommendation of George Cunningham, a staunch advocate of the Forward School.[5] In the first week of July 1947, Mountbatten announced that the Gilgit lease would be rescinded on 31 July 1947, so that the Maharaja of Kashmir would resume his authority over the Gilgit region. Meanwhile, Col Bacon, the political agent at Gilgit, had convinced Major General Scott (the British commander-in-chief of Jammu and Kashmir State Forces) and Maharaja Hari Singh of Kashmir to have the British officers Brown and Mathieson as commandant and assistant commandant of Gilgit Scouts, respectively.

When Col Bacon informed Major Brown that 'on 1 August 1947 the entire Gilgit Agency will be handed over to the Maharaja of Kashmir and we shall withdraw entirely',[6] Brown reacted describing it 'as monstrous thought that the Gilgit Agency should now be flung into the melting pot by handing it over to Kashmir'.[7] Brown was determined to have this frontier region under the sway of Pax Brittanica. He told Bacon:

> This step might quite well lead to a Soviet wedge being driven into the two new Dominions of the British Empire... All that Gilgit wanted was the peace and security afforded under Pax Brittanica, and the method by which this could have been continued, despite partition, would have been to have made the Gilgit Agency an Agency of the North West Frontier Province under H.E. the Governor.[8]

Mincing no words about his plan, Brown spontaneously agreed to go to Gilgit as commandant of the Gilgit Scouts.[9] According to the Bulletin of Military Historical Society of Great Britain, 'The broad post-partition plan had been discussed by [Major] Brown and the Colonel [Bacon] in June [1947]. And after Mathieson arrived (in Gilgit), as second in command, "the two British Officers refined contingency measures, should the Maharaja take his State over to India".'[10]

While Bacon, the last British political agent, arrived at Gilgit on 29 July 1947, Major Brown also arrived at Gilgit the same day by a small Harvad aircraft which took off from Peshawar.[11] Major General H.L. Scott (the chief of staff of Jammu and Kashmir State Forces), Brigadier Ghansara Singh (the new governor of Gilgit) and Captain Mohammad Said (Jammu and Kashmir State Forces) flew from Srinagar to Gilgit on 30 July 1947. Brigadier Ghansara Singh took over as the governor, being the representative of the Maharaja of Kashmir, and the Jammu and Kashmir state flag was hoisted on 1 August 1947, replacing the Union Jack. This was a fortnight before the independence of India and Pakistan. On the same day, the entire state of Jammu and Kashmir (including Gilgit) was illuminated to celebrate Kashmir's resumption of the civil and military administration of Gilgit. Major Brown claims to have been told in private by Col Bacon: 'I give the Kashmir administration three months in Gilgit. Then something will happen.'[12]

The die had been cast, and soon after taking over as commandant of Gilgit Scouts, Brown started organizing a rebellion of scouts and frontier tribes against Governor Ghansara

Singh. Brown visited Chilas, Gupis, Punial and Yasin, ostensibly to secure the oaths of their loyalty to the Maharaja of Kashmir. However, he actually took stock of the ground situation and firmed up his grip over the tribal chiefs and scouts. From day one, Brown was in a state of treacherous mutiny against Kashmir's Maharaja and his representative Ghansara Singh at Gilgit. While duping the Governor all the time, Brown worked out the brass tacks of his secret operation ensuring that the 6th Kashmir Infantry was kept at bay from the Gilgit Scouts. By the end of August 1947, Brown had tied up the loose ends co-opting all pro-Pakistan Muslims in the Gilgit administration and securing the support of frontier chiefs. The Kashmir battalion, which comprised of 500 well-trained and armed men (one-third Sikhs, one-third Dogras and one-third Muslims)[13], had been posted by Ghansara Singh at Jaglot Chowki and Pratap Pul. This posed a potential obstacle to Brown's plans.

In a late evening conversation with his assistant, Mathieson, Major Brown openly advocated armed rebellion against Kashmir's Maharaja to secure Gilgit for Pakistan. He stated:

> The Governor's (Ghansara Singh's) administration was hopeless and tolerable only if Kashmir remained independent or acceded to Pakistan. The ninety-nine per cent Muslim population unconditionally supported Pakistan. But the only way that the passive support could be converted into direct action would be if the Scouts joined the movement. I knew I had complete control over six platoons of the Scouts and could make them obey my will, whatever it might be. These were the three Hunza platoons, the Punial platoon, the Kuh Ghizar platoon and the Yasin platoon. I had no faith in the three Nagir platoons. The Gilgit platoon was unreliable. Unity in the Scouts was essential. A hint of disruption would lead to chaos, as the Governor would immediately order disbandment and would enforce the order through calling on the help

> of the 6th Kashmir Infantry from Bunji. I shuddered at the thought of the havoc which would follow a decision by the ruler of Kashmir to join India. I considered that the whole of Kashmir, including the Gilgit province, belonged undoubtedly to Pakistan in view of the fact that the population was predominantly Muslim. My sentiments dictated that if the Maharaja acceded to India, then I would forego all allegiance to him and I would not rest content until I had done the utmost in my power to ensure that not only the Gilgit province joined Pakistan, but the whole of Kashmir also. The Rubicon was crossed, and in the future all my actions were governed by these ideas.[14]

Captain Mathieson concurred with Brown and expressed his frank opinion: 'My sentiments dictate that I am bound to support any movement, the object of which is to make the Gilgit province and Kashmir for that matter, an integral part of Pakistan.' Brown replied: 'Yes, Jock, you are quite correct [...] We are going to get blind drunk for the last time until the Gilgit province has become a part of Pakistan.'[15]

Soon after hearing the news of accession of Jammu and Kashmir to India, Brown set in motion Operation Datta Khel. Mathieson started it in Chilas after receiving this signal code from Major Brown. On 30 October 1947, Brown met Governor Ghansara Singh alarming him about the accession of Swat and Chitral to Pakistan and their plans to invade Gilgit on the plea of liberating it.[16] Brown also stated that Khan Abdul Qayum Khan, the Premier of NWFP had pledged the support of all the Pathans in removing Dogra domination.[17] Brown proposed to Ghansara Singh to hold a referendum, which he believed would be in favour of Pakistan.[18] Ghansara Singh was also given an option to leave Gilgit along with his staff and the 6th Kashmir Infantry for Srinagar, so that Brown would become the governor in a bloodless coup. As Ghansara Singh did not oblige, Major Brown laid a siege along with 100 Gilgit Scouts to the Governor's residence on 31

October 1947. After a brief resistance, Ghansara Singh and his staff were imprisoned and the Gilgit Scouts took over. Brown telegraphed Khan Abdul Qayum Khan, the premier of the NWFP, about the pro-Pakistan revolution on 31 October 1947 in Gilgit.[19] Brown also wired Col Bacon, the political agent for Khyber based in Peshawar, about the success.[20] Hindu and Sikh soldiers of the 6th Kashmir Infantry put up a stout resistance, inflicting some casualties on the Gilgit Scouts. However, being outnumbered and with post and telegraph officials and some Muslim staff working for Brown, the fall of Gilgit was manipulated through subterfuge and treachery.

Hindu and Sikh shops and houses in Gilgit were looted and most of them were massacred. Pakistan's representative, Sardar Mohammad Alam, a tehsildar in NWFP, arrived at Gilgit on 16 November 1947 and took over as the political agent. Next day, on 17 November 1947, the Pakistan flag was hoisted on the flagpole of the Gilgit Agency house.[21] Major Aslam Khan, once deputy to Major Khurshid Anwar (one of the key Pakistani strategists who organized the armed invasion of Kashmir from the Muzaffarabad Road), also flew to Gilgit on 16 November 1947 and took over as the commandant of Gilgit Scouts. Major Brown and Captain Mathieson were relieved by Major Aslam Khan and Captain Mohammad Khan as the new commandant and deputy commandant, respectively. Interestingly, a British Air Force officer arrived in Gilgit from Risalpur bringing with him a wireless set for the use of Major Aslam Khan.[22] On 18 November 1947, the Mirs of Hunza and Nagar and Governors of Punial, Kuh-Ghizar, Ishkoman and Yasin arrived in Gilgit in response to a call made by Col Bacon and Major Brown.[23] They expressed their loyalty to Pakistan, after exchanging pleasantries with Mohammad Alam, the Pakistani political agent. The British, represented by George Cunningham and Col Bacon did not wish to see their officers (Brown and Mathieson) continuing to fight openly for Pakistan against India. With their mission accomplished, they were quickly moved out of Gilgit.[24]

All through this operation, Col Bacon served as the main link between Major Brown and the Pakistan government and with George Cunningham. After completing the Operation Datta Khel, Major Brown was called by Col Bacon to Peshawar for a briefing. Brown left Gilgit for Peshawar by air on 25 November 1947 and briefed Col Bacon, George Cunninghan, Khan Abdul Qayum Khan and Col Iskander Mirza (Pakistan's defence secretary).[25] Soon after, a detailed conference was held at Rawalpindi on 3 December 1947 in which Liaquat Ali Khan (PM of Paksitan), Col Iskander Mirza, Col Bacon, Khan Abdul Qayum Khan, Sardar Mohammad Ibrahim (president of Pakistan Occupied Kashmir government) and Major Brown participated. It was decided at this meeting that the territory of Gilgit would be held by Pakistan.[26]

Various contemporary accounts penned by key actors—Col Sayid Durrani (*Inqilab-i-Gilgit: Ek Mukhtasar Jaizah*), Col Ghulam Haidar (*Inqilab-i-Gilgit Meri Nazar Me*), Col Hassan Khan (*Jang-i-Azadi: Gilgit wa Baltistan*), Shah Rais Khan (*History of Gilgit*), William A. Brown (*The Gilgit Rebellion*) and noted Pakistani scholar A.H. Dani's *History of Northern Areas of Pakistan*—point to the lack of unanimity among the leaders of the Anti-Maharaja Movement. While being united in their opposition to the Hindu Maharaja of Kashmir, these leaders were pursuing their own agenda to seek positions of power. They formed the provisional government of Gilgit, which comprised of Shah Rais Khan (president), Captain Sayid Durrani (deputy leader), Captain Mirza Hassan Khan (commander-in-chief), Lt Ghulam Haidar (political agent), Raja Sultan Hamid (chief of police) and Subedar Major Babbar (quarter master).[27] None of the Mirs of Hunza and Nagar, Raja of Punial and Governors of Kuh-Ghizar and Yasin were included/represented in this provisional government. Besides, there was acrimony and mistrust among the local and Punjabi (Pakistani) officials and soldiers. The main unifying factors were their opposition to the Hindu Maharaja and Islamic fervour. The provisional government did not relish the arrival of Mohammad Alam on 16 November 1947 to take over as Pakistan's political agent of Gilgit. It also pressed for the replacement of Major William Brown and Captain Mathieson with Mirza Hassan Khan and Mohammad Sayid as commandant and assistant commandant of Gilgit Scouts, respectively.[28]

According to William Brown, Captain Mirza Hassan wanted to set up an independent Gilgit, which would have friendship with Pakistan, but have no allegiance to it.[29] Interestingly, the Mirs of Hunza and Nagar and Raja of Punial, who had come to Srinagar in July 1947 at the invitation of the Maharaja of Kashmir, were reported to have expressed their loyalty to the Maharaja and agreed to go along with whatever he decided.[30] The Raja of Punial had later come to Nagar along with his guards in an effort to defend Ghansara Singh.[31] While Shah Rais Khan of Gilgit aspired to establish himself as the Raja of Gilgit, the Mehtar of Chitral wished to extend his control over Yasin and Punial.[32] Captain Mirza Hassan Khan, who played a key role in the military operations against Kashmir's forces, aimed to secure a position of power in the new dispensation. Ironically, Hassan Khan and his family were ill-treated by the successive governments in Pakistan for raising their voice against the violations of civil and political rights of the people of Gilgit and Baltistan by the federal government. Hassan Khan's second son, Mirza Wajahat Hassan, has been living in exile in Europe for over a decade now.

The Mirs of Hunza and Nagar remained indifferent and sought to strengthen their positions in the crisis situation. In the words of Prof. A.H. Dani, 'the Rajas played a deliberate diplomatic game, except the Mehtar of Chitral who was out and out for Pakistan'.[33] Major William Brown claimed to have secured the letters of accession of the Mirs of Hunza and Nagar, governors of Kuh-Ghizar and Yasin and Raja of Punial to Pakistan on 3 November 1947.[34] One can safely say that there was no organized and united movement for Pakistan in Gilgit. It was essentially an Islamic current against the Hindu Maharaja. The operation of overthrowing Kashmir's control over Gilgit and its chiefships, and their handover to Pakistan on a platter would not have been successful but for the calibrated actions of the British officers positioned in Kashmir, Gilgit Agency and Peshawar along with the indifference and apathy of the newly independent GoI to the critical developments taking place at the vital and strategic Indian frontier.

Many records[35], leave no doubt about the British partisan policy of making the NWFP, Kashmir and particularly its frontier territory of Gilgit as part of Pakistan. The British High Commissioner to Pakistan Lawrence Grafftey-Smith, in his telegram of 29 October 1947 to Whitehall, described Indian acceptance of the accession of Kashmir as 'the heaviest blow yet sustained by Pakistan in her struggle for existence'. He argued:

> Strategically the frontier of Pakistan, which must be considered as requiring defence, is very greatly extended since India would gain direct access to the North West Frontier Province and tribal areas. Afghanistan policy will almost certainly change for the worse, and disturbances and disorders in Gilgit and the North West Frontier zone generally may...excite Russian interest and appetites.[36]

Grafftey-Smith's opinion weighed heavily on Whitehall, which believed that 'Indian control of the western areas of Jammu and Kashmir would imperil the very existence of Pakistan'.[37] Things became clear when in August 1948 the United Nations Commission for India and Pakistan (UNCIP) 'proposed the withdrawal of Pakistani troops that had entered Kashmir (which would include Pakistani withdrawal from Gilgit also)'[38] and the British opposed the proposal. The United States (US), which was inclined to support the proposal, was persuaded by the British against it. Ernest Bevin (the British foreign secretary) spoke to George Marshall (the US secretary of state) on 27 October 1948, when they were attending the UN General Assembly meeting in Paris.[39] Bevin explained: 'The main issue was who would control the main artery leading into Central Asia. The Indian proposals would leave that in their hands.'[40] As N.S. Sarila puts it, 'Bevin had let the cat out of the bag: that the issue concerning Gilgit was strategic and not of the legality or the presence or otherwise of the Pakistani forces there.'[41] The newly born Pakistan had the immense advantage of firm British support and guidance related to the strategic frontier region of Gilgit. While the well experienced British strategists like Olaf Caroe, George Cunningham and Col Bacon were steering the wheel, the British army officers Major Brown and Captain Mathieson were executing the plan on the ground. The GoI was unmindful of the gravity of the situation and took no measures to prevent the fall of Gilgit in November 1947 and even Baltistan in August 1948. In July 1948, England awarded the Most Exalted Order of the British Empire to Major Brown in recognition of his role in ensuring that this region went to Pakistan.[42]

In early 1958, when Pakistan requested the British government to share a copy of the confidential report of Major Brown's activities in Gilgit, the British authorities considered it inappropriate to give a copy to the Pakistan authorities. Being conscious of their complexity, the British foreign office believed (rightly so) that:

> The content of the report itself is somewhat explosive. Brown was at the time in question in the service of the Kashmir government, yet the report betrays his partiality towards Pakistan. The report highlights the contribution of the Gilgit Scouts under his command to secure Gilgit for Pakistan... The final disposition of the Gilgit Agency, like that of Kashmir is still before the Security Council, and it is incorrect to describe it as one of the 'areas now constituting Pakistan'.[43]

Brown was awarded Sitara-e-Pakistan posthumously by Pakistan, in recognition of his contribution on Pakistan's Independence Day, 1993.[44] Indian forces, supported by the people of Kashmir (led by Sheikh Abdullah, the popular leader of National Conference), pushed back Pakistani armed forces from the

Valley, Pakistan occupied Gilgit, Baltistan and adjoining frontier territories. When the ceasefire was declared in January 1949, the Kashmir Valley, Jammu, Ladakh and Kargil were left within India and Pakistan occupied a vast territory of Mirpur, Muzaffarabad and Gilgit–Baltistan. Later, 2,700 sq. miles of Gilgit–Baltistan were ceded by Pakistan to China in March 1963, in exchange for China's support. In an ironic twist of history, Pakistan, which was considered to be a bulwark against communism and Soviet Russia, became the all-weather and strategic partner of communist China. Both Pakistan and China have developed the main artery through Gilgit to Central Asia first as the KKH and now as CPEC, providing China easy access to the Persian Gulf.

Part III

NEW REALITIES

Fourteen

Migrations from Xinjiang to Kashmir

Thousands of Kashmiris, Balti, Bajaori, Afghan and Shikarpuri traders had taken up residence in Kashgar, Yarkand, Karghalik, Khotan, Aksu and other towns of Xinjiang to carry on their business. Most of them owned property in these places. Being devoid of robbers and free from any sort of political turmoil and due to their liking for India, the Yarkand–Ladakh–Kashmir route was preferred by the Muslims of Xinjiang for undertaking a Haj pilgrimage to Mecca. They braved all hazards of the strenuous journey over the mountains, the hot plains of India and the fatigue of sea travel. It provided a safe passage for the travellers from Xinjiang who mostly belonged to the rich strata of society and carried with them large quantities of bullion and precious items, like carpets and silks, for sale to defray their travel expenses. On numerous occasions, some members of the ruling elite of Xinjiang would come to India seeking safe hideouts, after they fell from grace or during times of political disorder in their country. Muslim migrations from Xinjiang to the neighbouring territory of Jammu and Kashmir took place between 1931 up to 1951, when that region witnessed a series of Muslim uprisings resulting in serious political disorder.

FIRST STREAM OF REFUGEES, 1932–34

By 1932, the Chinese authority in Xinjiang was successfully subverted by the Muslim rebellions of Tungans and Uyghurs. The Tungans had besieged Urumqi, the headquarters of the provincial administration. Khodja Niaz and Sabit Damulla had set up a Muslim administration in Kashgar under the name 'Turkish-Islamic Republic of East Turkestan (TIRET)'. Three Khotanlik brothers, Abdullah Boghra, Noor Ahmadjan Boghra and Mohammed Amin Boghra (known as amirs) held power from Yangi Hissar to Khotan in the southern part of Xinjiang under the title 'Committee for National Revolution' later renamed as the 'Khotan Islamic Government'. By 1934, the Chinese provincial administration was able to crush these Muslim rebellions with the Soviet military's support. The Tungan rebellion in Urumqi was crushed and they now shifted their headquarters to Khotan. There, they came into a head-on collision with the Amirs of Khotan. In the ensuing struggle, the Tungans were able to kill the two younger brothers (Abdullah and Noor Ahmadjan), while the eldest brother fled to India.

In the wake of serious political disorder in Xinjiang, which was accompanied by the massacres of Chinese and other non-Muslims, particularly the Hindu traders by the Muslim separatists, normal trade traffic with India (via Ladakh) was adversely affected. A number of Muslim refugees from Xinjiang (mainly from the elite class) and Indian traders (particularly the Hindus) fled towards India for safety, as all the Hindus trading in Posgam and Karghalik towns were massacred by the Muslim rebels and their property was looted.[1] In the years 1932 and 1933, a large number of Kashgaris came to Gilgit carrying with them gold and merchandise. Their sudden arrival caused problems of food and fodder in Gilgit. Many of these refugees set up shops in Gilgit to eke out a living. But the Kashmir government and British Indian authorities were not inclined to encourage such exodus, which was straining the limited resources of Gilgit. A partial check was imposed on the entry of Kashgar caravans into Gilgit. In August 1934, a Gilgit Scouts post was established at Murkushi along the Hunza–Xinjiang border to turn back any refugees coming from across the border.[2] By the autumn of 1935, all Muslim refugees who had come to Gilgit from the direction of Kashgar, were turned away.[3] Earlier in

May 1934, 22 Muslim soldiers who had been defeated by the Tungans at Kashgar and again at Tuskurghan, sought to enter India via the Misgar outpost. They too were not allowed to enter Indian territory.[4] Similarly, the Chief of Hunza who had been requested by his immediate neighbours in the Sarikol area of Xinjiang to help them against the Kyrgyz attacks, did not assist his Sarikoli friends, as he was advised by the British Political Agent in Gilgit to abstain from any involvement in the internal politics of Xinjiang.[5]

Mohammad Amin Boghra, the eldest brother of the Khotan Amirs was the political refugee of importance who escaped to India during the first phase of Xinjiang disturbances. He arrived at Leh on 1 October 1934, after having been forced out of Khotan by the Tungans.[6] He came to India ostensibly to go on a Haj pilgrimage but actually to seek British Indian support, including arms and ammunition, in his political struggle against the provincial authorities in Xinjiang. He made a formal request for such help to the British Resident in Kashmir through the office of the British Joint Commissioner in Ladakh, both of whom refused to entertain his pleas.[7]

However, in order to discourage him from staying in Ladakh, where he could easily communicate with other Muslim separatists in Xinjiang, Mohammad Amin was allowed to proceed to Mecca via Srinagar.[8] But instead of going on the Haj pilgrimage, he travelled in disguise to Chitral from where he entered Afghanistan.[9] There, he made several vain attempts to persuade the British Indian authorities to allow him to return to Xinjiang via Kashmir. In fact, his petitions sent to the British Legation at Kabul were not even acknowledged and he was not given a visa for re-entry into India.[10] From Kabul, Mohammad Amin travelled to Nanking seeking Kuomintang's support for his political aspirations. He returned to Xinjiang in 1946 as a member of the Kuomintang–East Turkestan Coalition Government led by Chang Chih-Chung as provincial chairman of Xinjiang.[11] Another important political figure Issa Effendi came to Kashmir during this period. However, he later made up with the Kuomintang and returned to join the Xinjiang provincial government at Urumqi (Tihwa).[12]

In the event of political disorder in Xinjiang and the consequent exodus of certain political refugees to India, the British GoI adopted a policy of discouraging both the Tungan and Khotan exiles in their struggle against the Chinese provincial authorities in Xinjiang. This was done with a view to establish good relations with the latter, and more so to discourage the provincial administration in Xinjiang from leaning heavily on Soviet support. In pursuit of this policy, the Indian authorities refused passage through India to any person who was known to be maintaining political interest in Xinjiang's affairs. Besides, a close watch was kept over the movements of Kashgari, Khotanese and Yarkandi traders who were engaged in business dealings at Leh, Srinagar and Amritsar. Not only that, instructions were issued to the postmaster at Gilgit not to allow copies of certain newspapers such as *Yash Turkestan*, *Ahwaz-i-Turkestan* and *Tien Shan* to pass through Gilgit (to Kashgar), as these papers published outside India contained inflammatory material against the Chinese provincial administration in Xinjiang.[13]

TURKI-TUNGAN REFUGEES, 1935–37

Notwithstanding the partial successes achieved by the Chinese provincial authorities in crushing the Muslim rebellions led by Khodja Niaz, Tungans and Khotan Amirs by 1934, new centres of Muslim resistance emerged following a realignment of the anti-government forces. While the authority of Tungans was now confined only to Khotan, Yarkand and adjoining areas, the eldest of the Khotan Amirs, while in exile in Kabul, tried to make common cause with his erstwhile foes, the Tungans, with a view to launch a joint struggle against the Soviet-backed Chinese authorities in Xinjiang. General Mahmud of Turfan, who was the chief military commander in TIRET headed by Khodja Niaz during 1933–34, later came to terms with the provincial administration that appointed him as commander of Muslim troops at Kashgar in July 1934.

The fragile Turko-Chinese alliance, which enjoyed Soviet support and held sway over Xinjiang since 1934 appeared to break down in 1937 when the pan-Turkic-Islamic forces started realigning themselves in a combined endeavour to oust the Chinese from the Xinjiang region. But both the Turkic forces, led by General Mahmud, and the Tungans, led by General Ma Hu-Shan, suffered a crushing defeat at the hands of government troops that received active military and aerial support from the Soviets. This was followed by a series of Chinese reprisals against the Muslim rebels, which resulted in a renewed exodus to India via Ladakh and Kashmir. The first group of about 400 Tungan refugees from Xinjiang came via western Tibet and crossed into Ladakh at the Demchok frontier in the winter of 1935. There, they were disarmed by Jammu and Kashmir state forces and were asked to stay in Ladakh for the winter. But the Tungans did not stay in Ladakh and moved on to cross the Zoji La Pass to enter Kashmir. On reaching Srinagar, they were lodged in a building. Later, the British Indian authorities evacuated all the Tungan refugees to the NWFP.[14]

General Mahmud, the erstwhile commander of Turki troops in Kashgar, his brother Mosul Mohammad Beg and 19 of his junior officers comprised the second stream of political refugees from Xinjiang who entered Ladakh in April 1937.[15] Mahmud was obliged to escape to India as he anticipated reprisals following his serious differences with the provincial authorities. As soon as the Indian government learnt about the arrival of Mahmud and his party at Leh, it decided (with the approval of the British Secretary of State for India) to disarm them and remove them to India,[16] where they could not intrigue against those in authority at Kashgar. General Mahmud and his followers reached Srinagar on 24 May 1937, carrying about 1,800 tolas (about 720 ounces) of gold and some money to defray their daily expenses. Though they wanted to stay in Kashmir due to its favourable climate, the British GoI was not inclined to accede to their request. In June 1937, Mahmud and some of his companions went to Calcutta to represent their case before the Chinese Consul General. In his meeting with the Consul General, Mahmud complained against the 'increasing Bolshevik influence' over Sheng Shih-ts'ai's administration in Xinjiang and sought the Nanking government's 'intervention to relieve our people of this grave danger to our lives and properties and above all to our religion'.[17] In July 1937, Mahmud returned to Srinagar where he continued to remain in touch with General Ma Hu-Shan, and other anti-government forces in Xinjiang.[18] Mahmud stayed in Srinagar till 14 October 1937, when he left for Punjab with the avowed object of proceeding to Mecca on Haj pilgrimage.[19] But during his stay in Lahore, Mahmud continued to send messages to the Muslim separatists in Kashgar. Finally, he along with some of his followers left India (via Karachi) on 23 January 1938, for Jeddah from where he wanted to go to Mecca or even to Constantinople to muster support for the Islamic movement against the Xinjiang provincial authorities.[20]

By mid-1937, the Tungan resistance to the provincial administration in Xinjiang faded away. With the departure of General Ma Hu-Shan in early September 1937 from Kashgar for India, the politico-military might of the Tungans in Southern Xinjiang was completely destroyed.[21] For the first time since its establishment, the Sheng Shih-ts'ai regime in Xinjiang was able to exercise effective control over the southern oasis. Ma Hu-Shan and his Tungan troops indulged in looting of property in Xinjiang in the course of their retreat and they escaped to India, bringing this loot chiefly in bullion. The Xinjiang provincial administration took a serious note of the successful flight of Turki and Tungan rebels to India via the Ladakh route and it sought the extradition of Ma Hu-Shan by the Indian government.[22] While the British GoI was unable to extradite Ma Hu-Shan in the absence of an extradition treaty, nonetheless, it issued orders for the confiscation of all property, including arms and money that was found in the possession of Ma Hu-Shan and his party. It also asked for his removal from Srinagar at the earliest, to minimize the chances of his intrigue against the Xinjiang government.[23] General Ma Hu-Shan and a party of about 64 Tungans, including his family and servants, arrived at Leh from Yarkand on 26 September 1937.[24] While the British GoI decided to send back the Tungan refugees as soon as the passes on the Leh–Karakoram–Yarkand route opened,[25] the Kashmir government insisted upon the removal of these refugees from Kashmir's territory at the earliest, as they were considered to be 'a menace to administration' and unnecessary strain on the meagre food supplies of the state.[26] Accordingly, 28 Tungan refugees were turned back from Leh towards Xinjiang and their arms and ammunition were confiscated by Kashmir's authorities.[27] Besides, about 4,600 ounces of gold in the form of bars, dust and ornaments worth about ₹4.5 lakh, which were found in the possession of Ma Hu-Shân and his followers, were confiscated and placed in the Kashmir Government's Treasury at Srinagar.[28] Soon after, in December 1937, Ma Hu-Shan and some of his followers met the Chinese Consul General at Calcutta to seek the Chinese central government's help in their movement against the Xinjiang provincial authorities. While Ma Hu-Shan and his companions left Calcutta for Canton in September 1938, 95 other Tungan refugees were subsequently repatriated by the Indian authorities to China proper.[29]

As regards to the disposal of confiscated gold brought by Ma Hu-Shan and his party, the British GoI agreed to hand over the same to the Xinjiang provincial administration after deducting the amount spent on the maintenance and repatriation of Tungan refugees from Kashmir to China, and payment of compensation to the Indian nationals who had suffered losses due to looting in Xinjiang during the Turki-Tungan uprising.[30] But the Chinese Central government raised objections and sought the transfer of the balance of this gold to them and not to the authorities in Xinjiang. The issue was finally resolved after the government in Xinjiang consented to the transfer of this gold to the Chinese Central government through its Consul General at Calcutta, to which the British agreed.[31] Out of the total ₹4.5 lakh worth of gold, an amount of about ₹2 lakh was spent on the maintenance and repatriation of Tungan refugees to China and compensation to Indian nationals who suffered losses during the 1937 uprising (who were later deported by the Xinjiang provincial authorities to India).[32] Finally, ₹3.5 lakh worth of gold was refunded to the Chinese Central government in 1943,[33] thereby acknowledging it to be the lawful owner of this property, which had been looted by the Tungan rebels in Xinjiang in 1937.

The Turki rebel leader General Mahmud's proceedings in India and his meetings with the representative of Central Nanking government at Calcutta, which had very little influence over the far-flung province of Xinjiang, evoked a sharp reaction from the provincial authorities. The Administrative Commissioner at Kashgar conveyed to the British Consul General his government's protest against the supposedly 'lenient' treatment meted out to the subversives of Xinjiang in India.[34] When the Tungan leader General Ma Hu-Shan and his party entered India via the Ladakh frontier, Xinjiang's authorities became more suspicious of possible British complicity in encouraging the Turki-Tungan uprising. So far as the British Indian government was concerned, it was in a fix, as the Chinese Consul General at Calcutta asked for transit facilities for Ma Hu-Shan and his party. Besides, the Kashmir government was maintaining a small garrison at Ladakh, which was not sufficient to turn back all the Tungan refugees from that territory.

However, both the Kashmiri and Indian authorities took certain steps to assuage the feelings of the Xinjiang authorities, such as the ejection of such refugees back to Xinjiang, the repatriation of the remaining ones to China proper and the confiscation of arms and property, particularly gold. The British Indian government even returned the balance amount of gold to the Chinese government in a bid to create goodwill with Xinjiang's administration. But this did not deter the provincial authorities from initiating repressive measures against the Indian settlers and traders in Xinjiang, including their deportation to India in miserable conditions. This anti-Indian attitude of the provincial authorities was mainly due to the flight of Mahmud and Ma Hu-Shan,[35] the leaders of the Turki-Tungan uprising, to India and the alleged involvement of certain Indian Muslim settlers from Southern Xinjiang in this rebellion.

THE KAZAKH EXODUS, 1941–42

A body of about 18,000 Kazakhs from the Tien Shan and Barkol areas in northern Xinjiang left their homes to escape the persecution of Muslim rebels by the Sheng Shih-ts'ai regime.[36] These Kazakh groups, which were led by their chiefs, Sultan Sharif and Hussain Taji, first took refuge in the uninhabited region near Gez Kol on the Xinjiang–Tsinghai–Kansu frontier.[37] Some of them moved after some time towards Kokonor lake in search of livelihood. By 1941, they had entered Tibetan territory where they were reported to have indulged in looting of monasteries, traders and passers-by. Due to their depredations, the Tibetan troops pushed the Kazakhs out of their territory, following which they made off towards Ladakh. Out of the original 5,000 Kazakhs who had left for Tibet, only about 3,000 were able to make their way to the Ladakh frontier.[38] It was in early October 1941 that a caravan consisting of about 3,000 horses and 1,000 camels entered Jammu and Kashmir territory through the Ladakh–Tibet frontier at Demchok.[39] On receipt of the information about the Kazakh exodus to Ladakh, Kashmir authorities reinforced the state military post at Demchok to prevent any such incursion.

On 6 October 1941, an armed clash took place between the state troops and the advance party of Kazakhs, which resulted in the death of six Kazakhs.[40] Since the Kazakh caravan heavily outnumbered the small contingent of 80 Dogra soldiers manning the Demchok frontier post, it became difficult for Kashmir's forces to stop the Kazakhs from entering Ladakh. However, the personal intervention of the Wazir of Ladakh, who went to the spot, and the gallant resistance put up by the Dogra soldiers prevented the situation from getting out of control. The Kazakhs were allowed to proceed to British India through the state territory only after they surrendered their arms [41] and undertook an oath to remain peaceful.[42] To ensure their proper conduct, the Kazakh caravan was accompanied by a strong contingent of Kashmir troops (especially brought from Srinagar) from Ladakh up to the camp set up at Muzaffarabad for their temporary stay.[43]

Such a massive immigration of Muslim Kazakhs from Xinjiang to Kashmir created a commotion among the official and public circles in India. While the Jammu and Kashmir government was against the prolonged stay of Kazakh refugees inside the state territory, the British Indian authorities found it impossible to eject such a huge number of refugees by force keeping in view the practical difficulties in doing so (mainly due to the onset of winter) and also on humanitarian considerations. However, public opinion in India, more particularly in Jammu and Kashmir, got polarized along communal lines on this issue. The Jammu and Kashmir Muslim Conference, the J&K National Conference (headed by Sheikh Abdullah) and the Muslim press[44], took an open stand in support of granting full amenities to these Muslim Kazakh refugees. Both the Muslim Conference and National Conference, the main political parties, did all in their means to overplay this humanitarian problem in a bid to widen their political base among the Muslim masses of the state. While the Muslim Conference voiced its demand to set up an enquiry commission to look into the circumstances leading to firing by state troops on Kazakhs at Demchok, the National Conference passed a resolution alleging the state government's indifference towards the Kazakh refugees and demanding full relief facilities for them on humanitarian grounds. The National Conference took up the task of providing relief to the Kazakh refugees[45], and a special 'Kazakh Refugees Relief Committee' was set up for this purpose. Sheikh Abdullah's assertion that the National Conference was not interested in the permanent settlement of Kazakh refugees in Kashmir in order to increase the ratio of Muslims in its population did not help in removing the suspicions entertained by non-Muslims on this account. The Hindu press, particularly *Chand*, *Sudarshan*, *Kashmir Times* and *Martand*, were sore about the manner in which the Muslim leaders of Kashmir were overzealously taking up the issue of Kazakh refugees.

On its part, the state government described the National Conference's allegations of indifferent governmental attitude towards Kazakhs as 'mischievous propaganda'.[46] It detailed the steps taken for setting up of a relief camp at Muzaffarabad, providing free provisions, medical facilities to these refugees and free fodder for their livestock, etc.[47] Meanwhile, the Bhotia traders of Almora pressed their claims with the GoI for compensation on account of losses suffered due to looting by Kazakhs in western Tibet before they entered Ladakh in October 1941. This matter was raised by several Indian members in the Central Legislative Assembly and the Foreign Department Secretary Olaf Caroe had to concede the demand for search of baggage of Kazakh refugees in Kashmir to recover stolen property from them.[48] In one instance, the British Indian authorities decided to pay ₹8,000 as compensation to an Indian trader Sher Singh, who had alleged that the Kazakh refugees had stolen some goods from him at the Leh Bazaar in Ladakh.[49] After deducting this amount, the Kashmiri government was reimbursed ₹106,708, 2 annas and 6 paise towards expenses incurred by Kashmir's government for the maintenance of Kazakhs while on Kashmir's territory.[50]

Eventually, the British Indian government took up the responsibility of maintenance of Kazakh refugees and it was decided to shift them away from Kashmir territory to Hazara district in the NWFP. The Kazakhs were transported at government expense to a camp at Tarnawa where they arrived on 2 May 1942.[51] Even though the Kazakhs were provided free ration, fuel, fodder and medical aid, about 650 refugees died due to disease, hardships of the journey and unfavourable climate during their one-year stay in Hazara.[52] The British Indian government, which was under constant pressure from several Muslim organizations to provide for the permanent settlement of Muslim Kazakh refugees in India, spent more than ₹5.5 lakh on their maintenance in India.[53] The states of Bhopal and Hyderabad agreed to have some of these refugees settled there. But only 588 Kazakhs agreed to shift to Bhopal, the rest having left the Tarnawa Camp in batches till it was fully vacated on 8 May 1943.[54] After one year of stay in Bhopal, the Kazakhs approached the Chinese Consul General in Calcutta for assistance. The Consul General acknowledged them to be Chinese nationals and took the responsibility of looking after those Kazakhs who wanted to return to China.[55] Tired of their wanderings for more than seven years, and finding life in the hot plains of India unsuitable to their nomadic way of life, most of the Kazakhs moved out of India in batches.

COMMUNIST TAKEOVER OF XINJIANG AND THE FINAL EXODUS, 1949–51

By the end of 1949, the PLA succeeded in establishing the authority of the CCP in Xinjiang after it crushed all elements of the Turkish-Islamic separatist movement and also the remnants of the Kuomintang government.[56] With the communist takeover, the remaining anti-communist forces in Xinjiang—represented by the adherents of the Kuomintang regime; the Turkish-Islamic separatists led by leaders like Mohammad Amin Bughra and Isa Yusaf Alaptekin; and the Kazakh separatists owing allegiance to chieftains like Yulbaz Khan, Usman Bator, Dalil Khan, Hussain Taji and Sultan Sharif—fled for safety. In the months of October 1949 to January 1950, nearly 789 Muslim refugees from Xinjiang crossed over into Ladakh via the Yarkand–Leh trade route.[57] Out of them, 154 persons returned to Xinjiang after arrival in Ladakh. The remaining refugees stayed in Leh and Srinagar. They included 377 men, 113 women, 111 children of school age and 34 children under the school age, 5 political leaders, 35 government officials, 12 religious leaders, 69 merchants, 42 skilled workers and 186 farmers.[58] Besides, almost all Indian traders (including Kashmiri Muslim and Shikarpuri Hindu traders) who had settled in the southern oasis towns of Xinjiang, returned to India following the sealing of Xinjiang's borders and the closure of Indian and Pakistani consulates there. However, there were numerous instances of Muslim refugees from Xinjiang having migrated to Pakistan via the Kashgar–Gilgit route.

Isa Yusuf Alaptekin (former secretary general of Xinjiang government) and Mohammad Amin Bughra (former vice governor of Xinjiang, who later spearheaded the movement for independence of East Turkestan from exile in Turkey) were among the first arrivals at Leh.[59] These refugees were lodged at Srinagar in the Yarkandi serai—the traditional abode of Central Asian traders and travellers in Kashmir. Once in India, Isa Alaptekin and Bughra enlisted the support of Sheikh Abdullah, the then chief minister of Jammu and Kashmir and other Muslim leaders like Maulana Azad (the then education minister of India). They also approached the Indian PM, Jawaharlal Nehru, seeking the GoI's permission for the temporary stay of Xinjiang's refugees in India. Bughra and Alaptekin met the Indian foreign secretary at New Delhi on 13 March 1950, requesting the GoI to secure exemption from the usual taxes levied by Saudi Arabia on the Xinjiang refugees (who were keen to go to Saudi Arabia for Haj pilgrimage and subsequently settle there).[60] Over 400 such refugees were reported to have already gone to Saudi Arabia and settled in the Chinese-Turks's colony in Mecca and Medina. Bughra and Alaptekin also sought arrangements to be made for the admission of refugee children in schools and also sought exemption from school fees. Subsequently, the Indian government approached the Saudi Arabian Consul at Bombay with the request to 'sympathetically consider the grant of exemption from usual levies made from pilgrims to Haj, in favor of refugees desirous of proceeding to Saudi Arabia for permanent settlement'.[61] The Indian Ministry of Education also agreed to assist children of these refugees to enter schools and colleges in India and to consider the exemption of their school fees.[62]

In May 1950, the GoI took up the matter of assistance to 600 Xinjiang refugees with the International Refugee Organization (IRO) at Geneva. But P. Jacobsen, assistant director general of IRO, in his reply of 12 June 1950, declined any help saying that since 'the majority of this group are Chinese "Turk Muslims", these persons cannot be considered as falling within the mandate of this organization, and are, therefore, not entitled to our assistance'.[63] Alaptekin met Indian Foreign Secretary K.P.S. Menon at Delhi on 18 August 1950 requesting for visas to be granted for at least two years's stay in India for the 117 refugees who still remained in the country.[64] In October 1950, the GoI sent its clearance to the Jammu and Kashmir government for the stay of these 117 refugees for a further period of six months in the first instance, 'provided these people do not act as a magnet for more refugees from Xinjiang'.[65] While the GoI provided its humanitarian assistance to Xinjiang's refugees during their stay in India, it was averse to their settlement in India and encouraged their departure from the country. Bughra, Alaptekin and Adam Sabri sent a joint letter on 8 March 1950 to PM Nehru, conveying their 'personal thanks for the great and practical sympathy shown by the GoI'[66] towards the refugees from Xinjiang. Since the members of this party belonged to elite and rich mercantile classes in Xinjiang, they found little difficulty in maintaining themselves in Kashmir. Most of these refugees proceeded to Saudi Arabia, Turkey or Formosa.

In early August 1951, another small caravan of 95 Kazakhs (including 37 women and 29 children), accompanied by their livestock, entered Ladakh from the direction of western Tibet.[67] When the State Border Police tried to push them back into Tibet, the Kazakh refugees refused to go.[68] They were disarmed and allowed to enter the state territory on humanitarian grounds, as most of them were women and children. This fresh exodus of Kazakhs to Ladakh followed the breakdown of the Kazakh resistance at the hands of PLA forces in eastern Xinjiang. When the Kazakh leaders like Usman Bator and Yulbaz Khan retreated to Gez Kol in the spring of 1950, they came in contact with those Kazakhs who had shifted there during the 1934–36 disturbances in Xinjiang.[69] But when the PLA forces launched a major offensive on 1 February 1951 against the Kazakhs in this area, they captured their leaders Usman Bator and Janim Khan (forcing the rest to flee towards India via Tibet).[70] While Yulbaz Khan escaped to Taiwan[71] via the Tibet–Darjeeling–Calcutta route, other Kazakh chieftains like Ali Beg Rahim, Hussain Taji, Dalil Khan and Sultan Sharif succeeded in evading Chinese pursuit. Then, together with a few hundred Kazakhs, they reached the frontiers of Ladakh in August 1951.[72]

Soon after the arrival of the first batch of 95 Kazakh refugees in Kashmir, the GoI asked Jammu and Kashmir's authorities not to accept any more refugees and to close the Tibet–Ladakh border, keeping in view the friendly relations between India and China.[73] Notwithstanding the ban on their entry, the Kazakhs continued to sneak into Ladakh through western Tibet. When a group of 175 refugees led by Dalil Khan arrived at the borders of Ladakh in September 1951, they were detained at the icy frontier for more than a month.[74] But following various representations made to Sheikh Abdullah by Bughra and Kazakh representatives, the Kashmir government gave permission to another caravan of Kazakh refugees to enter the state.[75] The plight of Kazakhs who narrated their sufferings at the hands of Chinese communists, generated sympathy among public circles in Kashmir and some quarters even pressed the Indian government to permit the Kazakhs to settle permanently in Kashmir.[76]

But the GoI was averse to any such proposal. Speaking in Indian Parliament on 21 September 1951, PM Nehru declared that the GoI policy was to 'stop their entry into Jammu and Kashmir and to send back as far as possible those who have already entered'.[77] While confirming that about 450 Kazakhs refugees had entered the state, Pandit Nehru explained that the 'government placed every difficulty'[78] in the way of Kazakhs settling down in Kashmir. However, with the Turkish government agreeing to settle Xinjiang's refugees permanently in Turkey, the problem of their rehabilitation in India was solved. They left Srinagar in batches for Turkey and the cost of their passage from Srinagar to Bombay and from Bombay to Turkey was borne by the Kashmir government and American World Church Society, respectively. The last of the Kazakh refugees left Srinagar on 12 June 1954 for Turkey.[79] However, some Muslim refugees from Xinjiang continued to live in Srinagar till late 1960s, when they finally shifted to Turkey. Due to their cultural, linguistic and racial ties with the Turkish people, the Xinjiang refugees did not encounter any difficulty in assimilating in Turkish society.

After the Chinese Revolution of 1911 and the consequent end of Qing rule, Xinjiang entered an era of warlordism, which lasted till the mid-1940s. All the successive provincial leaders were Han Chinese—Yang Tseng-Hsin (1911–28), Chin Shu-Jen (1928–33), Sheng Shish-ts'ai (1933–44)—whose authoritarian and exploitative policies acted as a catalyst for a series of Muslim uprisings that rocked Xinjiang from 1931 to 1949. Notwithstanding their thrust on pan-Islamic ideology and avowed hatred for Han Chinese, the leaders of the Muslim rebellions often worked at cross purposes. The Turkic Muslim leaders of Kumul, Khoja Niaz Haji and Yulbaz Khan, sought the assistance of Nanking in their struggle against the Chin Shu-Jen regime in Xinjiang. As against this, the Muslim uprisings in Southern Xinjiang were openly pan-Islamic and secessionist in character.

The establishment of TIRET between 1933–34, which was based on the principles of Islamic Sharia, was an abortive attempt to establish an Islamic theocracy in Xinjiang. But this experiment was doomed to fail as the Turkic Muslim leaders of Tarim Basin viewed Tungans (Chinese Muslims Huis) and Muslim leaders of the Kumul uprising as collaborators of Han Chinese. With the growing Turkic-Tungan hostility, a process of killings of Uyghurs by the Tungans and vice versa started. The political turmoil in Xinjiang took a serious turn with the recurrence of Muslim attacks on Han Chinese, which were followed by counter reprisals by the Chinese forces, whenever they had an upper hand. Such an anarchic situation resulted in several migrations of people (including defeated fugitives from Xinjiang) to adjoining territories, particularly after the retreating rebels were pursued by Chinese troops.

Whenever such migrations did take place to Kashmir (or its frontier territories of Gilgit, Hunza and Ladakh) the Indian government not only took firm steps to discourage such immigration but also refused to get involved in any manner in the internal politics of Xinjiang. This policy was dictated by the desire to maintain good relations with China and to discourage the provincial administration of Xinjiang from leaning heavily on Soviet support. It was in pursuit of this policy that the few Kashgari refugees, mainly traders who had arrived at Gilgit in 1932–33, were ejected later on and a strict check was imposed on any further ingress from across the border. The Chief of Hunza was not allowed to entertain requests for help from Sarikoli neighbours.

While the stray incidents of some fugitives entering India via Kashmir during the years 1932–34 and 1937 were adequately dealt with by the Indian government, the influx of about 3,000 destitute Kazakhs—mostly women and children—from Xinjiang into Ladakh via Tibet in 1941–42 created a commotion in public circles in India, particularly Kashmir. The state authorities were against their stay in Kashmir's territory, as the Kazakhs were considered to be a law-and-order problem besides being a drain on local resources. But the public opinion in the Muslim majority state was in favour of granting full relief facilities to the Kazakhs on humanitarian grounds. As mentioned previously, the main political parties—the National Conference and Muslim Conference—and the local Muslim press raised their voice in favour of the Kazakhs who had obviously succeeded in generating public sympathy in Kashmir. They described their woes of persecution at the hands of the Chinese authorities in Xinjiang. Apart from the Indian Muslim League, several Muslim organizations like the Red Crescent Society (Lahore), Kazakh Relief Committee (Abbotabad) and Kazakh Refugee Relief Committee (set up by the National Conference) played a key role in organizing relief for the Kazakh refugees. However, the Indian authorities took a calculated decision to shift the Kazakh refugees away from Kashmiri territory to Hazara district in the NWFP, thereby precluding any chance of their communication with the Muslim separatists in Xinjiang.

In late 1949 when the PLA forces were consolidating their position in Xinjiang, all Indian traders settled in the southern oasis towns of that province returned to India via the overland Yarkand–Leh route. Besides, a few hundred Muslim Uyghurs belonging to elite and rich trading classes came to Kashmir by the same route. Some Muslim separatist leaders like Alptekin and Bughra also used this occasion to escape from Xinjiang. But when the borders of Xinjiang were sealed to outside traffic following the establishment of the Chinese Communist Xinjiang Provincial government in December 1949, the Xinjiang traders and travellers already in Kashmir preferred to stay back. Two years later, some batches of Kazakh refugees entered Ladakh from the direction of Tibet. Though these refugees were lodged temporarily in Srinagar in the Yarkandi serai and were also provided some relief by the Kashmir authorities, the Indian government decided to discourage any further ingress of such refugees into India keeping in view the harmonious relations between India and China. PM Nehru, made a categorical statement that the GoI policy was to stop the entry of refugees from Xinjiang into Jammu and Kashmir and to send back as far as possible those who had already entered. Subsequently, almost all the Kazakh and Uyghur refugees from Xinjiang migrated to Turkey[80] for permanent settlement while some found their way to Saudi Arabia, Pakistan[81] and Taiwan. At no point of time, the GoI showed any interest in making any political capital of the deep hurt and sufferings of these refugees due to communist

Chinese takeover of Xinjiang. With the departure of Xinjiang's refugees from Kashmir to their new homes, an important chapter in the history of Kashmir's contacts with Xinjiang in modern times came to a close.

Fifteen

Karakoram Highway to CPEC

Soon after the takeover of Xinjiang by communist China, the Chinese embarked upon building a system of mountain routes linking Xinjiang with Tibet and the mountain regions of Gilgit–Baltistan controlled by Pakistan. This altered the geopolitical balance of power in the region. By 1957, China had completed the construction of a road through the Indian territory of Aksai Chin in Ladakh, providing a vital link between Xinjiang and Tibet. As China was preparing for war against India, it had reached an understanding with Pakistan in early 1961 to discuss and demarcate the border between Xinjiang and the contiguous area of Hunza (under the occupation of Pakistan). The Sino-Pakistan Boundary Agreement of 2 March 1963, by which the two countries agreed to delimit and demarcate the said boundary, laid the foundation of the all-weather friendship and strategic alliance between China and Pakistan. This was followed by agreements on trade, air links, building of roads, etc. Pakistan's membership of the western blocks of SEATO (Southeast Asia Treaty Organization) and CENTO (Central Treaty Organization) and close relations with the US, did not come in its way of building deep and long-lasting strategic relationship with communist China. The joint Sino-Pak project of KKH provided China 'with a logistical, political and diplomatic asset'.[1] To quote Mehnaz Ispahani, a noted Pakistani scholar, China's routing policies were 'closely linked to its military postures along its western and north-western borders'.[2]

THE KARAKORAM HIGHWAY

In 1959, the Pakistan Army Engineers started the construction of the 248-km-long Indus Valley Road connecting Havelian, Thakot, Besham and Pattan (up to Chilas).[3] Simultaneously, Gilgit Public Works Department took up the work of widening the 144-km-long stretch from Chilas to Gilgit.[4] The Indus Valley Road project thus became the precursor of the KKH project. In 1966, China and Pakistan concluded agreements for the construction of the highway linking Rawalpindi with Khunjerab Pass and for Chinese assistance and supply of bridging equipment and construction machinery.[5] The same year, Pakistan established the Frontier Works Organization (FWO) with headquarters in Gilgit, mobilizing seven battalions of Pakistan Army Engineers (10,000 men).[6] By 1971, FWO had completed the construction of 490-km-long stretch from Thakot to Hallehgush, and 156 km of the road between Hallehgush and Khunjerab Pass was built by the Chinese.[7] This phase of KKH was inaugurated on 16 February 1971 at Ganish. The opening ceremony was attended by General Abdul Hameed (chief of Pakistan army staff) and Yung Chih (China's minister of communications). Earlier, in August 1969, after about 20 years closure, a 50-camel caravan came from Kashgar crossing the Karakoram mountains at Mintaka Pass to reach Gilgit. It brought silk, carpets, pressure cookers and tea.[8] Both the Chinese and Pakistani traders were reported to have bartered goods worth US$16,667.[9]

In 1973, Pakistan and China signed an agreement for joint work on widening and converting the existing road into a two-lane international highway called the KKH to 'consolidate the economic, political and military links' between the two countries.[10] 15,000 Pakistani and 12,000 Chinese workers were moved to the Gilgit region to work on this mountain highway.[11] The KKH, also called the China–Pakistan Friendship Highway, was completed in 1978. It was inaugurated on 18 June 1978 at Thakot, by the then President of Pakistan General Zia-ul-Haq and the Chinese Vice

Premier Kang Piao who led a high-level Chinese delegation. The new, metalled, KKH is a 1,300-km-long road—887 km in Pakistan, known as Pakistan National Highway N-35, and 413 km in China, running across the Khunjerab pass in Gilgit to Kashgar in Xinjiang where it becomes China National Highway 314.

According to a renowned American journalist Seymour Topping, KKH provides China 'crucial overland links to the west and strengthens Pakistan against pressures from India and Afghanistan'.[12] Topping quoted the then Chinese Deputy PM Li Xunnian saying that the KKH 'allows us to give military aid to Pakistan'.[13] According to Indian defence experts, the 10-m-wide metalled road was built to take 5-tonne vehicles, light armoured cars, tanks, artillery guns, etc., aimed at augmenting Pakistan's operational and logistic capability in terms of Chinese supplies and reinforcements.[14] The KKH connects the main Pakistani towns of Rawalpindi, Hasan Abdal, Haripur, Abbotabad, Mansehra, Battagram, Besham, Pattan, Kohistan, Chilas, Jaglot, Gilgit, Nagar, Aliabad, Gulmit and Sust (a dry port along the Pak-China border). Pakistan's immigration and customs offices are based at Sust, from where the highway proceeds to Tashkurghan and Kashgar in the Xinjiang region of China. The KKH has facilitated Sino-Pak border trade, which, in 1985, was estimated to be around US$200 million.[15] The share of overland trade via KKH was reported to be a miniscule 4 per cent, the Chinese imports constituting about 83 per cent even when the Sino-Pak trade had reached US$7 billion.[16] However, Sino-Pak trade via the Khunjerab Pass was reported to have grown by about 47 per cent to US$856.3 million in 2019.[17]

The KKH has been more of strategic importance, as it enables Pakistan to extend its communications and transportation network and assert its physical possession of the mountainous territory of Gilgit–Baltistan (a disputed area claimed by India).[18] Besides, the feeder roads and bridges—built with Chinese help along Qala Panja, Mintaka and Wakhjir passes, and in Gupis, Yasin, Darel, Tangir and Shigar valleys—have strengthened Pakistan's military assets in these remote frontier areas and developed direct links between Gilgit–Baltistan and Afghanistan and Tajikistan.[19] China has also built a feeder road through Shaksgam, Raskam and Shimshal valleys to link 'Gilgit with Hotan, which is an important military base situated at the cross-section of Tibet-Xinjiang Highway and the Hotan-Golmud Highway', thereby connecting the military complexes in West Tibet with Xinjiang and Pakistan.[20]

THE CHINA–PAKISTAN ECONOMIC CORRIDOR (CPEC)

Due to its geo-strategic location being the crossroads of South Asia, Central Asia and West Asia, Pakistan provides shortest overland access to China and Central Asian republics to the sea. Soon after the independence of Central Asian republics, Pakistan strived to use the KKH as a corridor for the Chinese (Xinjiang) and Central Asian trade and traffic. Accordingly, a quadrilateral Agreement on Traffic in Transit was signed on 9 March 1995 by Pakistan, China, Kazakhstan and Kyrgyzstan, to open and promote overland traffic. This was followed by the signing of protocols on customs procedures for traffic in transit and visa regime (in July 1996) and on establishing a system of International Road Transit Permit for traffic in transit (in November 1996) among these four countries. The agreement could be operationalized only in 2004 due to delays in clearing immigration and customs procedures, etc. Meanwhile, in 2006, a memorandum of understanding was signed between Pakistan's National Highway Authority (NHA) and China's State-owned Assets Supervision and Administration Commission (SASAC), to widen the KKH from 10 m to 30 m and upgrade it for use by vehicles during extreme weather conditions. But in early 2010, a series of landslides near Atabad in Gilgit submerged about a 20-km-long stretch of KKH and blocked the Hunza River by creating a large lake, which halted usage of the highway. The upgrade of the highway and construction of tunnels was completed in 2018, after which traffic was restored on the KKH. Upgrading the highway from Raikot in Gilgit to Thakot in

Khyber Pakhtoonkhwa, has also been undertaken. Another road has been built from Havelian to Burhan in Punjab, so that the KKH intersects with the existing six-lane Peshawar–Islamabad highway. The reconstruction of KKH, which involves building new bridges and tunnels, and extending its connectivity to Pakistan's highway network, is aimed at reducing the distance and travel time from Khunjerab Pass on the Sino-Pak border to the CPEC.

When Pakistan's President Asif Ali Zardari visited China in July 2010, he sought Chinese assistance in upgrading the existing KKH and building a rail link along the route connecting Xinjiang with Gilgit–Baltistan. Pakistan urged China to tap the potential of Gwadar port, which has been built with Chinese assistance. In February 2013, Pakistan handed over the Gwadar port to the China Overseas Port Holding Company on a 43-year lease. The development of Gwadar includes building of roads, manufacturing and logistics hubs, warehouses, an international airport, a coal power plant and other infrastructure. Gwadar is integral to CPEC with proposed energy pipelines, road and rail links connecting it to Xinjiang through Gilgit–Baltistan via the KKH. The reconstruction and upgrading of KKH has been undertaken under the framework of the CPEC. While the CPEC is touted as the 'flagship' and 'frontrunner' project[21] of China's Belt and Road Initiative (BRI), the upgrade of KKH has formed the crucial component of CPEC.

CPEC is a 3,000-km-long corridor, connecting Gwadar port in Pakistan to Kashgar in Xinjiang (via the Pakistan-occupied territory of Gilgit–Baltistan). It is a collection of infrastructure, railways, roads, energy, hydel-power, communications projects and special economic zones (SEZs), originally estimated to cost about $46 billion, which has now increased to $62 billion. China and Pakistan began negotiations on the modalities and projects of CPEC in May 2013 during the visit of Chinese Premier Li Keqiang to Pakistan. The discussions were carried forward by Pakistan PM Nawaz Sharif during his visit to China in April

2014. The project was formally launched during the state visit of Chinese President Xi Jinping to Pakistan in April 2015. President Xi outlined the framework of CPEC in his signed article titled, 'China-Pak Dosti Zindabad', stressing the need to 'form a "1+4" cooperation structure with the CPEC at the centre and the Gwadar port, energy, infrastructure and industrial cooperation being the four key areas to drive development across Pakistan'.[22] During Xi Jinping's visit, China and Pakistan signed 51 cooperation agreements valued at $46 billion, to promote and accelerate the construction of CPEC.[23]

Xi Jinping had earlier, in September 2013, introduced the concept of One Belt One Road (OBOR) during his visit to Kazakhstan, stressing the importance of a Silk Road Economic Belt (SREB) that would include roads, railways, energy links and construction of a corridor along the ancient Silk Route connecting China to Europe (via Central Asia). CPEC is an important corridor being constructed as part of the OBOR/BRI. China is thus rebuilding the ancient Silk Route to boost its global reach and influence, ensure its energy security, enhance connectivity and to utilize its surplus human and material resources. In November 2015, China included the CPEC into its 13th five-year developmental plan. Both China and Pakistan approved a Long-Term Plan for CPEC (2017–30) to be implemented in three phases.[24] China hosted the first BRI Summit on 14–16 May 2017, which was attended by 29 countries including Pakistan. China used this occasion to highlight the goals of BRI as enhancing regional connectivity, deepening trade and economic relations and political cooperation among the countries covered by the BRI.

Pakistan projects CPEC as a 'game-changer' that could bring enormous economic benefits, create jobs and lead to the construction of mega energy and transport projects. However, doubts are being raised among sections of Pakistani society about the gap between such big promises and the actual ground reality. Dr Kaiser Bengali, the noted Pakistani economist, believes that CPEC will threaten local business, as Chinese companies bring everything from China rather than buying it locally in Pakistan. Pakistan's domestic products cannot compete with the influx of cheaper Chinese imports. The success of the project, particularly accrual of its economic benefits to Pakistan and its people, depends upon the success of the local manufacturing, industry, agriculture and services sectors of the economy. Dr Bengali opined that CPEC is being built purely for security purposes. CPEC is between two unequal partners and China will gain in both economic, military and strategic terms. Pakistan has deployed 16,000 security personnel as part of the Special Security Division (SSD) to protect projects under CPEC. The SSD forces have been deployed from Gwadar up to Gilgit–Baltistan.

Through CPEC, China has increased its communication footprint in Pakistan. Direct cross-border optic fibre cable has been laid from Tashkurghan in Xinjiang (across Khunjerab Pass) till Rawalpindi to deepen comprehensive strategic cooperation by establishing fast, reliable connectivity that is not routed through Europe or the US. It is poised to increase connectivity in remote but strategically important areas of Gilgit–Baltistan and Balochistan. It is also planned to provide the Central Asian republics a new, shorter and cost-effective route for connectivity. China's Digital Terrestrial Multimedia Broadcast (DTMB) technology is being brought into Pakistan to cover 90 per cent of its population. The communication plans include installation of surveillance cameras, explosives' detectors and scanners covering major roads, sensitive areas and crowded places. Tashkurghan (in Xinjiang) has been developed as a hub with a new airport. China has officially donated security vehicles with its banner (China Aid) to Pakistan for use in Gilgit–Baltistan. China has introduced yak-mounted cavalry to guard the Sino-Pak border. There are plans to build a railway running parallel to KKH from Havelian to Khunjerab, from where it will be linked to China's railway system at Kashgar. Gilgit–Baltistan functions mainly as a corridor between industrial centres and consumer markets in Xinjiang and Punjab (Pakistan). Plans are afoot to shift the Sust dry port in Gilgit to Havelian, which is being built on war footing. To conclude, CPEC is a strategic gain for China, as it will give the country access to oil-rich West Asia through Gwadar. Currently, 80 per cent of China's imported oil is transported over a distance of about 16,000 km through the Strait of Malacca to Shanghai, over three months. Once Gwadar Port becomes operational, it will reduce the distance to only about 2,500 km[25] providing China the shortest route and access to the Persian Gulf, Arabian Sea and the Indian Ocean. Heavy involvement of China in CPEC and Gilgit–Baltistan, Balochistan and Gwadar is a new security dimension to the situation in the region. Policymakers in Pakistan emphasize the importance of Gwadar and CPEC not only for Pakistan and China, but also for Central Asia, as it would provide the landlocked Central Asian republics an easy and short overland route to the sea. Former Pakistan President General Pervez Musharraf had highlighted 'Pakistan's potential to become the commercial hub for Central and South-West Asia and renew the ancient Silk Route'.[26] CPEC is viewed by Pakistan as yielding strategic dividends, as a counter to India and any inimical force in the neighbourhood. As Senge Sering (a Balti scholar) puts it, 'The Karakoram Corridor binds Central Asia, Afghanistan, Iran, Pakistan and China into a regional security bloc, which will be an anti-dote to counter Indian and Western influences in the region.'[27] One must also take into account the emerging equations of Pakistan with Turkey, Azerbaijan and even Russia.

India has been forthright in its opposition to CPEC, as it passes through the Pakistan-occupied territory of Gilgit–Baltistan, claimed by India. It violates Indian sovereignty and territorial integrity. Though China invited India to participate in the Belt and Road Forum (BRF) held in Beijing from 16–17 May 2017, India did not accept the same. Indian foreign ministry issued a statement on 13 May 2017 reiterating Indian position on the issue. It stated: '...Regarding the so-called "China-Pakistan Economic Corridor", which is being projected as the flagship project of the BRI/OBOR, the international community is well aware of India's position. No country can accept a project that ignores the core concerns of sovereignty and territorial integrity.'[28] The then China's Ambassador in India, Luo Zhaohui while speaking at the United Service Institute, New Delhi on 5 May 2017—few days before Beijing hosted the first BRF—acknowledged that, 'India still has reservations over the OBOR, saying that the CPEC passes through the Pakistan-controlled Kashmir raising sovereignty issues. China has no intention to get involved in the sovereignty and territorial disputes between the two countries. China supports the solution of the disputes between India and Pakistan through bilateral negotiations between the two countries'.[29] Indian Minister of State for External Affairs Shri Muraleedharan, while speaking in Indian Parliament on February 2020, said:

> Government's concerns arise in part from the fact that the inclusion of the so-called project of 'OBOR/BRI', directly impinges on the issue of sovereignty and territorial integrity of India. This so-called illegal CPEC passes through parts of the Union Territories of Jammu & Kashmir and Ladakh which are under illegal occupation of Pakistan. Government has conveyed its concerns to the Chinese side about their activities in areas illegally occupied by Pakistan in the Union Territories of Jammu & Kashmir and Ladakh and has asked them to cease such activities.[30]

Apart from violating Indian sovereignty, the deep Sino-Pak nexus poses a serious challenge to Indian security along its northern frontiers and beyond in Afghanistan and Central Asia. The creeping Chinese incursions in Galwan, Pangong, Depsang and other areas in Ladakh, and the resultant tension between the two countries, is a wake-up call for India to take concerted steps to assert its physical control over its remote frontiers and to adopt a calibrated diplomatic and military response to the looming threat. On its part, China is conscious of the legal-constitutional limbo in Gilgit–Baltistan, which is not recognized as part of Pakistan under its constitution. Though Pakistan renamed the region called 'Northern Areas' as Gilgit–Baltistan (by Giglit–Baltistan Empowerment and Self-Governance Order of 2009), it has not been integrated into Pakistan. China is keen to end the ambiguity over the constitutional status of Gilgit–Baltistan so that the legal glitch over the disputed character of this territory is removed. It remains to be seen if Pakistan goes ahead with the integration of Gilgit–Baltistan as its fifth province, which in turn will negate Pakistan's official stand over the disputed character of Kashmir, including Gilgit–Baltistan.

Sixteen

China's Policy in Xinjiang and Indian Experience in Kashmir

Abutting the borders of India, Pakistan, Afghanistan and Central Asian republics of Kazakhstan, Kyrgyzstan and Tajikistan, Xinjiang is the strategic frontier of China in its north-west. With main overland trade routes connecting China with Central and South Asia passing through Xinjiang, it is China's bridge to Central Asia and South Asia. Following the disintegration of the former Soviet Union and independence of Central Asian republics, China has been assiduously developing Xinjiang as the hub of Trans-Asian trade and traffic. Xinjiang is also vital for China's quest for energy security. China views Xinjiang as a continental bridge which 'extends China's reach to Central Asia and simultaneously serves as a security buffer to China proper'.[1] Besides being used as a site for nuclear testing, Xinjiang is a region of vast unexploited petroleum and mineral reserves and immense agricultural potential.

China has been following the time-tested policy of large-scale Han settlement in Xinjiang 'as a means to work towards regional stability and bring the new Central Asian republics and people of Xinjiang closer to China's world view'.[2] However, the main hurdle in achieving China's economic, political and strategic objectives in this region is the ethno-religious resurgence that feeds the Pan-Turkic and Islamic secessionist movement in Xinjiang. Though the 1980s and 1990s experienced numerous violent incidents in Xinjiang, including bomb blasts, arson, racial attacks and a hate campaign by Uyghur separatists against China's rule, past few years have witnessed an escalation in such campaigns and growing

Uyghur resistance spearheaded by the East Turkestan Islamic Movement (ETIM), World Uyghur Congress, etc. Though ETIM was designated as a terrorist organization by the US and UN in 2002, 'its members reconstituted as the jihadist *Turkestan Islamic Party* (TIP)',[3] which has been active in Syria and Afghanistan and seeks to establish an Islamic state in Xinjiang. Growing Uyghur demand for a separate homeland and violence have brought this region into focus of national and international attention.

On its part, the Chinese government has been quite conscious of the threat and has been pursuing a stringent policy of curbing the three evils of separatism, religious extremism and terrorism. China has also launched a slew of measures to uplift the economically underdeveloped region and bring the non-Han minorities into national mainstream and integrate them in economic, social and cultural realms.

AUTONOMY AND ADMINISTRATIVE RESTRUCTURING

Following the erstwhile Soviet Union, which was established as a multinational federation of various nationalities controlled by Moscow, 'China launched a campaign in the 1950s that recognized 56 nationalities having common territory, language, economic mode and culture'[4], and established various autonomous regions. However, the China model does not offer the formal right of political secession to its nationalities, as was provided in theory by the Soviet model.[5] Way back in 1955, China declared Xinjiang as an Uyghur Autonomous Region, in cognizance of its main Uyghur Muslim minority. It also established autonomous prefectures for Kazakh, Hui, Kyrgyz and Mongol populated areas; and autonomous counties for Kazakh, Hui, Mongolian, Tajik and Sibo dominated areas. Regional concentration of various ethno-religious groups has been consolidated by the Chinese policy of creating separate administrative divisions—autonomous prefectures, autonomous counties and towns within prefectures—where a particular ethnic or religious group is in majority. In this manner, China has set up necessary administrative mechanisms to take care of other non-Uyghur minority nationalities in Xinjiang.

China has successfully followed the policy of Han settlement in Xinjiang as a means of social and political stability, along with territorial integrity. The immigration and settlement of Hans, Huis and others from mainland China has resulted in an increase of the share of Han population from 6 per cent in 1953 to about 40 per cent in 2007, and sharp reduction of Uyghur population from 80 per cent in 1941 to about 46 per cent in 2007. Despite several attempts by local Uyghur Islamic radicals to intimidate and shoo away Han settlers in Xinjiang, the authorities have not only foiled such attempts but also managed to reinforce the Han presence in Xinjiang. The problem has been accentuated by a large concentration of Muslim Uyghurs in the southern part of Xinjiang (to the extent of about 90 per cent) while they constitute only about 46 per cent of total population in the entire province.

Through such administrative restructuring, China has sought to retain and further promote the distinct geocultural divisions in Xinjiang. While lofty mountain ranges of Altyn Tagh, Kuen Lun, Karakoram, Pamirs, Ala Tau and the Altai virtually encircle the region, the great Takla Makan desert to the east cuts it off from the mainland of China. The Tien Shan range of mountains cuts the region into two distinct but unequal parts, the northern region traditionally dominated by pastoral nomads and the southern region (or Tarim Basin) possessing numerous fertile oasis settlements dominated by Uyghurs. Different ethnic groups are settled in different geographical areas such as Uyghur Muslims dominating the southern parts of Xinjiang (Alty Shahr); Kyrgyzs settled in Kizilsu Prefecture in the south; Tajiks living in the mountainous Tashkurghan county; and Mongols, Kazakhs and Huis living in their distinct traditional habitats in northern Xinjiang. The Hans dominate both northern and eastern parts of Xinjiang. These ethnic groups retain their distinct ethno-cultural identity, which has been consolidated by the creation of separate autonomous prefectures and counties for the respective ethnic groups in their territorial loci within the overall framework of the Xinjiang Uyghur Autonomous Region of China. These ethnic groups speak different languages: Uyghur, Kyrgyz, Tajik, Kazakh, Mongol and Chinese Mandarin.

While Muslim Uyghurs are predominant in Southern Xinjiang—particularly in Kashgar, Khotan, Aksu and Turfan autonomous prefectures—Muslim Kazakhs are concentrated in Ili Kazakh Autonomous Prefecture (adjoining Kazakhstan); Mori Kazakh autonomous county of Changji Hui Autonomous Prefecture; and Barkol Kazakh autonomous county of Hami prefecture. Similarly, Muslim Kyrgyzs inhabit the Kizilsu Kyrgyz autonomous prefecture (adjoining Kyrgyzstan) and Muslim Tajiks have been provided an autonomous county of Tashkurghan (adjoining Tajikistan) within the Kashgar prefecture. Mongols reside mainly in Bayangholin and Bortala Mongol autonomous prefectures and Hoboksar Mongol autonomous county. In fact, these divisions were created during 1954, more than a year before Xinjiang was declared as the Uyghur Autonomous Region. Uyghurs are in majority in Southern Xinjiang (Kashgar, Khotan, Aksu) as well as in Turfan, which has turned this region into a centre of separatist forces. Hans are in majority in northern and eastern Xinjiang, mainly concentrated in urban areas. Notwithstanding their intra-ethnic differences, most of the non-Han population of Xinjiang are of Turkic stock and are Muslims by faith. They share their religion, Turkic language and culture with their counterparts in the neighbouring Central Asian countries. Given China's tenuous historical position in this region, any cross-border fraternization on ethno-religious grounds among the Muslims of Xinjiang with their Central Asian, Afghan and Pakistani neighbours is a potential source of instability for China at its strategic frontier.

Chinese scholars now advocate reconsideration of Chinese Nationalities Policy, which, they believe, is based on the Soviet (Marxist–Leninist) theory of nationalities that proved to be a failure with the disintegration of the former Soviet Union.[6] They argue that the Chinese Communist Party (CCP) adopted the Soviet nationalities policy, recognizing various ethnic groups of China as nationalities. Chinese scholars believe that the special policies and concessions in terms of family planning programmes, university admissions, administrative positions in autonomous areas and dual school system for local minorities, favouring ethnic minorities in China, are the roots of ethnic conflicts today as these have only strengthened minority group identity.

SECURITY MEASURES

The magnitude and intensity of ethnic clashes in Urumqi in July 2009 came as a rude shock to Chinese leadership. China's response to the crisis has been swift, tough and calibrated. They have taken security measures to control the situation by detaining hundreds of people, conducting summary trials and deterrent punishment to the convicted rioters, restricting internet and telephone communication, controlling the flow of information on the riots to the media and the outside world, taking steps to reassure Han Chinese settlers in Urumqi and reaching out to Muslim countries in Central and South Asia seeking their cooperation. At a high-level conference on Xinjiang held on 17–19 May 2010 at Beijing, former President Hu Jintao emphasized the importance of social stability and national unity in Xinjiang. China has secured its frontiers and neutralized this threat by consolidating its military presence in Xinjiang. China installed 50,000 CCTVs in 2009 in Urumqi alone, to monitor the movements of suspected Uyghur activists. On the diplomatic front, China has not only warded off any Islamic criticism of its policies in Xinjiang but has also succeeded in having its position legitimized and endorsed by Muslim countries like Iran, Pakistan, Central Asian republics and other West Asian countries. The Central Asian countries have even undertaken not to allow any anti-China movement by the Uyghurs living within their respective countries.

China is isolating the extremist and separatist elements from the general Uyghur population by removing economic disparities between Xinjiang and the rest of China. Since economic development is accompanied by the ingress of Hans, Huis and other nationalities, plans for changing the face of Southern Xinjiang have been set in motion.

Another important measure taken has been the policy of eliminating Uyghur Muslim ghettos, which have been centres of religious extremism and separatism. Many old houses in Southern Xinjiang have been demolished to create big public spaces, parks, roads and to construct high-rise residential buildings. Then, the concerned families are allotted flats in these buildings in a proportionate manner, so that a high-rise building has a mixture of various communities, which have equal stake in safety, security and welfare of their residential complex. Thus, this complex remains immune to any riots outside the complex.

The old and crowded Uyghur shops and slums around the Idgah Mosque in Kashgar have been cleared by the authorities. Now it has clean, calm and peaceful surroundings, with new shops/houses and multi-storied commercial complexes being built in a systematic manner. Beijing spent about 1.8 billion yuan in building a big artificial lake and park in Kashgar city. This lake serves as a place of recreation for the people. In another instance, some Uyghur boys were found picking pockets of pedestrians using an overhead foot bridge, opposite the National Library in Beijing. The problem persisted despite two police personnel being deployed at the two ends of the bridge. This was mainly because many Uyghur families lived in a ghetto nearby around Xinjiang Street (near the Central University of Nationalities, Beijing), as this was a cheaper area to live in. The authorities resolved this law-and-order problem by acquiring the land and houses in and around Xinjiang Street and built new multi-storied residential buildings, which were expensive and thus out of reach of the Uyghurs to buy or rent. Now, Xinjiang Street does not exist anywhere and the problem has been weeded out. According to a well-documented report by the Australian Strategic Policy Institute, '16,000 mosques have been damaged or destroyed and 8,450 mosques across Xinjiang have been entirely demolished since 2017.'[7]

After Xi Jinping came to power in March 2013, China has ramped up its efforts to deal with terrorism. In May 2014, Chinese authorities launched the Strike Hard Campaign against Violent Extremism in Xinjiang. In 2016, Chen Quanguo, who had overseen the increased securitization of Tibet, was appointed as the new party secretary in Xinjiang. Simultaneously, several national security laws were introduced. There have been frequent arrests and detention of suspected Muslim separatists and extremists, which has affected the daily life of indigenous people in Xinjiang. About 1 million Uyghurs and Kazakhs have been put in detention camps for the purpose of their political education, ideological training, Mandarin teaching and Chinese flag-raising ceremonies. Biometric data, voice samples and DNA testing of local people have been collected to identify, profile and track the suspected anti-China activists in Xinjiang. People are being filtered based on their profiling. Curbs on religious practices have also been enforced.

Though Haj pilgrimage is allowed, the new Administrative Measures for Islamic Haj Affairs, introduced in October 2020, stipulate that only the government-approved Islamic Association of China is authorized to organize Haj for Muslims (in accordance with the law).[8] The people are asked not to mix religion with education. Parents and teachers have been asked to keep their children away from religious teachings, etc. There is strict control over internet to curb propagation of religious fanaticism, radicalism and terrorism. In March 2017, a law was passed in Xinjiang to curb religious extremism, discourage wearing veils and to also discourage having 'abnormal' beards. Text books have been revised to have a 'correct' understanding of history of Xinjiang to build strong national ideological unity. Uyghur women are encouraged to remove veils and hijab, live a modern life and work in factories, etc.

Foreign visits of Uyghurs and Kazakhs are monitored and controlled. The police are authorized to scrutinize and control their foreign travel. Uyghur asylum seekers and refugees abroad are particularly being targeted and Chinese authorities seek their return/deportation to Xinjiang. For this purpose, China has listed 26 countries as 'sensitive'. These countries are: Afghanistan, Algeria, Azerbaijan, Egypt, Indonesia, Iran, Iraq, Kazakhstan, Kenya, Kyrgyzstan, Libya, Malaysia, Nigeria, Pakistan, Russia, Saudi Arabia, Somalia, South Sudan, Syria, Tajikistan, Thailand, Turkey, Turkmenistan, United Arab Emirates, Uzbekistan and Yemen. In July 2017, Egyptian authorities forced 20 Uyghur students to return to China. Thailand, Malaysia and Afghanistan have also deported groups of Uyghurs, as was sought by the Chinese authorities.

In October 2016, the Becoming Family Campaign was launched, which includes a compulsory home-stay programme. Han cadres spend at least five days every two months in the homes of Xinjiang residents, particularly in rural areas, to socialize with the Uyghur or Kazakh families. According to the Communist Party's official newspaper, at the end of September 2018, 1.1 million government workers had been deployed to the minorities' living rooms, dining areas and Muslim prayer spaces besides weddings, etc., under the Pair Up and Become Family programme. In this manner, Chinese authorities seek to promote inter-ethnic harmony and social stability[9]. However, all these measures are seen as intrusive and are proving to be counterproductive and further hurting local Muslim sentiments.

The Xinjiang Production Construction Corps (XPCC) or *bingtuan* (a military regiment), which was established in 1954, consists mainly of Han cadres. The XPCC currently employs 12 per cent of Xinjiang's population. It also has about 100,000 trained militia for frontier security. The XPCC dominates Xinjiang's agriculture (including the production of tomatoes, wheat, grapes and cotton), industry, local and urban development. It has established food processing, textile, iron, steel processing, building materials, chemical and coal mining industries.[10] XPCC has a military structure, along with a headquarters at Urumqi, 14 divisions, 176 regiments and a large number of companies, with the leaders being called commanders and commissars.[11] Though a nominal part of the Xinjiang Uyghur Autonomous Region (XUAR), XPCC conducts its own administrative and economic affairs with the support and under direct control of the central government.[12] The Han chief of XPCC 'wields power in the region second only to that of the leader of Xinjiang itself'.[13] China's President Xi Jinping has emphasized the important role of XPCC in the security and stability of Xinjiang.

The US and other Western countries have been vocal in their criticism of China's detention centres in Xinjiang. Permanent missions of the US, Germany, Netherlands, Canada and UK organized a high-level briefing at the UN Human Rights Council, Geneva on 13 March 2019 to address this issue. Kelley F. Curie, the US ambassador at large, who chaired the meeting, accused China of detaining more than one million people under horrific conditions in Xinjiang's internment camps. She alleged that China is using high-tech surveillance and collection of personal data.

Notwithstanding growing Western criticism over China's hardline measures against the indigenous Muslims of Xinjiang, Beijing has used its political and economic clout to muster support of many areas—mostly from Africa, Pakistan, Saudi Arabia and Russia—which commended China's achievements in the field of human rights. Several Muslim leaders and high-power delegations from Iran, Pakistan and Central Asian republics have visited Xinjiang and extended their support to China's policies against terrorism, Islamic extremism, ethno-religious separatism, drugs and arms trafficking. China has also institutionalized this process of cooperation through the Shanghai Cooperation Organisation (SCO). It is no surprise that China buys about a third of Iran's oil exports and about one-tenth of Saudi Arabia's oil exports.

Saudi Arabia, Russia and 35 other countries wrote a joint letter in July 2019 to the UN Human Rights Council supporting

China's policies in Xinjiang. They stated, 'Faced with the grave challenge of terrorism and extremism, China has undertaken a series of counter-terrorism and de-radicalization measures in Xinjiang, including setting up vocational education and training centres.'[14] This was a strong rebuttal to an earlier letter written by 22 (mostly Western) nations including Australia, Canada, France, Germany, Japan, England urging the UN Human Rights Council to investigate China's human rights violations in Xinjiang. They expressed concern about credible reports of arbitrary detention and widespread surveillance and restrictions in Xinjiang, particularly targeting Uyghurs and other minorities.

Brushing aside the condemnation by the US, European Union (EU) and others, Jinping is determined to control Xinjiang through a strategy of political indoctrination, demographic change and stringent security measures. Assimilation of Muslims is the key to China's policy in Xinjiang. The declining birth rate of Uyghurs is contributing to Han consolidation. Jinping, while addressing a gathering of officials on 25–26 September 2020, described his policies in Xinjiang as 'totally correct' and successful.[15] This was the first major party conclave since 2014, when Jinping adopted increasingly hardline measures including digital surveillance, mass internment (re-education camps), political indoctrination programmes, etc.

ECONOMIC DEVELOPMENT/SINIFICATION PROCESS

Soon after the incorporation of Xinjiang into China in 1949, the outlying periphery was brought close to the mainland by building roads. In fact, work on the Kashgar–Aksai Chin–Tibet highway was started in the 1950s.

China has followed a well-calibrated policy of development—railways, roads, telecommunications, buildings, high-rise residential apartments, industries, oil refineries, and so on in Xinjiang. The Chinese government has invested billions of dollars to upgrade transport infrastructure in Xinjiang and Tibet, with a dual purpose of integrating the two peripheral regions into the mainland, reducing both distance and time of travel, speeding up development along the new tracks and enhancing the PLA's mobility and capacity to bring troops to border areas. The PLA has also built a 'digital great wall' (a network of fibre-optics to improve PLA's command and control mechanism and communication) along the borders in Xinjiang and Tibet.

China has linked the mainland with the outlying and distant province of Xinjiang through rail link, thus overcoming the huge distance of the Taklamakan Desert. A rail route connects Beijing, passing through Lanzhou to Urumqi, and further the railway line goes across the border into Kazakhstan and beyond (via Alashankou), which has been developed as a big port to facilitate cross-border trade.

The main road from Kashgar Airport to the town is built in a manner that aircrafts can land on this road in case of an emergency security situation. The 2,540-km-long Beijing–Urumqi expressway has shortened the existing road between Beijing and Urumqi by nearly 1,300 km.

Even though vast deserts intervene between the settled oasis towns and cities, several settlements, small industries, hotels, restaurants and other service centres have come up along the railway line and highways (wherever there is some settlement/oasis). Most of these businesses, shops, hotels, services, etc. are manned by Han Chinese or even Hui Muslims. Many travel agencies and even taxis are run by Han Chinese. China Mobile, China Telecom, Sinopek, Petro China and many more major Chinese companies and banks have set up big establishments or high-rise buildings in various parts of Xinjiang. The Han Chinese run most of those offices, shops and establishments, with some Chinese- and English-speaking educated Uyghurs working there. While Urumqi, the capital of Xinjiang, is highly developed with massive industrialization, Uyghur-dominated regions of Southern Xinjiang like Kashgar and Khotan are also quite developed.

After the 2009 riots in Urumqi, China has taken all round view of the Uyghur unrest, keeping in mind the social, educational and economic issues in Xinjiang. Former President Hu Jintao stressed the need to reduce the gap between the GDP (gross domestic product) growth in Xinjiang and the rest of China. He emphasized the importance of social stability and national unity in Xinjiang. He urged national banks in China to invest in Xinjiang. After the conference, China announced a new development policy for Xinjiang. China has implemented its decision to charge new resource tax of 5 per cent on oil and gas produced in Xinjiang to boost Xinjiang's physical revenue by 25 per cent (about 5 billion yuan) for oil and 2 billion yuan for gas per year, which will be used for development projects in Xinjiang. The total quantity of oil produced in Xinjiang is over 27 million tonnes. Beijing plans to develop Kashgar as a second Shenzhen (which is the most advanced region in China).

China's largest petroleum company, Petro China, operates out of Xinjiang. Petro China, with a market value of US$220 billion, has been ranked 30th in the 2018 Forbes Global 2000.

China opened a new 1,833-km-long gas pipeline on 14 December 2009 connecting Turkmenistan, Uzbekistan and Kazakhstan with Xinjiang. This pipeline will deliver 55 billion tonnes of gas per year—more than half of China's current annual gas consumption—once it reaches full capacity.

Foreign companies investing in Xinjiang get more trade concessions than in Shanghai. Carrefoure (a French departmental store chain), which has several stores in Beijing and other parts of China, has opened several stores in Xinjiang as well. The Super 8 hotel chain, which is one of the world's largest economy lodging operators with almost 2,100 hotels worldwide, has three hotels in Xinjiang.

China evolved a 10-year (2011–2020) partner assistance programme, involving 19 affluent regions including coastal and central provinces and big cities, to accelerate the socio-economic development of various areas in Xinjiang.[16] For instance, Beijing Municipality is spending 7.26 billion yuan (about US$1.06 billion) for housing and protecting agriculture in Khotan city, Khotan county, Moyu county and Lop county of Khotan prefecture over a period of five years. Anhui province along with Beijing and Tianjin municipalities are investing in the construction of railways, roads, fruit processing and protected agriculture in Khotan. Guangdong province allotted 9.6 billion yuan (US$1.41 billion) for infrastructure and public services in Kashgar prefecture.

Hebei Province is partnering with No. 2 Division of the XPCC and Bayingolin Mongol autonomous prefecture with an investment of 1.8 billion yuan (about US$263.62 million) in agricultural technologies, housing, employment and education. Hubei province is also developing agriculture, tourism and education in Bole city, Jinghe and Wenquan Counties of Bortala Mongol autonomous prefecture in partnership with No. 5 Division of the XPCC. Jiangxi province is investing 2.03 billion yuan ($303.16 million) in Akto county of Kizilsu Kyrgyz autonomous prefecture. The three north-eastern provinces of Heilongjiang, Jilin and Liaoning will partner with Tacheng and Altay in northern Xinjiang as they have similar climatic conditions. They will invest in mining, flood preventions, disaster relief and job training.

All of this means direct involvement of experts, officials and other Hans from mainland China in giving their professional expertise and economic support to develop and implement various projects in Xinjiang. This practice not only enables other provinces/Han experts to acquire direct first-hand knowledge of Xinjiang's affairs but also promotes cross-regional contacts, besides paving the way for Han penetration into the Uyghur-dominated areas. That XPCC is the local partner/implementing agency in most of these programmes. It ensures that overall Chinese security concerns and objectives are met in the process of execution of such projects in Xinjiang.

According to a Xinhua report (25 September 2019), Xinjiang's GDP increased 200 times from 791 million yuan (US$111 million) in 1952 to 1.22 trillion yuan in 2018. Xinjiang's foreign trade rose to US$20 billion in 2018, about 1,481 times to that in 1950, mainly due to increased economic exchanges with the neighbouring countries due to the BRI. In 2018, Xinjiang attracted over 150 million tourists from home and abroad, which marked an increase of 40 per cent a year. Xinjiang produces 70 per cent of all of China's tomatoes and China exports 700,000 metric tonnes of tomatoes every year (mainly to Russia, Italy, etc.) China produces 20 per cent of the world's cotton, most of which comes from Xinjiang. However, in response to the petition by World Uyghur Congress and the Coalition to End Uyghur Forced Labour, the US Customs and Border Protection (CBP) recently banned all cotton and tomato products produced in Xinjiang.

CULTURAL POLICY

China and its people are acutely conscious of history, politics and importance of Xinjiang, which has remained embedded in Chinese memory and consciousness since ancient times. Various Chinese annals have recorded numerous episodes of forays and feats in this remote, north-western border area. Chinese cultural policy in Xinjiang has the following main features.

1. To preserve, sustain and promote all those objects, historical and cultural sites and episodes in the history of Xinjiang which demonstrate China's administrative and political jurisdiction in this area throughout history.
2. Accordingly, numerous sites which have been ascribed cultural and national importance, are appropriated and presented as treasured part of ancient Chinese civilization and its presence in the region.
3. To promote Uyghur shrines and tourist spots as places of cultural tourism, rather than of ethno-religious importance. Many Chinese tourists from the mainland and from Hong Kong, Taiwan etc., besides Uyghur pilgrims visit these places.
4. Uyghur handicrafts such as brass ware, musical

instruments, knives, wooden articles, besides dance are tolerated. Typical Central Asian bazaars are functioning and cater to the needs of the local people, in every town and city in Xinjiang. The Central Asian bazaars in Kashgar and Urumqi have developed as centres of international trade with adjoining countries in Central Asia and South Asia (Pakistan and Afghanistan).

5. Uyghur music and dance is sought to be promoted at the national level, in a bid to showcase it as part of the mainstream and also to create better social and cultural understanding between Uyghur and Han communities. Uyghur girls and boys perform their dance in several forms at intervals at the National Stadium.
6. Chinese cuisine has been introduced into Xinjiang in a big way. Apart from the Hui Muslim restaurants (which follow Chinese food style), several Chinese hotels and restaurants exist across the region. Quan Ju De—the famous roast duck restaurant of Beijing—has opened its branch in Urumqi, which is the exact replica of the original one. Peking ducks served in the Urumqi restaurant are brought in from Beijing. This is the unique Chinese way of 'Sinicising' the local food.

Despite the rapid development, Uyghurs in Xinjiang continue to nourish aspirations of ethno-political independence and have not come closer to the Chinese national mainstream. This is notwithstanding the economic development due to increased Chinese and foreign investments and flourishing border trade. The large-scale Han migration has further contributed to the resentment and discontent among the Uyghurs, leading to violence against Hans. Uyghurs being dispersed across a vast region, comprising one-sixth of the territory of China, and their weakness in terms of leadership (unlike in the case of Dalai Lama for Tibetans); lack of international support; and China's political determination, economic prowess and international clout, have made an uphill task of moving forward in their ethno-political goal of achieving an independent East Turkestan. The Xinjiang issue is not only complicated, but it is also dynamically changing due to the sustained, long-term and calibrated policy and administrative measures by China. With Xinjiang becoming the hub of Trans-Asian trade and traffic and due to its rich energy resources, the Muslims of Xinjiang are poised to assert their ethno-political position. This poses a serious challenge to China in the region. Whether it is China's grand initiatives like BRI or SCO, or China's relations with the adjoining Central Asian countries and also the Muslim world at large, the Xinjiang situation needs a constant watch and a comprehensive view.

COMPARISON WITH THE INDIAN EXPERIENCE IN KASHMIR

Since Xinjiang has close parallels to Kashmir in terms of its geographical and ethno-religious setting—besides the political history of religious extremism and separatism—it is instructive to make a comparative study of China's policies in Xinjiang with the Indian experience in Kashmir.

In order to ensure tranquility along its strategic frontier, China has resolved outstanding border disputes with the Central Asian republics of Kazakhstan, Kyrgyzstan and Tajikistan, albeit on its own terms. So, China does not have any hostile and belligerent neighbour that could destabilize Xinjiang. Due to its geo-strategic location—abutting the borders of China, Pakistan and Afghanistan and being in close proximity to Central Asia—Jammu, Kashmir and Ladakh is the strategic frontier of India in its north. Ladakh offers India the only overland access to Central Asia. However, independent India lost the opportunity of having direct overland access to Xinjiang and Central Asia after Pakistan illegally occupied the vital strategic territory of Gilgit and Baltistan spanning an area of 73,000 sq. km in 1947–48. While Aksai Chin, with an area of 37,555 sq. km, in eastern Ladakh is under the occupation of China,

5,180 sq. km of Shaksgam and Muztagh Valley in north Ladakh was ceded by Pakistan to China in 1963. As such, India has been living with festering disputes with Pakistan and China since 1947, having fought wars in 1947–48, 1962, 1965, 1971 and 1999. Since 1989, Kashmir has been suffering the brunt of Pakistan-sponsored cross-border terrorism, religious extremism and secessionism.

As mentioned previously, the Xinjiang region of China presents a case of geocultural diversity. The northern region has been traditionally dominated by pastoral nomads and southern region (possessing numerous fertile oasis settlements) is dominated by Uyghurs. China has followed a calculated policy to consolidate the diverse and distinct ethno-cultural identities in Xinjiang by creating separate autonomous prefectures, regions and counties for the respective ethnic groups in their respective territorial loci within the overall framework of Xinjiang Uyghur Autonomous Region. From the geocultural perspective, the erstwhile Jammu and Kashmir state of India presents a heterogeneous mix of geography and ethno-cultural groups. Distinct geographical zones are inhabited by distinct ethno-cultural groups like Dogras in Jammu, nomadic Gujjar tribes in the hills, Kashmiris in the Valley, Baltis (Shia Muslims) in Kargil and Baltistan, Ladakhis (Buddhists) in Ladakh, Dards in Gurais and Dardistan (Gilgit, Hunza etc.) and Mirpuris or Potoharis in the Muzaffarabad–Mirpur region. Different ethnic groups speak different languages—Dogri, Gojri, Kashmiri, Balti, Ladakhi and Mirpuri/Potohari/Punjabi.

From the historical point of view, mainland China has had a tenuous relationship with its distant periphery in Xinjiang. While its Chinese connection dates back more than 2,000 years, Xinjiang has remained under effective control of imperial China intermittently for about five centuries. Long distance, the intervening Taklamakan Desert and lack of adequate means of communication (besides shifting balance of power in the mainland), were the contributory factors for China's weak control over Xinjiang for a considerable period in history. Whenever the centre was strong in China, it exerted its control over Xinjiang.

Whenever the centre was weak, local chieftains, Mongol Khans, Khojas, Muslim chiefs and warlords assumed control over their territorial strongholds. However, the chiefs of Hami and Turfan in the eastern part of Xinjiang, being in proximity to China, maintained a sort of tributary relationship with the centre, while retaining their autonomy.

Kashmir has remained an inalienable part of Indian civilizational and political system since ancient times. It was a Hindu kingdom till the fourteenth century and as such was an integral part of Hindu historical past. In fact, Kashmir acted as the fountainhead of Indian civilization, as most classical Indian works on art, aesthetics, religion, philosophy, literature, poetics, dramaturgy, history, etc., were written and produced in Kashmir. It has been the main centre of Buddhism and Shaivism as well. Even after the introduction of Islam, Kashmir produced its indigenous rishi order synthesizing the local Shaivite and Buddhist traditions with the new Sufi thought, brought in by the immigrant Syeds and Sufis from Central Asia and Persia. In medieval times, Kashmir was part of the Mughal empire in India. But in post-independent India, the government and administrative setup of Jammu and Kashmir—being controlled by the local Muslim bureaucracy and political elite—have promoted and projected Islamic identity and heritage of Jammu and Kashmir by obliterating its glorious ancient Hindu and Buddhist heritage. This heritage exists in the form of hundreds of temples, archeological sites, shrines and artefacts. This obliteration has been done to weaken the deep civilizational connect between Kashmir and the rest of India.[17] Over 500 Hindu temples are reported to have been destroyed and over 50,000 *kanals* (8,250 acres) of land has been encroached upon by the Islamist extremists and terrorists in Kashmir over the past 30 years.[18] Even the local Kashmiri language, spoken by nearly 57 per cent of people, was neglected by declaring Urdu as the official language even though it was spoken only by 0.16 per cent of the population (as per 2011 census). It is only recently in September 2020, after 73 years, that local languages—Kashmiri, Dogri and

Hindi—have been accorded their due by including them in the list of the official languages of Jammu and Kashmir, in addition to the existing Urdu and English.[19] Concrete steps must be taken by the new government of the Union Territory of Jammu and Kashmir to restore the ancient Hindu and Buddhist shrines, temples and monuments in order to keep the ancient civilizational heritage alive.

From the cultural and racial point of view, Uyghurs and other Muslim groups like Kazakhs and Kyrgyzs belong to Turkic Islamic groups and they see Chinese Hans and even Chinese Hui Muslims as the 'other' ethnic group and race. Local Muslims speak Turkic (Uyghur, Kazakh, Kyrgyz) languages, whereas Chinese Hans and Huis speak Mandarin. There is a communication gap between Han Chinese and local Turkic racial groups. The Han Chinese are seen by the locals as colonialists and even today local Muslims eat in their own Muslim restaurants (*chaikhanas*), as they abhor pork. Chinese Hans are not uncomfortable in eating at the Chinese Hui Muslim restaurants, as Huis, though Muslim by faith, speak the Chinese language and have Chinese cuisine. However, pork and beef are openly sold in the bazaars, though in South Xinjiang one can predominantly find lamb meat in the cuisine. All Uyghur, Kazakh and Kyrgyz Muslims in Xinjiang observe local Xinjiang time (which is two hours behind Beijing time). This is in marked contrast to various offices and institutions and Han Chinese people settled in Xinjiang, who observe Beijing time. Few Uyghurs and Kazakhs can speak Chinese and very few Chinese know the local language. There exist separate hostels for Han and Muslim students in universities and institutes as well. Similarly, there are exclusive restaurants for Muslims and Hans. In Muslim restaurants, smoking or drinking are not allowed. Over 300,000 Uyghurs and Kazakhs are scattered in mainland China (Beijing, Henan and some other places) working mainly in restaurants, bakeries and as labour. They continue to live in ghettoes even while staying outside Xinjiang. Some have been involved in petty crimes and in extremist and terrorist activities.

From the cultural and racial point of view, except for their religious differences, Kashmiri Muslims and Kashmiri Hindus speak the same language and have had the same dressing and cuisine. A sizeable number of Kashmir Muslims still retain the Kashmiri Pandit surnames like Kaul, Raina, Mattoo, Bhat, Kichloo, Bakshi, Durrani, Wangnoo and so on. However, since Islamic radicalization in the Valley, many Muslims have been adopting more Arabicized names under the influence of radical Wahhabi Islam. And after the forced expulsion of the Kashmiri Hindu minority population in 1989–90, the Valley has been turned into a mono-ethnic territory, with Islamic radicalism ruling the roost. While, in the recent past, the local Muslim population abhorred eating pork, in the same manner as Kashmiri Hindus shunned eating beef, now the latter is openly sold in the markets across the Valley as a symbol of Islamic triumph over the secular and composite ethno-cultural heritage and traditions. Kashmiri Muslims are living, working/studying in various parts of India particularly, Delhi, Gurugram, Uttar Pradesh, Uttarakhand, Kolkata, Chennai, Goa, Kerala, Mumbai and other metropolitan cities doing business in sale/export of handicrafts, travel and tourism, services and other professions. In fact, after the onset of militancy in Kashmir in 1989, Kashmiri Muslim professionals have chosen to work in various places of India, leading to their integration in the Indian mainstream. The vibrant and resurgent economy of India and large number of educational professional institutions, coupled with encouraging policies towards the Muslim minority, offer a big attraction to Kashmiri Muslim youth availing of these avenues. However, some secessionist elements among the floating Kashmiri Muslim population, have been found involved in terrorist and anti-state activities in various parts of India.

Even before the Xinjiang Uyghur autonomous region was founded on 1 October 1955, in cognizance of its main Uyghur nationality, China had designated over 50 per cent of Xinjiang's land area as autonomous prefectures for Kazakh, Hui, Kyrgyz,

Khalkas and Mongol nationality areas; autonomous counties for Kazakh, Hui, Mongolian, Tajik and Xibo; besides numerous autonomous townships for other nationalities settled in other minority ghettos, in recognition of their distinct ethno-cultural characteristics. In this manner, China has set up necessary administrative mechanisms to take care of other non-Uyghur minority nationalities in Xinjiang. China has also encouraged the immigration and settlement of Hans, Huis and others from mainland China, which has resulted in the increase of the share of the Han population from 6 per cent in 1953 to 40 per cent in 2000, and a sharp reduction of the Uyghur population from 80 per cent in 1941 to 45.2 per cent in 2000. China has successfully followed the policy of Han settlement in Xinjiang as a means to social and political stability, and territorial integrity. Despite several attempts by the local Uyghur Islamic radicals to intimidate and shoo away the Han settlers in Xinjiang, the authorities have not only foiled all such attempts but even reinforced the Han presence in Xinjiang.

Post-Independence India accorded unique autonomy to Jammu and Kashmir through Article 370 of the Indian Constitution. Jammu and Kashmir also had its separate constitution. Under Article 370 and Article 35-A, no non-state subject and Kashmiri woman who had married outside the state can buy or own land or any property in Jammu and Kashmir. As such, there has been no immigration from other parts of India into the state. However, there has been out-migration of Hindu minorities from the Valley to other parts of India due to economic and political deprivation. The population of Hindus in Kashmir province registered only 6.75 per cent decadal growth during 1971–81, as against the growth rate of 27.29 per cent for the Valley as a whole. Notwithstanding the presence of Indian security forces, over 90,000 Kashmiri Hindu-minority families, comprising over 450,000 persons, were forced to leave the Valley during and after 1989–90 due to targeted terror strikes and violent hate campaigns. Ironically, several hundred Muslim refugees from Tibet and several thousand

Afghans (presently clustered in Gotli Bagh, Kashmir) were granted state subjects's status by the state authorities. As such, the Valley turned into a mono-ethnic Islamic stronghold, breeding and sustaining separatism and extremism.[20]

The people of Ladakh and Kargil were granted the Leh and Kargil Autonomous Hill Development Councils in 1995 and 2002, respectively, to promote the socio-economic development of these remote and backward areas. Besides, Muslim nomadic Gujjars and Bakarwals and the indigenous Buddhist and Balti (Shia Muslims) population in Ladakh and Kargil have been granted Scheduled Tribe status. This provides them enormous opportunities through quotas in admission into colleges, professional institutions and the elite Indian Civil Services.

It is after over 70 years that the GoI woke up on 5 August 2019, when the Indian Parliament passed the Jammu and Kashmir Reorganisation Bill, 2019, which bifurcated the state and created UTs of Jammu and Kashmir, and Ladakh, each to be administered by the president of India through a lieutenant governor. Article 370 granting special status to Jammu and Kashmir was revoked and Article 35-A (which allowed the state to define permanent residents and their rights and privileges, and to restrict settlement in the state and acquire immoveable property) was repealed. In doing so, the GoI met the long-standing demand of the people of India for the revocation of Articles 370 and 35-A and of Ladakh receiving UT status. This helped enable Ladakh's people to realize their political aspirations and to preserve and promote their distinct historical, ethnic, linguistic and eco-cultural heritage and identity.

Notwithstanding this major policy correction by the GoI regarding Kashmir, there has been no progress in the return and settlement of Kashmiri Pandit displaced persons in their homeland or in the acquisition of property by a non-Kashmiri. Instead, the terrorists began 2021 by gunning down a Punjabi, Hindu settler in Kashmir (Satpal Nischal), after he got a domicile certificate and purchased a shop and house in the capital city of

Srinagar.[21] A terrorist group The Resistance Front (TRF) while claiming responsibility for this attack warned that everyone other than indigenous Kashmiris would be treated as occupiers if they acquired property in the state.[22] There have been several targeted killings of Kashmiri Pandits, who had stayed put in the Valley despite terrorism during 2021–22, which has spurred the exodus of few hundred Kashmiri Pandits who were doing odd jobs in different areas, for safety to Jammu.

Xinjiang is very rich in oil, gas and mineral resources. It possesses high quality oil reserves, which accounts for 30 per cent of China's oil reserves. It has natural gas reserves of trillions of cubic metres, accounting for 34 per cent of China's natural gas reserves. Xinjiang has coal reserves of 2 trillion tonnes, accounting for 47 per cent of China's coal reserves. Xinjiang ranks second in China's wind energy resources. In 2008, Xinjiang ranked second in China by producing 27.22 million tonnes of crude oil; and first by producing 24 billion cubic meters of natural gas.[23] It also produced 3 million tonnes of cotton in 2008, ranking first in China.[24]

The wine-making industry is making rapid progress in Xinjiang. The local revenue of Xinjiang crossed 36 billion yuan in 2008.[25] With the revised resource tax of 5 per cent being levied on prices (instead of production volume), from mid-2010, CNPC and Sinopec, China's top two oil companies, expected to generate an additional 5 billion yuan (US$732 million) in annual tax revenue for Xinjiang.[26] The per capita income of rural households in Xinjiang was 3,503 yuan in 2008, which was less than the national average of 4,140 yuan. The per capita income of urban residents was 11,432 yuan as compared with the national average of 15,780 yuan. The Chinese government has acknowledged the imbalance due to the lower standard of living in Xinjiang than in other parts of China.

As regards to Jammu and Kashmir, no such rich natural resources like oil, gas, minerals etc., have been found there, which, coupled with the ban on purchase of land by the non-state subjects, are the main causes of lack of major industries in the state. The local economy is mainly based on agriculture, horticulture, handicrafts, government employment and tourism sectors. Jammu and Kashmir has the distinction of receiving the largest provincial assistance (90 per cent as grants-in-aid) from the central government. In 2009–10, Jammu and Kashmir received ₹13,252 crores from the Centre, which constituted nearly 60 per cent of the state's total expenditure. During the two decades of 1989–90 and 2009–10, Jammu and Kashmir received grants amounting to ₹94,409 crore, which is much above Jammu and Kashmir's share of India's population (a mere one per cent).[27]

Over a 15-year period (2004–19), Jammu and Kashmir received 10 per cent of federal grants amounting to ₹2.77 lakh crore (about US$ 40 billion) despite having only 1 per cent of population of India. The annual budget allocation of the financial year (FY) 2020–21 was ₹100,000 crore, which is over and above other central government schemes.[28] The income tax revenue in Kashmir was only about ₹200 crore in the FY 2009–10.[29] Jammu and Kashmir employs about 500,000 people making it a ratio of over 50 government employees to every thousand persons. A decade ago, the total bill for salary, pension and other allowances of the state's employees amounted to ₹11,525 crores, which was more than three times the state's total annual income of ₹3,600 crores.[30] Jammu and Kashmir has achieved the distinction of having the lowest rate of poverty in India. Only 3.7 per cent of rural Kashmiris and 1.19 per cent of urban residents in Kashmir live below the poverty line as against 27.09 and 23.02 per cent respectively in the rest of India.[31] An average household in the state owns assets worth over ₹1 million, which is the highest in India.[32]

Xinjiang, being the only Muslim majority province in China, has been home to ethno-religious separatist movement for a long time. While the Uyghur resentment against the Han Chinese presence in Xinjiang is increasing, China's sovereignty is also being challenged by Uyghur Muslim separatists. The 2009 riots in Urumqi—in which over 150 people, mostly Hans, were killed—

sent shockwaves across China. The Uyghur diaspora settled in the US, Europe, Middle Eastern and Central Asian countries, with the backing of some foreign agencies, keeps on raising the issue of the violation of human rights of Uyghurs and the independence of East Turkestan. The Taliban, Lashkar-e-Taiba, Pakistan's Jamaat-e-Islami, Hizb ut-Tahrir, ETIM and other organizations have been training and funding the Uyghur separatist cadres to wage an armed struggle against the Chinese in Xinjiang.

Jammu and Kashmir is the only Muslim majority province in India. The state has been the focus of national and international attention ever since October 1947, when Pakistani raiders launched an armed attack on the state in 1947. The Kashmir issue remained at the centre stage of UN Security Council debates, particularly due to deep Anglo-US involvement and biased approach against India during the height of the Cold War. However, things settled down in 1972 after the creation of Bangladesh and the conclusion of the Shimla Agreement between India and Pakistan in 1972. But after 1989–90, Kashmir has witnessed the rise of Islamic extremism, armed insurgency and terrorism bringing the issue into the limelight once again. After 9/11, terrorism and violent religious movement are not accepted by the international community. The new strategy of the separatists is to transform the Kashmiri Muslim separatist movement from the violent Islamist movement to a mass civil disobedience movement. This explains the upsurge in Kashmir with stone throwers coming out in streets across the Valley during 2018–19, as a means to seek international attention and support.

In Xinjiang, Uyghur extremists used modern means of communication, internet services etc., to spread anti-Han hate mails and separatist agenda during the course of Urumqi riots in July 2009. Soon after, China snapped all communication links in Xinjiang, which has 7 million internet users, to prevent the expansion and recurrence of violence as the riots were fanned and orchestrated by the Uyghur separatists via the Internet, text messages and long-distance telephone calls. Internet and mobile services were resumed in Xinjiang in May 2010—10 months after the July 2009 riots. In China, very few commentators write on Xinjiang's affairs and its reporting is done with official consent. As such, no public discussion or debate of Xinjiang's affairs can be seen, except for the projection of the official position. This was done during the May 2010 Beijing Conference on Xinjiang's Development to highlight peaceful anniversary of July 2009 Urumqi riots.

In Kashmir, too, the Internet, mobile text messages and telephone communication have been used by Muslim separatists to send provocative messages, agendas for agitation and violence. Dozens of YouTube-based news channels and websites, operated from Pakistan, have been running openly in Kashmir, airing provocative and anti-India programmes. Besides, both the local and national media have been used skilfully by their local correspondents to project the local, pro-separatist and more often anti-government reports, thereby feeding and sustaining the secessionist movement. In India, the Kashmir issue has become a sort of industry, with so many ill-informed people commenting, writing and publishing provocative, and often pro-separatist views without any knowledge of history, language, culture and politics of the region.

China allows legitimate and normal religious activities in Xinjiang, which has about 25,000 registered mosques and 29,000 imams, etc. About 3,000 Muslims from Xinjiang go to the Haj pilgrimage each year. However, all religious activities, including speeches/sermons of imams, are monitored by the government under its law on Prescriptions on the Management of Religious Activities in Xinjiang. Using Islam for politicization and interference in the government, society, administration, judiciary and other activities is not allowed. The Xinjiang Islamic Institute has been established to train imams and religious preachers for various mosques in Xinjiang within the prescribed norms. The Haj pilgrimage is allowed but is organized by the state and its approved Islamic Association of China. Since 1996, only 50,000

Muslims of Xinjiang have made the Haj pilgrimage to Mecca.[33]

In case of Jammu and Kashmir, there exists absolute freedom of religion, which has been grossly misused by vested political interests to the detriment of social stability, peace and harmony. The number of mosques, madrassas and preachers runs into tens of thousands in the Valley. The number of Kashmiri Muslims making Haj pilgrimage each year is over 6,000, each person receiving government subsidy in travel and other expenses. In fact, Islam in Kashmir is thriving—having transformed from a traditional form into a resurgent and radicalized Islam. Ironically, over 600 traditional and local Kashmir Muslim imams from various mosques across the Valley were gradually and systematically replaced in the 1980s by extremist non-Kashmiri imams who were trained in radicalized Islamic institutes in Uttar Pradesh and Bihar, through the network of Jamaat-e-Islami mosques, madrassas and cadres. This ushered in a process of radicalization of Islam at the grassroots in the Valley, leading to the Islamization of politics in Kashmir. These new Imams have been utilizing the pulpit of the mosques to propagate hate and anti-government venom among their followers. Now, open calls for the establishment of Nizam-e-Mustafa (Islamic government based on Sharia) are made as was witnessed in the spate of violent demonstrations by the stone pelting mobs after 1990. The Islamic radicals have used the Indian democratic system of free press, judiciary and other mechanisms to propagate their radical and separatist ideas freely, without any fear of deterrent punishment by the law-and-order machinery.[34]

As in case of other provinces, the Xinjiang region of China is governed by the CCP. Though Uyghurs are members of the CCP, the party secretary, who wields authority at provincial or the district level, has always been a Han.

Jammu and Kashmir has held elections to the 87-member Legislative Assembly every five–six years, 11 times since 1951, and 12 times to the Lok Sabha since 1967. Though there have been complaints about the rigging of elections in the past, elections of 1977, 2002, 2008 and 2014 have been acclaimed as free, fair and transparent. During the period 1948–2019, the state government was headed by the chief minister, who was elected from the party winning a majority of the seats. Right from 1947–48, the state chief minister has been a Muslim from the Valley, with some of his cabinet ministers representing Jammu and Ladakh provinces. Similarly, the people of Jammu and Kashmir elected six representatives through ballot to the Indian Parliament. The Muslim-dominated Valley of Kashmir has had a large share of political presence in the central government at Delhi. Heavyweight politicians like Syed Mir Qasim, Mohammad Shafi Qureshi, Mufti Mohammad Syed, Ghulam Nabi Azad, Saifudin Soz, Dr Farooq Abdullah and his son Omar Abdullah, have held key portfolios of home affairs, external affairs, tourism, civil aviation, food supplies, environment, renewable energy, etc., in the central government at various points. In effect, these Kashmiri politicians have successfully moulded Indian government policies in tune with the interests of their constituencies in the Valley. During the period between 1948–2019, the central government catered to the interests of regional *satraps* from the Valley, rather than dealing with the masses of Jammu and Kashmir covering all ethnic, regional and religious groups (which has been the bane of India's policy in Kashmir).[35]

The abrogation of Article 370 dealt a blow to the regional satraps and their dirty politics. The three-tier system of grassroots-level democracy has been established in the UT of Jammu and Kashmir through elections—and by devolution of power to panch and sarpanch of panchayats, block development councils (BDCs) and district development councils (DDCs)—to ensure the empowerment of people and comprehensive development at the grassroots. Elections to 4,483 panchayats (local bodies at village level) were held in November–December 2018. About 5.8 million voters exercised their right to choose from over 25,000 candidates of sarpanch of the panchayats. Election of chairpersons of over 310 BDCs of Jammu and Kashmir was held in October 2019. Elections to 280 DDCs were held in November 2020, each council having

Acknowledgements

This book is a follow-up to my study of Xinjiang during the nineteenth century, which was completed in 1980 as part of my M. Phil research programme at the then newly established Centre of Central Asian Studies (CCAS), University of Kashmir, Srinagar. My deep gratitude to late Prof. S. Maqbool Ahmad, the founder director of CCAS and a well-known scholar of West Asian studies, for including me in the first batch of M. Phil scholars at his centre. This study has evolved over a period of 40 years, which I spent collecting relevant materials and conducting field studies in Xinjiang.

Late Shri R.K. Kak (1911–88), the veteran journalist—who started his career with *Statesman* in 1939, and was with *The Indian Express* between 1970s and '80s—was the doyen of Kashmiri journalism. Kak Saheb had covered in person the events before 1947, the wars of 1947–48, 1962, 1965, 1971 and all other important events in Kashmir's politics. He had extensively covered the influx of refugees from Xinjiang to Kashmir in 1940s, and had detailed interviews with Uyghur leaders like Isa Yusuf Alaptekin and Mohammad Amin Bughra. Kak Saheb unveiled to me intricate details of Xinjiang politics in 1940s; China's policy and incorporation of Xinjiang in communist China in 1949; and the travails of refugees from Xinjiang. This important dimension of China's frontier politics stuck with me and propelled me to delve deeper into the subject. I cherish the memories of my close interaction with Kak Saheb for nearly a decade from the late 1970s to the 1980s.

Late Shri P.N. Jalali (1928–2006) was a freedom fighter and a follower of communism. He participated in the Quit Kashmir Movement led by Sheikh Abdullah in 1942. Later, Jalali took to journalism and worked for *Blitz* (Bombay) and *Patriot* (New

Delhi). He later worked with Press Trust of India from the 1960s till his retirement as its Jammu and Kashmir Bureau Chief. Jalali Saheb pushed me to take up the study of Central Asia, particularly its links with Kashmir, at Kashmir University in 1979. I remain grateful to him for his encouragement.

During my initial study of the subject, I came across the names of Shikarpuri traders who had not only traded with Yarkand but also resided there representing their parent companies. After some efforts, I established contact with Shri Bihari Lal Parashar of Gagret, Hoshiarpur in 1983. Parashar had gone to Yarkand in September 1937 as a trade agent of the Hoshiarpuri merchant Shadi Lal Dwarkanath. He stayed in Yarkand until 1951, for over 14 years, conducting trading activities for his company. Parashar was one of the last Indians who returned to India via the Yarkand–Leh route in 1951 after the establishment of Chinese control in Xinjiang. In a series of meetings with late Shri Bihari Lal Parashar during 1983–84, I got details of trade between Yarkand and Ladakh. His was an important authoritative account, which intensified my quest for a detailed and holistic study of Kashmir–Xinjiang links. I feel privileged to have interacted with Parashar ji.

A chance meeting with Khwaja Abdul Wahid Radho (1918–2011) at Srinagar in 1982, led me a to a treasure of information and rich personal experiences of the great caravaneer who had taken part in the Lapchak Mission (trading caravan) in 1942, as the worthy descendant of Radhos who had the monopoly of Lapchak caravans for several generations. Abdul Wahid Radho who did his schooling at Tyndale Biscoe Mission School, Srinagar and graduated from Aligarh Muslim University, had a sharp intellect and grasp of the complex geopolitics of Tibet and Xinjiang. I am indebted to him for sharing his insightful experiences and also some rare literature on Xinjiang with me.

Late Prof. Devendra Kaushik (1934–2020), the doyen of Soviet/Central Asian studies in India, was my research supervisor during my doctoral research on Central Asia at Jawaharlal Nehru University. He remained a true guru and mentor to me, guiding me through varied discourses on Central Asia and supporting me in my research pursuits. I remain highly obliged to Prof. Kaushik for his unflinching support, all through my association with him since 1980 till his last breath.

I acknowledge with thanks the help received from Dr Zhao Shuqing, former director of the Institute of Ethnic Minority Groups Development Research, Beijing and his team for facilitating my field studies in Xinjiang during 2010 and 2011.

Prof. Vimla Rama Rao, former head of the department of English, Bangalore University has been kind enough to go through many of my draft chapters. My sincere thanks to the staff of National Archives of India, Nehru Memorial Museum and Library, Central Secretariat Library (all in New Delhi); and School of Oriental & African Studies and India Office Records (both in London), for facilitating my work on their archives and collections.

This book has come to fruition during my two years Senior Fellowship of Nehru Memorial Museum and Library (April 2019–March 2021), which pushed me to complete the work after intensive study of records, archives and research materials. I am grateful to the director of Nehru Memorial Museum and Library for enabling me to complete this important task. Finally, my thanks to Mr Kapish Mehra of Rupa Publications for bringing out this book under his banner.

List of Abbreviations

BRI:	Belt and Road Initiative
CENTO:	Central Treaty Organization
CPC:	Communist Party of China
CPEC:	China–Pakistan Economic Corridor
CPSU:	Communist Party of Soviet Union
DTMB:	Digital Terrestrial Multimedia Broadcast, China
EIC:	East India Company
ETIM:	East Turkestan Islamic Movement
EU:	European Union
FWO:	Frontier Works Organization
GoI:	Government of India
IOR:	India Office Library & Records, London
KKH:	Karakoram Highway
NHA:	National Highway Authority of Pakistan
NWFP:	North-West Frontier Province
OBOR:	One Belt One Road
OSD:	Officer on Special Duty
PLA:	People's Liberation Army
SASAC:	State-owned Assets Supervision and Administration Commission, China
SCO:	Shanghai Cooperation Organization
SEATO:	Southeast Asia Treaty Organization
SEZ:	Special Economic Zone
SREB:	Silk Road Economic Belt
SSD:	Special Security Division
TIRET:	Turkish-Islamic Republic of Eastern Turkestan
UN:	United Nations
UNCIP:	United Nations Commission for India and Pakistan
US:	United States of America

USSR: Union of Soviet Socialist Republics
UT: Union Territory
XPCC: Xinjiang Production and Construction Corps
XUAR: Xinjiang Uyghur Autonomous Region

Notes

Chapter 1

1 Nizami, K.A., 'India's Cultural Relations with Central Asia during the Medieval Period', *Central Asia Movements of Peoples and Ideas from Times Pre-historic to Modern*, Amlendu Guha (ed.), ICCR and Vikas Publishers, New Delhi, 1970, p. 158.

2 Yusuf, Suhail, 'Threatened Rock Carvings of Pakistan', *Dawn*, 18 May 2011, https://tinyurl.com/etdyfhh7. Accessed on 31 July 2023.

3 Ibid.

4 Bapat, P.V., *2500 Years of Buddhism*, Publications Division, Ministry of Information and Broadcasting, Government of India, 1976, p. 58.

5 Shen, Fuwei, *Cultural Flow between China and outside World throughout History*, Foreign Languages Press, 1996, p. 49.

6 Ibid. 56.

7 Mir, G.M., *China and Kashmir: Ancient Political and Cultural Relations*, Mirpur, 2002, p. 45.

8 Naudou, Jean, *Buddhists of Kashmir*, Agam Kala, 1980, p. 3.

9 Ibid.

10 Ibid.

11 Kaul, Advaitavadini, *Buddhist Savants of Kashmir: Their Contribution Abroad*, Utpal Publication, 1987, p. 24; Khosla, Sarla, *History of Buddhism in Kashmir*, Sagar Publications, 1972, p. 195.

12 Ibid.

13 Kaul, Advaitavadini, *Buddhist Savants of Kashmir: Their Contribution Abroad*, Utpal Publication, 1987, p. 24.

14 Ibid. 25.

15 Ibid. 27.

16 Ibid. 26.

17 Ibid. 28.

18 Chung, Tan, 'Ageless Brotherhood between India and China', *Indian Horizons*, Vol. 43, Nos 1–2, 1994, p. 15.

19 Shen, Fuwei, *Cultural Flow between China and outside World throughout History*, Foreign Languages Press, 1996, p. 103.
20 Ganhar, J.N., and P.N. Ganhar, *Buddhism in Kashmir & Ladakh*, New Delhi, p. 177.
21 Ibid. 180.
22 Mir, G.M., *China and Kashmir: Ancient Political and Cultural Relations*, Mirpur, 2002, p. 34.
23 Ibid.
24 Ibid.
25 Ibid.
26 Ibid.
27 Ibid.
28 Khosla, Sarla, *History of Buddhism in Kashmir*, Sagar Publications, 1972, p. 62.
29 Sen, Tansen, *Buddhism, Diplomacy and Trade: The Realignment of Sino-Indian Relations, 600-1400*, Manohar, 2004, p. 102.
30 Ibid. 27.
31 Panikkar, Sardar K.M., and Sunil Chandra Ray, *Early History and Culture of Kashmir*, Munshiram Manoharlal, 1973, p. 44.
32 Ibid. 44–45.
33 Sen, Tansen, *Buddhism, Diplomacy and Trade: The Realignment of Sino-Indian Relations, 600-1400*, Manohar, 2004, p. 30.
34 Ibid. 32.
35 Stein, M.A., *Ancient Khotan: Detailed Report of Archaeological Explorations in Chinese Turkestan*, Calderon Press, Oxford, 1907, p. 165.
36 Kalhaṇa, *Kalhaṇa's Rājataraṅgiṇī A Chronicle of the Kings of Kaśmīr*, Volume 1, M.A. Stein (trans.), A. Constable and Comp., London, 1900, pp. 143–44.
37 Ibid. 311.
38 Ibid. 357.
39 Rafiqi, A.Q., *Sufism in Kashmir from the Fourteenth to the Sixteenth Century*, Bharatiya Publishing House, Varanasi, 1972, p. 17.
40 Ibid. 43.
41 Parmu, R.K., *History of Muslim Rule in Kashmir*, People's Publishing House, Delhi, 1969, p. 226.

42 Warikoo, K., *Central Asia and Kashmir: A Study in the context of Anglo-Russian Rivalry,* Gian, New Delhi, 1989, p. 102.

43 Ibid.

Chapter 2

1 Klimburg-Salter, D.E., *The Silk Route and the Diamond Path: Esoteric Buddhist Art on the Trans-Himalayan Trade Route*, UCLA Art Council, 1982, p. 27.

2 'Census of India, 1941, Vol. XXII', *Census of India,* 1943, p. 481.

3 Desideri, Ippolito, *An Account of Tibet: The Travels of Ippolito Desideri of Pistoia, S. J., 1712-1727*, Filippo de Filippi (ed.), George Routledge & Sons, 1937, p. 78.

4 Rizvi, Janet, *Trans-Himalayan Caravans: Merchant Princes and Peasant Traders in Ladakh,* Oxford University Press, 2001, p. 184.

5 Macartney, G., Received by First Assistant to the Resident in Kashmir, 10 March 1916, Foreign. Est. B., National Archives of India, New Delhi, January 1918, No. 240.

6 Metcalfe, H.A.F, Received by Under Secretary of State for India, 5 January 1938, R-2/1076 (232), India Office Library & Records, 1938, No. 22-C.

7 Montgomerie, T.G., Received by the Lt Governor, Punjab, 6 April 1871, Foreign Political A., National Archives of India, New Delhi, June 1871, Nos 560–597.

8 Cunningham, Alexander, *Ladāk, Physical, Statistical, and Historical: With Notices of the Surrounding Countries,* W.H. Allen and Company, 1854, p. 149.

9 Kennion, R.L., Received by A.C. Talbot, 16 August 1900, Foreign Extl. B., National Archives of India, New Delhi, February 1901.

10 Joldan, E., *Harvest Festival of Buddhist Dards of Ladakh and Other Essays,* Kapoor Bros., 1985, pp. 64–65.

11 Warikoo, K., 'Ladakh's Trade Relations with Tibet under the Dogras', *China Report,* Vol. 26, No. 2, 1990, p. 143.

12 Drew, Frederic, *The Jummoo and Kashmir Territories: A Geographical Account Part 73*, E. Stanford, 1875, p. 363.

13 Francke, A.H., *Antiquities of Indian Tibet Vol. 2,* Asian Educational Services, New Delhi, pp. 116–17.

14 Ibid. 40.

15 Ibid. 55–56.

16 Hedin, Sven Anders, *Trans-Himalaya: Discoveries and Adventures in Tibet, Volume 1,* Macmillan, 1909, p. 57.

17 Ibid. 59.

18 Ibid. 58.

19 For further details, see: Note given by the Ministry of External Affairs, New Delhi, to the Embassy of China in India, 24 September 1959; *India, Ministry of External Affairs, Notes, Memoranda and Letters Exchanged between the Governments of India and China, September to November 1959,* White Paper II, New Delhi, 1959, pp. 88–96.

20 According to a contemporary estimate about, 10,000–12,000 people participated in this fair. See: Gerard, Alexander, *Account of Koonawur in the Himalaya, Etc.*, George Lloyd (ed.), James Madden, 1841, p. 145.

21 Strachey, H., *Account of Ladakh Trade,* Foreign S.C., National Archives of India, New Delhi, 12 September 1851, pp. 153–56; For further details, see: Warikoo, K., 'Ladakh's Trade Relations with Tibet under the Dogras', *China Report,* Vol. 26, No. 2, 1990, pp. 133–44.

22 Ibid.

23 Ibid.

24 Rizvi, Janet, *Trans-Himalayan Caravans: Merchant Princes and Peasant Traders in Ladakh,* Oxford University Press, 2001, p. 174.

25 Ibid.

26 Strachey, H., *Account of Ladakh Trade,* Foreign S.C., National Archives of India, New Delhi, 12 September 1851.

27 Ibid.

28 Cunningham, Alexander, *Ladāk, Physical, Statistical, and Historical: With Notices of the Surrounding Countries,* W.H. Allen and Company, 1854, p. 251.

29 Moorcroft, William, and George Trebeck, *Travels in the Himalayan Provinces of Hindustan and the Panjab: In Ladakh and Kashmir; In*

Peshawar, Kabul, Kunduz, and Bokhara Volume 1, J. Murray, 1841, p. 253.

30 Ibid. 252.

31 From: Foreign Pol. A., National Archives of India, New Delhi, September 1875, Nos 21–24.

32 Ibid.

33 Ibid.

34 From: Foreign. Pol. A., National Archives of India, New Delhi, September 1878, Nos 45–69.

35 From: Foreign Pol. Frontr. B., National Archives of India, New Delhi, November 1921, Nos 16–18.

36 Joldan, E., *Harvest Festival of Buddhist Dards of Ladakh and Other Essays*, Kapoor Bros., 1985, p. 54.

37 Rizvi, Janet, *Ladakh: Crossroads of High Asia,* Oxford University Press, 1983, p. 103.

38 Colvin, E.G., Received by the Secretary to Government of India, Foreign Department, 17 May 1904, Foreign, Frontr. A, National Archives of India, New Delhi, June 1904, Nos 110–111.

39 Ibid.

40 Ibid.

41 Cunningham, Alexander, *Ladāk, Physical, Statistical, and Historical: With Notices of the Surrounding Countries,* W.H. Allen and Company, 1854, p. 23.

Chapter 3

1 Davies, R.H., *Report on the Trade and Resources of the Countries on the North Western Boundary of British India,* Government Press, 1862, p. ccxxvi.

2 Rizvi, Janet, *Trans-Karakoram Caravans,* Oxford University Press, 1999, p. 211.

3 *Ladakh Trade Report for 1882,* National Archives of India, New Delhi.

4 *Report of the Indian Hemp Drugs Commission 1893-94,* Government Central Printing Office, Calcutta, 1894, pp. 1–2.

5 Aitchison, J.E.T, *Hand-Book of the Trade Products of Leh, with the Statistics of the Trade from 1867 to 1872 Inclusive*, Wyman, 1874, p. 54.
6 Ibid.
7 *Report of the Indian Hemp Drugs Commission 1893-94*, Government Central Printing Office, Calcutta, 1894, p. 141.
8 Ibid. 139.
9 Ibid. 44, 47, 48.
10 Ibid. 360.
11 From: Foreign Frontier A., National Archives of India, New Delhi, February 1896, Nos 105–115.
12 Ibid.
13 Ibid.
14 From: Foreign. Est. B., National Archives of India, New Delhi, January 1918, No. 240.
15 Foreign Secretary, GoI, Received by Secretary, Political Department, India Office, London, 25 May 1936, L/RS/12/2378, India Office Library & Records, Nos 12/38.
16 *Kashgar Diary*, 15 April 1898, National Archives of India, New Delhi.
17 Ibid.
18 From: Foreign. Secret F., National Archives of India, New Delhi, June 1898, Nos 501–504.
19 Dy. Foreign Secretary, GoI, Received by Resident in Kashmir, 19 October 1909, Foreign Front. A., National Archives of India, New Delhi, November 1909, Nos 10–14.
20 Aitchison, J.E.T, *Hand-Book of the Trade Products of Leh, with the Statistics of the Trade from 1867 to 1872 Inclusive*, Wyman, 1874, pp. 10, 218–19.
21 Mercer, T.W., Received by Secretary to Punjab Government, 12 July 1861; Davies, R.H., *Report on the Trade and Resources of the Countries on the North Western Boundary of British India*, Government Press, 1862, p. 39.
22 Aitchison, J.E.T, *Hand-Book of the Trade Products of Leh, with the Statistics of the Trade from 1867 to 1872 Inclusive*, Wyman, 1874, p. 218.
23 *Ladakh Trade Report for 1875*, National Archives of India, New Delhi.

24 In the 1880s, Chinese authorities in Sinkiang had imposed a prohibition on the import of Indian tea for sale within Xinjiang in a bid to encourage the use of Chinese tea there. While the Kashgarian or Indian traders could not trade in Indian tea, the Kokandi, Andijani or Russian traders were free to import the same via Xinjiang but for sale in Russian Central Asia. These traders were obliged to come personally to Ladakh to purchase Indian tea required for consumption in their homeland. To ensure that no Indian tea was sold off partly or fully while in transit within Xinjiang, the Chinese guards used to accompany such trading caravans up to the Russian frontier at Irkishtam.

25 During 1893–94 and 1894–95, 399 pieces of Kokandi silk (valuing ₹1,197) and 841 pieces of Bukhara silk (valuing ₹2,523) were imported into Ladakh from Yarkand, respectively; *Ladakh Trade Reports for 1893–94, 1894–95*, National Archives of India, New Delhi.

26 G.T. Vigne, who travelled through Kashmir and Ladakh in late 1830s, mentions gold coins of Bukhara as one of the imports from Yarkand into India via Ladakh. See: Vigne, G.T., *Travels in Kashmir, Ladak, Iskardo, the Countries Adjoining the Mountain-Course of the Indus, and the Himalaya, North of Panjab: With Map and Other Illustrations*, Henry Colburn, 1842, p. 344.

27 Strachey, H., *Report on Geographical and Statistical Information and Commerce of Ladakh,* National Archives of India, New Delhi, 21 May 1851, p. 378.

28 Ibid.

29 Ibid.

30 Aitchison, J.E.T., *Hand-Book of the Trade Products of Leh, with the Statistics of the Trade from 1867 to 1872 Inclusive*, Wyman, 1874, p. 250.

31 *Ladakh Trade Report for 1884*, National Archives of India, New Delhi.

32 It becomes amply clear from the fact that the value shown for each gold coin imported from Xinjiang into Ladakh during 1875 to 1882 is shown as ₹5 only as against ₹5.5 during the year preceding 1875.

33 These were rated at only ₹5 per coin in Ladakh and were thus considered an unprofitable item for trade

34 *Ladakh Trade Report for 1890–91*, National Archives of India, New Delhi.

35 Macartney, G., Received by Resident in Kashmir, 4 July 1900, Foreign. Frontier B., National Archives of India, January 1901, Nos 84–85.

36 Vigne, G.T., *Travels in Kashmir, Ladak, Iskardo, the Countries Adjoining the Mountain-Course of the Indus, and the Himalaya, North of Panjab: With Map and Other Illustrations*, Henry Colburn, 1842, p. 344.

37 Strachey, H., *Report on Geographical and Statistical Information and Commerce of Ladakh*, National Archives of India, New Delhi, 21 May 1851, p. 380.

38 Aitchison, J.E.T., *Hand-Book of the Trade Products of Leh, with the Statistics of the Trade from 1867 to 1872 Inclusive*, Wyman, 1874, pp. 32, 349.

39 For instance, in 1854, Xinjiang exported raw materials worth 1,601,400 roubles to Russia importing therefrom goods valuing 652,100 roubles only. However, in 1890s, this trade is reported to have become more or less balanced. See: Sladkovsky, M.I., *The Long Road: Sino-Russian Economic Contacts from Ancient Times to 1917*, Progress Publishers, Moscow, 1981, pp. 228–31.

40 The Treaty of St Petersburg allowed the Russians to trade free of duty in the towns and other places of Ili, Tarbagatay, Kashgar, Urumchi and other districts that lay both on the northern and southern slopes of the Tian Shan range, thus providing free access to the Russian traders in Kashgaria.

41 Macartney, G., *Report on Trade between India and Chinese Turkestan 1900–01*, National Archives of India, New Delhi.

42 Macartney, G., *Report on Trade between India and Chinese Turkestan 1909–10*, National Archives of India, New Delhi. As per the *Ladakh Trade Report for 1909-10*, Russian gold coins valuing ₹78,279 were imported into Ladakh from Xinjiang that year, whereas the quantity of Chinese yambus and Khotan gold dust imported during the same period represented amounts of ₹168,815 and ₹93,997, respectively. This shows that the Indian traders preferred to remit their money to India in Chinese silver and gold dust rather than in roubles, which were dearer.

43 Macartney reported that the exchange value of a rouble in Chinese silver had risen to 0.875 tael during 1909 as against 0.6025 tael two years before that.

44 The import of Russian gold coins into Ladakh during 1905–06 was valued at ₹243,335 as against ₹427,505 in the preceding year. See: *Ladakh Trade Reports for 1904-05, 1905-06*, National Archives of India, New Delhi. During the Russo-Japanese war, India received little supplies of Japanese silk, thereby raising its price. That is why Indian traders in Kashgaria brought bulk quantities of Khotan silk to earn more profits from reselling it in India at exorbitant prices.

45 During 1915–16 gold roubles worth ₹22,784 only were imported into Ladakh, which represented less than one-sixth of such import in the preceding year; *Ladakh Trade Reports for 1914–15, 1915–16*, National Archives of India, New Delhi.

46 Macartney, G., *Report on Indo-Chinese Turkestan Trade for 1904–05*, National Archives of India, New Delhi.

47 *Ladakh Trade Reports for 1919–20*, National Archives of India, New Delhi.

48 *Ladakh Trade Reports for 1920–21*, National Archives of India, New Delhi.

49 Thomson Gleaver, J.W., *Kashgar Trade Report for 1933*, Foreign & Political (External), National Archives of India, New Delhi, 1934, No. 415-X; Thomson Gleaver, J.W., *Report of Trade of Chinese Turkestan with India, 1934*, Foreign & Political (External), National Archives of India, New Delhi, 1935, No. 287-X.

50 Ibid.

51 Yu-fen, Chiang, Received by H.H.J. Johnson, 8 April 1939, L/P&S/12/ 2394, India Office Library & Records, Coll. 12/51.

52 Hugel, C.B.V., *Kashmir Under Maharaja Ranjit Singh*, Atlantic Publishers & Distributors, 1984, p. 61.

53 Davies, R.H., *Report on the Trade and Resources of the Countries on the North Western Boundary of British India*, Government Press, 1862, p. 38.

54 Thomson Gleaver, J.W., *Kashgar Trade Report for 1933*, Foreign & Political (External), National Archives of India, New Delhi, 1934, No.

14 members from each district with sufficient powers and funds to supervise, implement and sponsor health, welfare, education, public works and development at the local district level.

The political turmoil and anarchic situation in Xinjiang resulted in several migrations of refugees, including the fugitives from Xinjiang to Kashmir. Whenever such migrations did take place to Kashmir (or its frontier territories of Gilgit, Hunza and Ladakh) the Indian government not only took firm steps to discourage such immigration, but also refused to get involved in any manner in the internal politics of Xinjiang. This policy was dictated by the desire to maintain good relations with China and to discourage the provincial administration of Xinjiang from leaning heavily on Soviet support. At no point of time has the post-Independence GoI showed interest in making any political capital of the deep hurt and sufferings of these refugees due to the communist Chinese takeover of Xinjiang. A few years ago, India denied visas to a few Uyghur activists who desired to visit India for participation in a conference in Himachal Pradesh. The GoI has followed a consistent policy of being sensitive to Chinese concerns over Xinjiang and has never used the Uyghur card to counter Chinese provocations, whether on Kashmir, Masood Azhar (the terrorist) or border incursions in Ladakh. The foregoing conclusions drawn after a micro-study of Kashmir–Xinjiang relations, provide some lessons to both India and China to bridge their differences in the interest of regional peace, tranquility and security.

415-X; Thomson Gleaver, J.W., *Report of Trade of Chinese Turkestan with India, 1934*, Foreign & Political (External), National Archives of India, New Delhi, 1935, No. 287-X.

55 Ibid.

56 Aitchison, J.E.T., *Hand-Book of the Trade Products of Leh, with the Statistics of the Trade from 1867 to 1872 Inclusive*, Wyman, 1874, pp. 190–91.

57 Ibid.

58 Ibid.

59 Moorcroft, William, and George Trebeck, *Travels in the Himalayan Provinces of Hindustan and the Panjab, in Ladakh and Kashmir, in Peshawar, Kabul, Kunduz, and Bokhara, by Mr William Moorcroft and Mr. George Trebeck, from 1819 to 1825, Vol. 2 of 2*, J. Murray, 1841.

60 Aitchison, J.E.T, *Hand-Book of the Trade Products of Leh, with the Statistics of the Trade from 1867 to 1872 Inclusive*, Wyman, 1874, pp. 14, 16, 150, 152; Strachey, H., *Account of Ladakh Trade*, Foreign S.C., National Archives of India, New Delhi, 12 September 1851, Nos 153–56; Davies, R.H., *Report on the Trade and Resources of the Countries on the North Western Boundary of British India*, Government Press, 1862, p. 68.

61 In May 1897, B.E.M. Gurdon, the then assistant political agent in Chitral, brought to the notice of his government that 70 pony-loads of Russian goods, mainly drill-cloth and chintzes, used to be imported there annually, Foreign. Sec. F., National Archives of India, New Delhi, August 1897. Nos 216–251. See also: *Chitral Diaries 25-31 October 1899, 1–7 November 1899*, Foreign. Sec. F., National Archives of India, New Delhi, February 1990, Nos 10–11.

62 A Badakhshi merchant was reported to have arrived in Hunza on 19 March 1895, bringing Russian cotton-cloth. See, *Gilgit Diary*, 17–25 March 1895.

63 Macartney, G., Received by Erskine, 31 May 1911, Foreign Frontier. B., National Archives of India, New Delhi, Nos 57–59.

Chapter 4

1 Davies, R.H., *Report on the Trade and Resources of the Countries on the North Western Boundary of British India*, Government Press, 1862, p. 6.

2 From: *Ladakh Trade Reports for 1888–89*, National Archives of India, New Delhi.

3 British Joint Commissioner, Ladakh, Received by Resident in Kashmir, 30 October 1888, Foreign. Frontier A., National Archives of India, New Delhi, December 1888, Nos 106–133.

4 Macartney, G., *Note on Leh Trade Report, 1893-94*, National Archives of India, New Delhi, 16 March 1895.

5 Ibid.

6 Macartney, G., *Report on Trade with Chinese Turkestan for 1897–98*, National Archives of India, New Delhi.

7 Forster, G., *A Journey from Bengal to England, through the Northern Part of India, Kashmire, Afghanistan, and Persia, and into Russia, by the Caspian Sea: Vol. II*, R. Faudler, London, 1798, p. 20.

8 Kerim Boukhary, Mir Abdoul, *Histoire de L'Asie Centrale (Afghanistan, Boukhara, Khiva, Khokand) Depuis les Dernieres Annees du Regne Nadir Shah 1153, Jusqu'en 1233 de l'Hegire (1740-1818)*, C. Schefer (trans.), Ernest Leroux, Paris, 1876.

9 Moorcroft, William, Received by G. Swinton, 12 November 1822, Foreign. Political., National Archives of India, New Delhi, 10 October 1823, No. 29.

10 Ibid.

11 Burnes, A., *Travels into Bokhara: Being the Account of a Journey from India to Cabool, Tartary, and Persia; Also, Narrative of a Voyage on the Indus, from the Sea to Lahore, with Presents from the King of Great Britain; Performed under the Orders of the Supreme Government of India, in the Years 1831, 1832, and 1833, Volume 2*, John Murray, 1834, p. 435.

12 From: Foreign. S.C., National Archives of India, New Delhi, 24 November 1854, Nos 1–54.

13 Khan, Nazir Ibrahim, *Account of Journey to Bukhara in 1869–70*, Foreign Poitical. B., National Archives of India, New Delhi, November 1871, No. 31.

14 Aitchison, J.E.T, *Hand-Book of the Trade Products of Leh, with the Statistics of the Trade from 1867 to 1872 Inclusive*, Wyman, 1874, p. 193.

15 Ibid.

16 Macartney, G., Received by Resident in Kashmir, 31 March 1902; Macartney, G., *Report on Indo-Yarkand trade via Ladakh 1907-08*, Foreign Frontr A., National Archives of India, New Delhi, January 1904, Nos 137–144.

17 Macartney, G., *Report on Trade with Chinese Turkestan for 1897–98*, National Archives of India, New Delhi.

18 Macartney, G., Received by Resident in Kashmir, 31 March 1902; Macartney, G., *Report on Indo-Yarkand trade via Ladakh 1907-08*, Foreign Frontr A., National Archives of India, New Delhi, January 1904, Nos 137–144.

19 Macartney, G., *Report on Indo-Chinese Turkestan trade 1904-05*, National Archives of India, New Delhi.

20 *Ladakh Trade Report for 1918-19*, National Archives of India, New Delhi.

21 Macartney, G., *Report on Indo-Yarkand trade for 1905-06*, National Archives of India, New Delhi.

Chapter 5

1 Moorcroft, William, Received by C.J. Metcalfe, 19 May 1821, Foreign. Political., National Archives of India, New Delhi, 10 October 1823, Nos 21–22.

2 Ibid.

3 Clark, George, Received by Maddock, 25 August 1840, Foreign. S.C., National Archives of India, New Delhi, 1 March 1841, No. 126.

4 Ibid.

5 Clark, George, Received by GoI, Foreign. S.C., National Archives of India, New Delhi, 25 January 1841, No. 91.

6 Clark, George, Received by H. Maddock, 2 January 1841, Foreign. S.C., National Archives of India, New Delhi, 25 January 1841, No. 90.

7 From: Foreign. Secret C., National Archives of India, New Delhi, 21 June 1841, No. 15.

8 Lamb, Alastair, *Britain and Chinese Central Asia,* Routledge, 1960, p. 52.

9 Clark, George, Received by Maddock, 23 September 1841, Foreign. S.C., National Archives of India, New Delhi, 18 October 1841, Nos 67–92.

10 Ibid.

11 Purwanah from Lahore Durbar, Received by Rai Gobind Joo (vakil waiting on George Clark), Foreign. S.C., National Archives of India, New Delhi, 18 October 1841, Nos 67–72.

12 Ibid.

13 Governor General, Received by George Clark, 18 October 1841, Foreign. S.C., National Archives of India, New Delhi, 18 October 1841, Nos 67–72.

14 For the full translation of the Persian text of this treaty, see: Foreign. Secret F., National Archives of India, New Delhi, September 1889, Nos 211–17 (K.W.3); *Gulab Nama of Diwan Kirpa Ram,* S.S. Charak (trans.), Light & Life Publishers, New Delhi, 1983, pp. 234–35; For a translation of the Tibetan text, see: Shakabpa, Tsepon W.D., *Tibet: A Political History,* Potala Publications, 1982, pp. 327–28.

15 Ibid. 328.

16 For further details see: Warikoo, K., 'Ladakh's Trade Relations with Tibet under the Dogras', *China Report,* Vol. 26, No. 2, 1990.

17 From: Foreign. P.C., National Archives of India, New Delhi, 1 August 1838, Nos 32–33; Wade had received this information from Abdul Rahim, the Bukharan news agent in Kashmir. Before forwarding it to the British GoI, Wade confirmed it from other sources including Dr Falconer (the superintendent of Company's Garden at Saharanpur) who was then at Leh.

18 Ibid.

19 Ibid. G.T. Vigne's attempts to explore the roads to Yarkand through Nubra were also thwarted by Gulab Singh. See: Vigne, G.T., *Travels in Kashmir, Ladak, Iskardo, the Countries Adjoining the Mountain-Course of the Indus, and the Himalaya, North of Panjab: With Map and Other Illustrations,* Henry Colburn, 1842, p. 350.

20 From: Foreign. P.C., National Archives of India, New Delhi, 1 August 1838, Nos 32–33.

21 From: Foreign. S.C., National Archives of India, New Delhi, 24 November 1854, Nos 1–25.

22 Ibid.

23 Nakshbandi, Ahmad Shah, Received by Johan Lawrence, Foreign. S.C., National Archives of India, New Delhi, 30 November 1855, Nos 33–34.

24 Ibid.

25 From: Foreign. S.C., National Archives of India, New Delhi, 30 November 1855, Nos 27–34.

26 From: Foreign. Secret., National Archives of India, New Delhi, 27 March 1857, Nos 21–22.

27 *Faiz Buksh's Papers*, Foreign. Political A., National Archives of India, New Delhi, December 1872, Nos 592–593.

28 From: Foreign. Political A., National Archives of India, New Delhi, August 1865, Nos 139–141.

29 Ibid.

30 Governor General, Received by Lt Governor, Punjab, 24 August 1865, Foreign. Political A., National Archives of India, New Delhi, August 1865, Nos 139–141.

31 From: Foreign. Political A., National Archives of India, New Delhi, August 1865, Nos 139–141.

32 From: Foreign. Political A., National Archives of India, New Delhi, December 1865, Nos 223–225.

33 Ibid.

34 From: Foreign. Political A., National Archives of India, New Delhi, September 1866, Nos 61–62.

35 From: Foreign. Political A., National Archives of India, New Delhi, December 1865, Nos 223–225.

36 From: Foreign. Secret., National Archives of India, New Delhi, April 1878, Nos 155–158.

37 Henderson, P.D., Received by the Maharaja of Kashmir, 22 October 1877, Foreign. Secret., National Archives of India, New Delhi, April 1878, Nos 155–158.

38 *Ladakh Diary*, 16–30 September 1880, Foreign. Political A., National Archives of India, New Delhi, October 1880, Nos 127–131.

39 From: Foreign. Political A., National Archives of India, New Delhi, 8 December 1866.

40 Ibid.

41 Ibid.

42 Ibid.

43 Ibid.

44 Cayley, H., Received by T.H. Thornton, Leh, 4 August 1868, Foreign. Political A., National Archives of India, New Delhi, September 1868, Nos 216–217.

45 Cayley, H., Received by T.H. Thornton, Leh, 12 October 1869, Foreign. S.I., National Archives of India, New Delhi, 1869, Nos 350–361.

46 Cayley, H., Received by T.H. Thornton, 17 August 1869, Foreign. S.I., National Archives of India, New Delhi, 1869, Nos 156–172.

47 Ibid.

48 *Cayley's Report*, Foreign. S.I., National Archives of India, New Delhi, September 1869, Nos 184–188.

49 Cayley, H., Received by T.H. Thornton, 7 September 1869, Foreign. S.I., National Archives of India, New Delhi, 1869, Nos 156–172.

50 Nakshbandi, Ghafur Shah, Received by Lt Governor, Punjab, 18 October 1871, from: Foreign. Political A., National Archives of India, New Delhi, February 1872, Nos 173–197.

51 Ibid.

52 Secretary, Punjab Government, Received by Foreign Secretary, GoI, 13 March 1873, Foreign. Secret., National Archives of India, New Delhi, April 1873, Nos 59–60.

53 From: Foreign. Political A., National Archives of India, New Delhi, August 1870, Nos 242–255.

54 Forsyth, T.D., *Report of a Mission to Yarkand, 1870*, 2 December 1870, Foreign. Political A., National Archives of India, New Delhi, January 1871, Nos 382–386.

55 *Faiz Buksh's Papers*, Foreign. Political A., National Archives of India, New Delhi, December 1872, Nos 592–593.

56 Ibid.

57 Ibid.

58 Forsyth, T.D., Received by Secretary, Punjab Government, 3 October 1870, Foreign. Secret., National Archives of India, New Delhi, December 1872, Nos 375–376.

59 Ibid.

60 Forsyth, T.D., Received by T.H. Thornton, 24 July 1870, Foreign. Political A., National Archives of India, New Delhi, January 1871, Nos 351–381.

61 Ibid.

62 Ibid.

63 Ibid.

64 Ibid.

65 From: Foreign. Secret., National Archives of India, New Delhi, April 1873, Nos 59–60.

66 *Ladakh Diaries 1–16 January and 15–28 February 1878*, Foreign. Political A., National Archives of India, New Delhi, May 1878, Nos 256–275.

67 From: Foreign. Political A., National Archives of India, New Delhi, June 1882, Nos 355–388.

68 From: Foreign. Political A., National Archives of India, New Delhi, October 1881, Nos 313–321.

69 Johnson, Received by Maharaja of Kashmir, 3 December 1872, Foreign. Political A., National Archives of India, New Delhi, January 1873, Nos 101–110.

70 Ibid.

71 From: Foreign. Political A., National Archives of India, New Delhi, January 1873, Nos 101–110.

72 From: Foreign. Political A., National Archives of India, New Delhi, March 1873, No. 302.

73 From: Foreign. Secret., National Archives of India, New Delhi, March 1873, Nos 220–233.

74 Ibid.

75 Ibid.

76 Ibid.

77 Ibid.

78 From: Foreign. Secret., National Archives of India, New Delhi, January 1874, Nos 108–136.

79 Ibid.

80 From: Foreign. Secret., National Archives of India, New Delhi, June 1874, Nos 81–87.

81 Ibid.

82 Ibid.

83 From: Foreign. Secret., National Archives of India, New Delhi, May 1875, Nos 118–124.

84 Ibid.

85 Ibid.

86 Ibid.

87 From: Foreign. Secret., National Archives of India, New Delhi, June 1878, Nos 35–44.

88 Ibid.

89 Layard, A.L., Received by Viceroy of India, 29 April 1878, National Archives of India, New Delhi.

90 *Minute by Lord Lytton, the Viceroy of India*, 13 April 1878, National Archives of India, New Delhi.

91 Foreign. A Political E., National Archives of India, New Delhi, October 1882, Nos 7–25.

92 Foreign. External B (Print)., National Archives of India, New Delhi, October 1921, Nos 320–322.

93 Ibid.

94 Ibid.

95 Ibid.

Chapter 6

1 Muller-Stellrecht, Irmtraud, *Hunza und China, 1761-1891*, Steiner, 1978.

2 Lin, Hsiao-ting, 'The Tributary System in China's Historical Imagination: China and Hunza, ca. 1760-1960', *Journal of Royal Asiatic Society. Third Series*, Vol. 19, No. 4, October 2009, pp. 489–507.

3 Dani, A.H., *History of Northern Areas of Pakistan: Upto 2000 AD*, Sang-e-meel Publications, Islamabad, 2001.
4 Ibid.
5 Ibid.
6 Muller-Stellrecht, Irmtraud, *Hunza und China, 1761-1891*, Steiner, 1978, p. 136.
7 Ibid.
8 Warikoo, K., 'China and Central Asia: A Review of Ch'ing Policy in Xinjiang, 1755–1884', *Ethnicity and Politics in Central Asia*, K. Warikoo and Dawa Norbu (eds), South Asian Publishers, New Delhi, 1992, pp. 3–4.
9 Lin, Hsiao-ting, 'The Tributary System in China's Historical Imagination: China and Hunza, ca. 1760-1960', *Journal of Royal Asiatic Society. Third Series*, Vol. 19, No. 4, October 2009, p. 492.
10 Ibid.
11 Ibid.
12 Ibid. 493.
13 Thornton, T.H., Received by Captain J. Biddulph, 22 September 1877, Foreign. Political A., National Archives of India, New Delhi, February 1878, Nos 117–137.
14 *Gilgit Diary*, 5–13 April 1878, National Archives of India, New Delhi.
15 Ibid.
16 *Gilgit Diary*, 21–28 April 1878, National Archives of India, New Delhi.
17 Ibid.
18 Ibid.
19 McMahon, A.H., Received by the Resident in Kashmir, 10 May 1898, Foreign. Secret F., National Archives of India, New Delhi, July 1898, Nos 306–347.
20 Ibid.
21 Ibid.
22 McMahon, A.H., Received by the Resident in Kashmir, 10 May 1898, Foreign. Secret F., National Archives of India, New Delhi, July 1898, Nos 306–347.
23 Ibid.

24 *Kashgar Diary*, 15 March 1896, National Archives of India, New Delhi.

25 Younghusband, F.E., Received by W.J. Cunningham, 17 November 1897, Foreign. Secret F., National Archives of India, New Delhi, January 1898, Nos 160–169.

26 'Narrative of Grombchevsky's Expedition,1889', *Proceedings of Russian Imperial Geographical Society*, Vol. 26, No. 1, 1890.

27 Ibid.

28 Hamid, S. Shahid, *Karakorum Hunza: The Land of Just Enough*, Maaref Ltd, 1979, p. 35.

29 Lin, Hsiao-ting, 'The Tributary System in China's Historical Imagination: China and Hunza, ca. 1760-1960', *Journal of Royal Asiatic Society. Third Series*, Vol. 19, No. 4, October 2009, p. 494; Hamid, S. Shahid, *Karakorum Hunza: The Land of Just Enough*, Maaref Ltd, 1979, p. 31.

30 Letter and enclosures from British Political Agent, Gilgit, Received by Resident in Kashmir, 21 January and 4 February 1892, Foreign. Secret F., National Archives of India, New Delhi, September 1892, Nos 396–472.

31 Ibid.

32 Ibid.

33 Ibid.

34 Ibid.

35 Lin, Hsiao-ting, 'The Tributary System in China's Historical Imagination: China and Hunza, ca. 1760-1960', *Journal of Royal Asiatic Society. Third Series*, Vol. 19, No. 4, October 2009, p. 496.

36 Hamid, S. Shahid, *Karakorum Hunza: The Land of Just Enough*, Maaref Ltd, 1979, p. 54.

37 Ibid. 55; *The Autobiography of Muhammad Nazim Khan, K.C.I.E., Mir of Hunza*, Khan Bahadur Maseh Pal (trans.), Mohd. Jamal Khan, 1936, p. 33.

38 Ibid. 34.

39 Ibid.

40 Ibid. 36.

41 Ibid.

42 From: Foreign. Secret F., National Archives of India, New Delhi, October 1888, Nos 102–104.

43 Ibid.

44 Ibid.

45 Ibid.

46 Hamid, S. Shahid, *Karakorum Hunza: The Land of Just Enough*, Maaref Ltd, 1979, pp. 59–60.

47 *The Autobiography of Muhammad Nazim Khan, K.C.I.E., Mir of Hunza,* Khan Bahadur Maseh Pal (trans.), Mohd. Jamal Khan, 1936, pp. 45–49.

48 Hamid, S. Shahid, *Karakorum Hunza: The Land of Just Enough*, Maaref Ltd, 1979, p. 67.

49 *The Autobiography of Muhammad Nazim Khan, K.C.I.E., Mir of Hunza,* Khan Bahadur Maseh Pal (trans.), Mohd. Jamal Khan, 1936, p. 52.

50 Ibid.

51 Ibid.

52 Ibid. 53.

53 Ibid. 53, 59.

54 Ibid. 58.

55 Walsham, John, Received by Marquess of Salisbury, London, 25 February 1892, Foreign. Secret F., National Archives of India, New Delhi, May 1892, Nos 1–38.

56 Ibid.

57 Sanderson, T.H., Received by Under Secretary of State, India Office, London, 5 March 1892, National Archives of India, New Delhi.

58 Ibid.

59 Marquess of Salisbury, Received by Sieh Tajen, 14 May 1892, National Archives of India, New Delhi.

60 Ibid.

61 Marquess of Salisbury, Received by Sieh Tajen, 11 July 1892, Foreign. Secret F., National Archives of India, New Delhi, August 1892, Nos 156–198.

62 Viceroy, Shimla, Received by Secretary of State, 29 June 1892, National Archives of India, New Delhi.

63 Secretary of State, London, Received by Viceroy, Shimla, 2 July 1892; from Foreign. Secret F., National Archives of India, New Delhi, August 1892, Nos 156–198.

64 From: Foreign. Secret F., National Archives of India, New Delhi, September 1892, Nos 69–95.

65 *The Autobiography of Muhammad Nazim Khan, K.C.I.E., Mir of Hunza,* Khan Bahadur Maseh Pal (trans.), Mohd. Jamal Khan, 1936, p. 61.

66 British Resident in Kashmir, Received by Secretary, Foreign Department, British GoI, 21 August 1892, Foreign. Secret F., National Archives of India, New Delhi, September 1892, Nos 69–95.

67 Secretary, Foreign Department, British GoI, Received by Resident in Kashmir, 24 August 1892.

68 From: Foreign. Secret F., National Archives of India, New Delhi, December 1892, Nos 136–148.

69 Lin, Hsiao-ting, 'The Tributary System in China's Historical Imagination: China and Hunza, ca. 1760-1960', *Journal of Royal Asiatic Society. Third Series*, Vol. 19, No. 4, October 2009, p. 499.

70 Ibid.

71 Napier, A.P., Received by Political Agent, 5 November 1893, Foreign. Secret F., National Archives of India, New Delhi, January 1894, Nos 41–54.

72 *Kashgar Diary,* 1–15 March 1896, Foreign. Secret F., National Archives of India, New Delhi, June 1896, Nos 27–37.

73 Ibid.

74 Taotai's letter, 8 March 1896, Foreign. Secret F., National Archives of India, New Delhi, June 1896, Nos 175–180.

75 Ibid.

76 From: Foreign. Secret F., National Archives of India, New Delhi, October 1896, Nos 533–541.

Chapter 7

1 McMahon, A.H., Received by the Resident in Kashmir, 10 May 1898, Foreign. Secret F., National Archives of India, New Delhi, July 1898, Nos 306–347.

2 Ibid.

3 Ibid. Macartney in his *Kashgar Diary*, 17–31 March 1898, confirmed that the Yarkand Amban was ordered to proceed with Brigadier General Chang to the Raskam Valley and divide the lands between the Kyrgyzs and the Kanjutis. See: Foreign. Secret F., National Archives of India, New Delhi, July 1898, Nos 464–467.

4 Ibid.

5 Ibid.

6 *Kashgar Diary*, 30 June 1898, National Archives of India, New Delhi.

7 *Kashgar Diary*, 31 July 1898, National Archives of India, New Delhi.

8 Younghusband, F.E., Received by R.P. Nisbet, 24 October 1889, from: Foreign. Secret F., National Archives of India, New Delhi, February 1890, Nos 59–77.

9 Ibid.

10 Ibid.

11 Ibid.

12 From: Foreign. Secret F., National Archives of India, New Delhi, September 1892, Nos 396–472.

13 *Gilgit Diary*, 21–27 February 1892, Foreign. Secret F., National Archives of India, New Delhi, July 1892, Nos 271–292.

14 Ibid.

15 From: Foreign. Secret F., National Archives of India, New Delhi, July 1892, Nos 130–177.

16 Ibid.

17 *Kashgar Diary*, 15 April 1898, Foreign Sec. F., National Archives of India, June 1898, Nos 464–467.

18 Ibid. Macartney, the British consul at Kashgar, learnt about this exchange of letters from his Chinese Munshi who had read the Futai's reply addressed to Petrovsky.

19 *Kashgar Diary*, 15 January 1899, Foreign Sec. F., National Archives of India, New Delhi, April 1899, Nos 119–125.

20 *Kashgar Diary*, 30 April 1899, Foreign. Secret F., National Archives of India, New Delhi, August 1899, Nos 168–201.

21 Ibid.

22 From: Foreign Sec. F., National Archives of India, New Delhi, August

1899, Nos 168–201.

23 Ibid. The Amban had, in his letter dated 7th of the 3rd month of the 25th year of Kuangshu 1316, even proposed to annually supply grain to such people from Hunza as would be sent to Yarkand for the purpose, in consideration of the food requirements of Hunza.

24 Ibid.

25 Scott, C., Received by Salisbury, 17 May 1899, Foreign Sec. F., National Archives of India, August 1899, No. 183.

26 Secretary of State, London, Received by Viceroy, 1 July 1899, Foreign Sec. F., National Archives of India, New Delhi, August 1899, Nos 168–201.

27 From: Foreign Sec. F., National Archives of India, New Delhi, September 1899, pp. 210–40.

28 Secretary of State, London, Received by Viceroy, 1 July 1899, Foreign Sec. F., National Archives of India, New Delhi, August 1899, Nos 168–201.

29 From: Foreign Secret F., National Archives of India, New Delhi, September 1899, No. 216.

30 Ibid.

31 Bax-Ironside, Received by the Foreign Office, London, 20 May 1899, National Archives of India, New Delhi.

32 From: Foreign. Secret F., National Archives of India, New Delhi, August 1899, Nos 168–201.

33 Ibid.

34 Ibid.

35 The Kashgar Taotai's letter of 2 July 1899 addressed to the Mir of Hunza is indicative of the Chinese official opinion about the MacDonald proposals, Foreign. Secret F., National Archives of India, New Delhi, August 1899, Nos 168–201.

36 From: Foreign Secret F., National Archives of India, New Delhi, September 1899, No. 233.

37 From: Foreign Secret F., National Archives of India, New Delhi, No. 21; Telegram from the Governor of Xinjiang, Received by G. Macartney, 8 November 1899. It informs about the decision of the Tsungli Yamen to allot only five plots to be leased to Hunza, exclusive

of those at Azghar and Ursur, Foreign. Secret F., National Archives of India, New Delhi, February 1900, Nos 141–151.

38 From: Foreign. Secret F., National Archives of India, New Delhi, February 1900, Nos 141–151.

39 Ibid.

40 Cunningham, W., Received by B.E.M. Gurdon, 11 January 1900, Foreign. Secret F., National Archives of India, New Delhi, February 1900, Nos 141–151.

41 Macartney, Received by Political Agent, Gilgit, 27 December 1899, Foreign. Secret F., National Archives of India, New Delhi, June 1900, Nos 83–95.

42 From: Foreign. Secret F., National Archives of India, New Delhi, June 1900, Nos 83–95.

43 Ibid.

44 Ibid.

45 Satow, E., Received by Chinese Plenipotentiaries, 29 May 1901, Foreign Secret F., National Archives of India, July 1902, No. 56.

46 Lamb, Alastair, *The Sino-Indian Border in Ladakh*, Canberra, 1973, p. 59.

47 Foreign. Sec. F., National Archives of India, New Delhi, September 1903, Nos 104–110.

48 Ibid.

49 Lamb has adroitly described the situation as: 'Petrovsky saw the Hunza move into Raskam as the thin edge of a British wedge. He was in all probability, just as concerned at the prospect of the British turning the flank of the 1895 line in the Pamirs, as were the British at the prospect of the similar attempt by the Russians.' See: Lamb, Alastair, *The Sino-Indian Border in Ladakh*, Canberra, 1973, p. 40.

50 From: Foreign. Secret F., National Archives of India, New Delhi, May 1901, Nos 79–90.

51 Viceroy of India, Received by Secretary of State, London, 13 March 1901, Foreign. Secret F., National Archives of India, New Delhi, May 1901, Nos 79–90.

52 From: Foreign. Secret F., National Archives of India, New Delhi, May 1901, Nos 79–90.

53 Secretary of State, London, Received by Viceroy of India, 16 April 1901, Foreign. Secret F., National Archives of India, New Delhi, May 1901, Nos 79–90.

54 From: Foreign. Secret F., National Archives of India, New Delhi, May 1901, Nos 79–90.

55 Ibid.

56 Ibid.

57 From: Foreign. Secret F., National Archives of India, New Delhi, July 1902, Nos 54–73.

58 From: Foreign. Secret F., National Archives of India, New Delhi, October 1904, Nos 42–109.

59 From: Foreign. Frontier B., National Archives of India, New Delhi, October 1902, Nos 533–534.

60 From: Foreign. Frontier B., National Archives of India, New Delhi, November 1910, Nos 101–105.

61 From: Foreign. Secret F., National Archives of India, New Delhi, March 1913, Nos 3–7.

62 In fact, Curzon was strongly in favour of implementing the MacDonald proposals of 14 March 1899 so that the connection between Hunza and China could be severed once and for all. In doing so, Curzon was influenced by the fear of Russian domination of Xinjiang, which, in turn, would result in Russia staking claim over Hunza, and by the possibility of Safdar Ali's settlement in Raskam by the Chinese authorities in Kashgar, which would be a real source of discomfiture for the new Mir of Hunza.

63 From: Foreign. Secret F., National Archives of India, New Delhi, February 1905, Nos 165–202.

64 Ibid.

65 Ibid.

66 Ibid.

67 Ibid.

68 Ibid.

69 Ibid.

70 Ibid.

71 From: Foreign. Secret F., National Archives of India, New Delhi,

January 1906, Nos 56–63.

72 Secretary, Foreign Department, British GoI, Received by E.G. Colvin, Resident in Kashmir, 7 July 1904.

73 *Tashkurghan Diary*, 6 August 1904; *Sarikol Diary*, 15–24 July 1908; *Gilgit Agency Political Diary*, August 1913, Foreign. Secret F., National Archives of India, New Delhi, October 1916, Nos 21–23.

74 *Gilgit Agency Politial Diary*, August 1913, Foreign. Secret External., National Archives of India, New Delhi, April 1914, Nos 92–103.

75 Ibid.

76 Political Agent, Gilgit, Received by British Consul General, Kashgar, 2 December 1913.

77 Macpherson, A.D., Received by H.V. Cobb, 6 May and 19 May 1915, Foreign. Secret Frontier., National Archives of India, New Delhi, October 1915, Nos 6–20.

78 Lorimer, D.L.R., *Gilgit Agency Diary*, June and August 1922, National Archives of India, New Delhi.

79 *Gilgit Diary*, September 1923, National Archives of India, New Delhi.

80 Lorimer, D.L.R., *Gilgit Diary*, May and November 1923, National Archives of India, New Delhi.

81 Political Agent, Gilgit, Received by Secretary, Foreign Department, British GoI, 28 September 1923, Foreign. Political., National Archives of India, New Delhi, 1923, No. 618-F.

82 Political Agent, Gilgit, Received by Secretary, Foreign Department, British GoI, 5 October 1923, Foreign. Political., National Archives of India, New Delhi, 1923, No. 618-F.

83 Foreign. Political, National Archives of India, New Delhi, 1923, No. 618-F.

84 Ibid.

85 Ibid.

86 Loch, P.G., *Gilgit Political Diary*, November 1924, National Archives of India, New Delhi.

87 *Kashgar Diary*, July 1925, August 1926, October–November 1925, Foreign. Political 280-X (Secret), National Archives of India, New Delhi, 1927; *Gilgit Diary*, October 1925, July 1926, April 1927, Foreign. Political. 276-X (External), National Archives of India, New

Delhi, 1925.

88 *Kashgar Diary*, October–November 1927, National Archives of India, New Delhi.

89 Political Agent, Gilgit, Received by Assistant to Resident in Kashmir, 26 May 1933, L/P&S/12/3292, India Office Library & Records, No. 24/10.

90 Ibid.

91 Ibid.

92 Ibid.

93 Gillian, G.V.B., Received by Resident in Kashmir, Srinagar, 24 August 1933.

94 Ibid.

95 *Kashgar Diary*, January 1935, September 1937, Foreign. Political (External). 108-X (Secret), National Archives of India, New Delhi, 1935.

96 Deputy Secretary, Foreign Department, GoI, Received by Resident in Kashmir, 17 June 1914; Telegram from Secretary, Foreign Department, GoI, Received by Resident in Kashmir, 8 June 1924.

97 Caroe, O.K., Received by Lt Col L.E. Lang, 22 June 1935, L/P&S/12/3292, India Office Library & Records, No. 24/10.

98 Ibid.

99 L/P&S/12/3292, India Office Library & Records, No. 24/10.

100 Ibid.

101 Menon, K.P.S., Received by Resident in Kashmir, 7 December 1936.

102 Ibid.

103 Mir of Hunza, Received by Political Agent, Gilgit, 5 April 1937.

104 Telegram from GoI, Received by Secretary of State, 16 April 1938; Telegram from Secretary of State, London, Received by GoI, 6 May 1938.

105 From: Foreign. Political. 84-X (Secret), National Archives of India, New Delhi, 1935.

106 Lin, Hsiao-ting, 'The Tributary System in China's Historical Imagination: China and Hunza, ca. 1760-1960', *Journal of Royal Asiatic Society. Third Series,* Vol. 19, No. 4, October 2009, p. 504.

107 Ibid.

108 Ibid.
109 Ibid.
110 Ibid.
111 Ibid. 506.
112 Kak, B.L., *The Fall of Gilgit*, Light & Life Publishers, 1977, p. 30.
113 Ibid. 31.
114 Ibid.
115 Khan Afridi, Manzoor, and Abdul Zahoor Khan, 'Pak-China Boundary Agreement: Factors and Indian Reactions', *International Journal of Social Science Studies* Vol. 4, No. 1, November 2015, pp. 2–3.
116 Ibid.
117 Ibid.
118 Ibid.
119 Ibid.
120 Ibid. 4.
121 *Report of the Officials of the Government of India and People's Republic of China on the Boundary Question*, Indian Ministry of External Affairs, New Delhi, 1961, p. 56.
122 Sering, Senge H., *Expansion of the Karakoram Corridor*, IDSA, 2012, p. 10.

Chapter 8

1 Moorcroft had taken with him English piece goods—such as cotton, broadcloth and hardware—worth about £4,000 on behalf of M/S Palmer & Co. and Mackillop and Co. of Calcutta with a view to create demand for British goods in Central Asia. See: Moorcroft, William, and George Trebeck, *Travels in the Himalayan Provinces of Hindustan and the Panjab: In Ladakh and Kashmir; In Peshawar, Kabul, Kunduz, and Bokhara Volume 1*, J. Murray, 1841, p. 103.
2 Kashmiri traders residing in Yarkand and Ladakh made repeated attempts to influence the authorities in these places to deny trading facilities to British merchants, fearing the erosion of their monopoly over the shawl wool trade. Their machinations in Yarkand succeeded in preventing Moorcroft's entry into the region.

3 Moorcroft, William, and George Trebeck, *Travels in the Himalayan Provinces of Hindustan and the Panjab: In Ladakh and Kashmir; In Peshawar, Kabul, Kunduz, and Bokhara Volume 1*, J. Murray, 1841, p. 255.

4 Ibid. 257.

5 Ibid. 420.

6 Foreign Secret., National Archives of India, New Delhi, 25 November 1831, Nos 1–3.

7 Ibid.

8 Burnes, A., Received by W.H. McNaughten, 15 March 1838, Foreign P.C., National Archives of India, New Delhi, 18 July 1838, Nos 59–60.

9 Burnes, A., Received by W.H. McNaughten, 1 February 1838, Foreign Secret, National Archives of India, New Delhi, 1 August 1838, Nos 14–15.

10 Ibid.

11 From: Foreign S.C., National Archives of India, New Delhi, 24 November 1854, Nos 1–5.

12 Ibid.

13 Ibid.

14 Ibid.

15 Ibid. In opposition to Lawrence's contention, Dalhousie ordered that these native officers would receive half pay upto a period of five years in India over and above their allowances in Kokand.

16 From: Foreign S.C., National Archives of India, New Delhi, 30 November 1855, No. 27. Two British officers Lt Hodson and G.O. Mayes who had offered their services to the Kokand envoy were not permitted by the government to go there.

17 Ibid. The envoy was also provided with ₹10,000 as expenses of his journey other than daily allowances and presents for the Khan of Kokand.

18 From: Foreign. Political A., National Archives of India, New Delhi, January 1867, Nos 171–180.

19 These sentiments were repeated in the Viceroy's letter dated 24 January 1867 sent to the Amir of Bukhara through this envoy.

20 From: Foreign Secret, National Archives of India, New Delhi,

September 1872, Nos 186–192. The Bukhara ruler had conveyed his desire to the British Ambassador at Constantinople, on 5 July 1872, through his envoy there.

21 Major Macgregor was the first OSD so appointed.

22 Edwardes, Received by GoI, 17 August 1848, Foreign Secret, National Archives of India, New Delhi, 27 October 1849, Nos 27–46.

23 *Governor General's Minute*, 24 August 1848, Foreign Secret, National Archives of India, New Delhi, 27 October 1849, Nos 27–46.

24 Lawrence, H.M., Received by Maharaja Gulab Singh, 17 September 1849, Foreign Secret, National Archives of India, New Delhi, 27 October 1849, Nos 27–46. Basti Ram was later absolved of these charges by Lawrence.

25 *Minute by H.M. Lawrence*, 1 November 1851, Foreign F.C., National Archives of India, New Delhi, 20 February 1852, Nos 99–04; *Governor General's Minute*, 16 February 1852, Foreign F.C., National Archives of India, New Delhi, 20 February 1852, Nos 99–104.

26 From: Foreign. S.C., National Archives of India, New Delhi, 24 November 1854, Nos 1–25.

27 Forsyth, T.D., Received by Punjab Government, 18 July 1866, Foreign. Political A., National Archives of India, New Delhi, September 1866, Nos 50–53.

28 From: Foreign. Political A., National Archives of India, New Delhi, November 1868, No. 82.

29 Secretary of State, Received by British GoI, 15 February 1868, Foreign. Political A., National Archives of India, New Delhi, March 1864, No. 144.

30 In October 1868, the Maharaja of Kashmir sent these proposals to the Governor General through his confidential Minister Jawalla Sahai. See: Foreign. Political A., National Archives of India, New Delhi, November 1868, No. 82.

31 Ibid.

32 From: Foreign. Political A., National Archives of India, New Delhi, January 1870, No. 136.

33 Aitchison, C.U., *A Collection of Treaties, Engagements, and Sunnuds Relating to India and Neighbouring Countries, Volume 12*, Government

of India, Central Publication Branch, 1929, pp. 26–29.

34 Cayley, H., Received by GoI, 20 September 1869, Foreign. S.I., National Archives of India, New Delhi, September 1869, Nos 184–188. These rumours were discounted by Robert Shaw, according to whom Russian and Yakub Beg's forces were separated by three days' journey across snowy ranges and not merely by the Naryn River.

35 Alder, G.J., *British India's Northern Frontier 1865-95: A Study in Imperial Policy*, Royal Commonwealth Society, 1963, p. 28.

36 Foreign. Secret., National Archives of India, New Delhi, August 1876, Nos 73–75.

37 Foreign. Secret., National Archives of India, New Delhi, March 1875, Nos 19–29.

38 Secretary, Foreign Department, GoI, Received by Secretary, Punjab Government, 12 September 1873, Foreign. Secret., National Archives of India, New Delhi, March 1875, Nos 19–29.

39 Foreign. Secret., National Archives of India, New Delhi, March 1875, Nos 19–29.

40 Telegram of the Secretary of State, Received by the Viceroy of India, 12 November 1873, Foreign. Secret., National Archives of India, New Delhi, March 1875, Nos 19–29.

41 Telegram of the Secretary of State, Received by the Viceroy of India, 27 November 1873, Foreign. Secret., National Archives of India, New Delhi, March 1875, Nos 19–29.

42 Davies met the Maharaja at Jammu on 5 and 6 December 1873 with regards to this.

43 Davies, Received by Northbrook, 7 December 1873, Foreign. Secret., National Archives of India, New Delhi, March 1875, Nos 19–29.

44 Foreign. Secret., National Archives of India, New Delhi, March 1875, Nos 19–29.

45 Oliver St John took over as OSD in Kashmir from F. Henvey on 1 January 1883.

46 Ghosh, D.K., *Kashmir in Transition,1885-93*, World Press, 1975, p. 21.

47 Secretary of State, Received by the Government of India, 23 May

1884, Foreign Secret E., National Archives of India, New Delhi, December 1885, Nos 192–245.

48 Ibid.

Chapter 9

1 In 1876, Russia occupied Kokand and Britain went on another war with Afghanistan in 1878.

2 Macgregor, Charles, *The Defence of India: A Strategical Study*, Government Central Branch Press, 1884.

3 Ibid.

4 Ibid. 221.

5 John Keay, *The Gilgit Game: The Explorers of the Western Himalayas, 1865-95*, Oxford University Press, 1990, p. 160.

6 Ibid. 208–09.

7 Kaushik, D., *Central Asia in Modern Times: A History from the Early 19th Century*, Progress Publishers, 1970, p. 59.

8 Alder, G.J., *British India's Northern Frontier 1865-95: A Study in Imperial Policy*, Royal Commonwealth Society, 1963, p. 11.

9 *Memo of Conversation Held at Madhopore on 17 and 18 November 1876 between the Viceroy and Maharaja of Kashmir*, Foreign. Secret., National Archives of India, New Delhi, July 1877, No. 34–60B.

10 Ibid.

11 Lytton, Received by Salisbury, 11 June 1877, Foreign. Secret., National Archives of India, New Delhi, July 1877, No. 34–60B.

12 Ibid.

13 Thornton, T.H., Received by J. Biddulph, 22 September 1877, Foreign Pol. A., National Archives of India, New Delhi, February 1878, Nos 117–37.

14 Leaving Gilgit on 17 May 1878, Shah Khushwakt took his route via Darel, Tangir, Maidan, Kabul, Mazar-i-Sharif, Bukhara, Samarkand, Khojend, Kokand, Marghilan, Osh, Andijan, Namangan, Karategin, Kolab, Wakhan, Hunza, Chitral, Darel and back to Gilgit. See: Foreign Secret, National Archives of India, November 1879, Nos 152–191.

15 Ibid.

16 Foreign Secret, National Archives of India, New Delhi, January 1879, Nos 24–3.

17 Ibid.

18 See: Alder, G.J., *British India's Northern Frontier 1865-95: A Study in Imperial Policy*, Royal Commonwealth Society, 1963, p. 133.

19 Ibid. 138.

20 Secretary of State, Received by British GoI, 16 September 1881, Foreign Sec., National Archives of India, New Delhi, January 1882, Nos 741–776.

21 King of Afghanistan, Received by General Amir Ahmed Khan, 20 March 1882, Foreign Secret, National Archives of India, New Delhi, April 1882, Nos 353–360.

22 In his reply to General Amir Ahmad dated 3 May 1882, the Secretary, Foreign Department British GoI (C. Grant) made it explicitly clear that, 'Government of India is under a solemn engagement to acknowledge the suzerainty of the Maharaja of Kashmir over Chitral and to afford His Highness countenance and material aid, if necessary, in defending and maintaining his rights over that country.'

23 Panjdeh is famous for the Panjdeh Crisis of 1985, when Britain and Russia came close to a war over a skirmish that occurred on 25 March 1985. The Russian forces seized the Afghan territory around an oasis at Panjdeh, south of the Oxus River. However, the war was averted through diplomatic means after Russia kept the Merv Oasis and relinquished other areas, besides promising to uphold the territorial integrity of Afghanistan. Following this incident, the Anglo-Russian Boundary Commission was established to delineate the northern frontier of Afghanistan and the border was finally laid down giving the border town of Kushka to Russia.

24 Ghosh, D.K., *Kashmir in Transition, 1885-93*, World Press, 1975, p. 159.

25 Ibid. 160.

26 British GoI, Received by the Secretary of State, 28 August 1885, Foreign Sec. F., National Archives of India, New Delhi, December 1885, Nos 118–124.

27 Alder, G.J., *British India's Northern Frontier 1865-95: A Study in Imperial Policy*, Royal Commonwealth Society, 1963, p. 155.

28 From: Foreign Sec. F., National Archives of India, New Delhi, January 1888, Nos 115–118.

29 Ibid.

30 Ibid.

31 From: Foreign Sec. F., National Archives of India, New Delhi, January 1888, pp. 115–18.

32 Ghosh, D.K., *Kashmir in Transition, 1885-93*, World Press, 1975, p. 166.

33 Durand, H.M., Received by the Resident in Kashmir, 18 October 1887, Foreign Sec. F., National Archives of India, New Delhi, January 1888.

34 Ibid.

35 Ibid.

36 Ibid.

37 Durand, H.M., Received by Captain A.G.A. Durand, 22 June 1888, National Archives of India, New Delhi.

38 Durand, A.G.A., *Report on the Present Military Situation in Gilgit*, Shimla, 5 December 1888, p. 14.

39 Ibid. 45.

40 Ibid. 14.

41 Ibid.

42 Durand, A.G.A., *Making of a Frontier: Five Years' Experiences & Adventures in Gilgit, Hunza, Nagar, Chitral & the Eastern Hindu-Kush*, Murray, 1899, p. 120.

43 Ibid. 123. By virtue of a notification issued by the foreign department, GoI, on 6 August 1889, Captain Durand was appointed as the British Agent at Gilgit with effect from 17 July 1889.

44 Dispatch from Secretary of State, Received by GoI, 28 June 1889, Foreign Sec. F., National Archives of India, New Delhi, October 1889, Nos 104–132. In their letter of 6 May 1889 to the Secretary of State, the GoI sought his approval to this proposal in view of the Russian advance 'up to the frontiers of Afghanistan and recent development of her military power in Asia'.

Chapter 10

1 Afanas'evich Kotov, Fedot, Filipp Sergeevich Efremov and Rap'iel Danibegašvili, *Russian Travellers to India and Persia 1624-1798, Kotov*, P.M. Kemp (trans.) (ed.), Jiwan Prakashan, Delhi, 1959. p. 120.

2 Davies, R.H., *Report on the Trade and Resources of the Countries on the North Western Boundary of British India*, Government Press, Lahore, 1862, p. cclvi.

3 Mehta Sher Singh, *Safar Nama: Report of a Tour into Central Asia, 1866–67*, Persian Records, J&K Archives, 1923–24, No. 379 of Samwat, Folios 69–70; Haward, G.W., 'Journey from Leh to Yarkand and Kashgar', *Journal of Royal Geographical Society*, Vol. 40, 1870, p. 49; Henderson, George, and Allan D. Hume, *Lahore to Yarkand: Incidents of the Route and Natural History of the Countries Traversed by the Expedition of 1870, under T.D. Forsyth*, L. Reeve, London, 1873, p. 98; Forsyth, T.D., *Report of a Mission to Yarkand in 1873*, Foreign Department Press, Calcutta, 1875, pp. 3, 37, 59.

4 Mehta Sher Singh, *Safar Nama: Report of a Tour into Central Asia, 1866–67*, Persian Records, J&K Archives, 1923–24, No. 379 of Samwat, Folio. 13.

5 Mehta Sher Singh, *Safar Nama: Report of a Tour into Central Asia, 1866–67*, Persian Records, J&K Archives, 1923–24, No. 379 of Samwat, Folios 69–70.

6 Ibid.

7 Forsyth, T.D., *Report of a Mission to Yarkand in 1873*, Foreign Department Press, Calcutta, 1875, p. 3.

8 Vice President of Kashmir State Council, Received by Resident in Kashmir, 16 April 1892, Foreign Secret F., National Archives of India, New Delhi, September 1892, Nos 1–5.

9 Ibid.

10 Ibid.

11 Mehta Sher Singh returned to Leh from Shahidulla on 16 September 1873, Foreign. Political A., National Archives of India, New Delhi, October 1873, Nos 392–400.

12 Resident in Kashmir, Received by Vice-President of Kashmir State

Council, 21 July 1892; from Foreign. Political A., National Archives of India, New Delhi, October 1873, Nos 392–400.

13 Elias, Ney, Received by Secretary, Foreign Department, GoI, 26 July 1885, Foreign, Sec. F., National Archives of India, New Delhi, November 1885, Nos 12–14; *Memo by Captain F.E. Younghusband*, 31 January 1890, Foreign Sec. F., National Archives of India, New Delhi, July, 225–245.

14 Henderson, P.D., Received by T.H. Thornton, 11 September 1877, Foreign Secret., National Archives of India, New Delhi, April 1878, Nos 189–195.

15 Henvey, F., Received by A.C. Lyall, 23 November 1878, Foreign. Secret., National Archives of India, New Delhi, February 1880, Nos 2–3.

16 Memo by N. Elias, 23 November 1878; from Foreign. Secret., National Archives of India, New Delhi, February 1880, Nos 2–3.

17 Ibid.

18 Foreign. Secret., National Archives of India, New Delhi, February 1880, No. 2.

19 Elias, Ney, Received by Secretary, Foreign Department, GoI, 26 July 1885, Foreign Secret. F., National Archives of India, New Delhi, November 1885, Nos 12–14.

20 Ibid.

21 Elias, Ney, Received by Secretary, Foreign Department GoI, 5 August 1885; British GoI, Received by OSD in Kashmir, 1 September 1885, Foreign Secret. F., National Archives of India, New Delhi, November 1885, Nos 12–14.

22 Ramsay, H., Received by the Resident in Kashmir, 27 September 1886, Foreign Secret. F., National Archives of India, New Delhi, June 1887, No. 169.

23 Ibid.

24 Crawford, J.A.C, Received by Resident in Kashmir, 9 April 1887, National Archives of India, New Delhi.

25 *Minute of Lord Lansdowne*, 28 September 1889, Foreign Sec. F., National Archives of India, New Delhi, October 1889, Nos 182–197.

26 *J&K Annual Administration Report, 1889-90*, Jammu, 1891.

49 From: Foreign Secret F., National Archives of India, New Delhi, January 1893, Nos 500–510.

50 Ibid.

51 Secretary, Foreign Department, GoI, Received by Resident in Kashmir, 16 January 1893.

52 From: Foreign. Secret F., National Archives of India, New Delhi, January 1893, Nos 500–510.

53 Ibid.

54 O'Conor, Received by Earl of Rosebury, 13 June 1893, Foreign. Secret F., National Archives of India, New Delhi, August 1894, Nos 26–33.

55 O'Conor, Received by Earl of Rosebury, 3 April 1894, National Archives of India, New Delhi.

56 Fowler, H.W., Received by GoI, 15 June 1894, National Archives of India, New Delhi.

57 Earl of Dunmore, *The Pamirs: Being a Narrative of a Year's Expedition on Horseback and on Foot through Kashmir, Western Tibet, Chinese Tartary, and Russian Central Asia, Volume 1*, J. Murray, 1893, pp. 228–29.

58 Fisher, M.W., Leo E. Rose and R.A. Huttenback, *Himalayan Battleground: Sino-India Rivalry in Ladakh*, Praeger, 1963, p. 114.

59 Ibid.

60 *Report of the Officials of the Government of India and the People's Republic of China on the Boundary Question*, Ministry of External Affairs, Government of India, New Delhi, 1961, pp. 75–76.

61 Ibid.

Chapter 11

1 Morgan, Gerard, *Ney Elias: Explorer and Envoy Extraordinary in High Asia*, George Allen & Unwin, 1971, p. 121.

2 Foreign. Secret F. Proceedings, National Archives of India, New Delhi, July 1885, Nos 570–639.

3 Ibid.

4 Ibid.

5 Ibid.

6 Elias, Ney, Received by Lord Dufferin, 4 October 1885, Foreign. Secret F. Proceedings, National Archives of India, New Delhi, July 1885, Nos 570–639.

7 Ibid.

8 Ibid.

9 Ibid.

10 Ibid.

11 British GoI, Received by Secretary of State, 18 June 1886, Foreign. Secret F., National Archives of India, New Delhi, December 1886, Nos 1–17.

12 Secretary of State for Foreign Affairs, London, Received by John Walsham, 11 September 1886, National Archives of India, New Delhi.

13 British GoI, Received by Secretary of State, 16 August 1889, Foreign. Secret F., National Archives of India, New Delhi, July 1890, Nos 225–245.

14 Ibid.

15 Ibid.

16 From: Foreign. Secret F., National Archives of India, New Delhi, February 1893, Nos 161–210.

17 Ibid.

18 Ibid.

19 Cunningham, W.J., Received by Younghusband, 23 June 1890, Foreign. Secret F., National Archives of India, New Delhi, July 1890, Nos 214–224.

20 Skrine, C.P., and Pamela Nightingale, *Macartney at Kashgar: New Light on British, Chinese and Russian Activities in Sinkiang, 1890-1918*, Methuen & Co., 1973, p. 3.

21 From: Foreign. Secret F., National Archives of India, New Delhi, July 1890, Nos 214–224.

22 From: Foreign. Frontier A., National Archives of India, New Delhi, September 1891, Nos 277–278.

23 British GoI, Received by Viscount Cross, 7 May 1892, Foreign. Secret F., National Archives of India, New Delhi, February 1893, Nos 161–210.

24 Taqjen, Sieh, Received by T.H. Sanderson, 18 May 1892, National Archives of India, New Delhi.

25 From: Foreign. Secret F., National Archives of India, New Delhi, February 1893, Nos 161–210.

26 Ibid.

27 Ibid.

28 Ibid.

29 Ibid.

30 British GoI, Received by Secretary of State, 16 November 1895, Foreign. Secret F., National Archives of India, New Delhi, June 1896, Nos 201–211.

31 Ibid.

32 MacDonald, C., Received by Marquis of Salisbury, 22 September 1896, Foreign. Secret F., National Archives of India, New Delhi, December 1896, Nos 56–71.

33 From: Foreign. Secret F., National Archives of India, New Delhi, September 1903, No. 104.

34 Ibid.

35 From: Foreign. Secret F., National Archives of India, New Delhi, December 1904, Nos 1–36.

36 Ibid.

37 Ibid.

38 Prince Ch'ing, Received by E. Satow, 7 May 1904, National Archives of India, New Delhi.

39 Ibid.

40 From: Foreign. General B., National Archives of India, New Delhi, September 1908, Nos 90–91.

41 Jordan, J.N., Received by Edward Grey, 6 July 1908, Foreign. Secret F., National Archives of India, New Delhi, October 1908, Nos 129–166.

42 *Kashgar Diary*, 21–31 August 1908, National Archives of India, New Delhi.

43 *Kashgar Diary*, 1–10 September 1908, National Archives of India, New Delhi.

44 Skrine, C.P., and Pamela Nightingale, *Macartney at Kashgar: New*

Light on British, Chinese and Russian Activities in Sinkiang, 1890-1918, Methuen & Co., 1973, p. 233.

45 F. 51(49) AII/53, GoI, Ministry of External Affairs, National Archives of India, New Delhi, 1953.

46 GI/54/1111/1202, GoI, Ministry of External Affairs, National Archives of India, New Delhi, 1954.

47 Skrine, C.P., and Pamela Nightingale, *Macartney at Kashgar: New Light on British, Chinese and Russian Activities in Sinkiang, 1890-1918*, Methuen & Co., 1973, p. 260.

48 Waugh, Daniel C., *Etherton at Kashgar: Rhetoric and Reality in the History of the 'Great Game'*, Bactrian Press, 2007, p. 14.

49 Ibid. 60.

50 GI/54/1111/1202, GoI, Ministry of External Affairs, National Archives of India, New Delhi, 1954.

Chapter 12

1 Stanwood, F., *War, Revolution and British Imperialism in Central Asia*, Ithaca Press, 1983, p. 107.

2 Ibid. 74.

3 Imam, Zafar, *Colonialism in East-West Relations: A Study of Soviet Policy Towards India and Anglo-Soviet Relations, 1917-1947*, Eastman Publications, 1969, p. 113.

4 According to a report, the British had supplied the Amir of Bukhara with 20,000 rifles in April 1919 and 8,000 rifles in May 1919. Similarly, the number of British instructors in the Emirate of Bukhara had reached 600 by the spring of 1919. See Kaushik, D., *Central Asia in Modern Times: A History from the Early 19th Century*, Progress Publishers, 1970, p. 157.

5 In early 1919, the Territorial Committee of the Russian Communist Party (Bolshevik), Tashkent, had an agency for conducting propaganda work among Persians, Turks, Afghans, Chinese, Uyghurs and Indians. Later on, a separate Council for International Propaganda (Sovienterprop) was established in Turkestan with the object of uniting all available revolutionary organizations of

the contiguous countries operating both in and outside Turkestan. The council strove to train clear and able agitators and organizers in the East. Persits, M.A., *Revolutionaries of India in Soviet Russia: Mainsprings of the Communist Movement in the East*, Progress, 1973, p. 100.

In early 1920, a special training school for Indian revolutionaries was set up in Tashkent by the Tashkent branch of the Soviet Commissariat for Foreign Affairs. The school was soon taken over by the Tashkent Bureau of the Communist International, headed by M.N. Roy. Several Indian Muhajirs were provided training in the school. But following the Anglo-Soviet Accord, the Tashkent School was closed. See: W. Spain, James, *The Pathan Borderland*, Hague, Mouton, 1963, p. 250.

6 The mass protest against the passage of Rowlatt Bill Act of 1919 was described by *The Times*, London, dated 20 March 1919, as part of the 'Bolshevik plans to raise revolution in India'.

7 Telegram from G. Buchanan, Received by the Foreign Office, London, 5 December 1917, Foreign. War B (Secret), National Archives of India, New Delhi, October 1918, Nos 1–82.

8 Ibid.

9 The Order of Star of Bukhara presented to General Malleson by the Amir of Bukhara in appreciation of his service for preventing all of Turkestan being overrun by Bolsheviks in 1918 naturally lost its relevance when the Soviet People's Republic was established in Bukhara in late 1920. From: Foreign Int. B., National Archives of India, New Delhi, June 1919, No. 296.

10 Bailey, F.M., *Mission to Tashkent*, Jonathan Cape, 1946, p. 15.

11 Ibid. 22. The other route, a longer one, from India to Kashgar was via Srinagar, Leh, Karakoram Pass, Shahidulla and Yarkand.

12 Ibid. 15.

13 From: Foreign Est B., National Archives of India, New Delhi, July 1918, Nos 53–58; during the year 1918–19, the Bailey Mission spent about ₹116,225, which was far in excess of the original sanctioned provision of ₹1 lakh for the purpose, Foreign. Est. B., National Archives of India, New Delhi, May 1921, Nos 240–261.

14 Bailey, F.M., *Report of Kashgar Mission,* 1918–20, Foreign. Sec. Extl., National Archives of India, August 1920, Nos 253–256.

15 Ibid.

16 Bailey arrived at Delhi on 9 February 1920.

17 Bailey, F.M., *Mission to Tashkent,* Jonathan Cape, 1946, p. 15; Swinson, A., *Beyond the Frontiers: The Biography of Colonel F.M. Bailey Explorer and Special Agent*, Hutchinson, 1971, p. 226.

18 Glancy, C.B.J., Received by the Chief Minister, J&K Archives, 23 December 1919.

19 Ibid.

20 Ibid.

21 Telegram from Chief of General Staff, Shimla, Received by General Officer Commanding, Northern Command, Murree, 11 May 1920, Foreign. Pol. 48 (III) M., National Archives of India, New Delhi, 1924.

22 O.E.R. 31/31-C, J&K Archives, 1919.

23 Glancy, B.J., Received by the Chief Minister, 29 February 1920, O.E.R. 31/31-C, J&K Archives, 1919.

24 O.E.R. 31/31-C, J&K Archives, 1919.

25 From: Foreign. Frontr. B., National Archives of India, New Delhi, August 1920. Nos 4–11.

26 Bannerman, A.D.A., Received by Major G.D. Ogilvie, 19 January 1920.

27 *Ladakh Trade Report 1919-20,* National Archives of India, New Delhi. Due to this prohibition, the import of Russian rouble notes into India via Xinjiang and Kashmir dropped to an insignificant number of 750 (valuing only ₹70) in 1920–21 from an impressive figure of 58, 44, 439 (value ₹8, ₹10, ₹484) during 1919–20.

28 From: Foreign, Sec. Intl., National Archives of India, New Delhi, August 1920, Nos 8–26.

29 From: Foreign. Frontr. B., National Archives of India, New Delhi, February 1919, Nos 69–71.

30 Telegram by British Consul General, Kashgar, Received by the Resident in Kashmir, 27 June 1919, Foreign and Political. 48 M., National Archives of India, New Delhi, 1924, No. 86.

31 Ibid.

32 Ibid.

33 Foreign & Political, 48-M., National Archives of India, New Delhi, 1924, No. 132.

34 Ibid.

35 Ibid.

36 Foreign & Political, 48-M., National Archives of India, New Delhi, 1924, No. 118.

37 Ibid.

38 Telegram by Resident in Kashmir, Received by Secretary, Foreign Department, GoI, 30 October 1919, Foreign & Political. 48-M, National Archives of India, New Delhi, 1924, No. 173.

39 Deputy Secretary, Foreign Department, GoI, Received by Resident in Kashmir, 22 November 1919, Foreign & Political, 48-M., National Archives of India, New Delhi, 1924, No. 200.

40 Persits, M.A., *Revolutionaries of India in Soviet Russia: Mainsprings of the Communist Movement in the East*, Progress, 1973, p. 78.

41 Rafiq Ahmad, who was one among this group of Indians, has narrated his experiences of travelling through difficult mountainous regions and later his convictions at Peshawar. See: Ahmad, Muzaffar, *Communist Party of India and its Formation Abroad*, National Book Agency, 1962, pp. 12–55.

42 Between 1921 and 1924, four successive communist conspiracy cases were launched under Section 121-A of the Indian Penal Code in Peshawar and another was launched in Meerut in 1927. All the Indian revolutionaries who had come to India from Central Asia were arrested and later sentenced to rigorous imprisonment for a period ranging from one to seven years.

For additional details about the Peshawar conspiracy cases, see: Kaye, Cecil, *Communism in India: With Unpublished Documents from National Archives of India, 1919-1924*, South Asia Books, 1971; Āhamada, Mujaphphara, *Myself and the Communist Party of India 1920-29*, Prabhas Kumar Sinha (trans.), National Book Agency, 1970.

43 Foreign. Frontr B., National Archives of India, New Delhi, July 1921, Nos 139–140.

44 Pratap, Raja Mahendra, *My Life story of Fifty Five Years (December 1886 to December 1941)*, M. Pratap, 1947, pp. 63–64.

45 It was as early as 27 March 1920 that the Director of British Intelligence, London, informed his government about the stoppage of Indian propaganda by the Bolsheviks. In his opinion, the Soviet government intended to use it as a great concession to England in the course of future negotiations. See: Kaye, Cecil, *Communism in India: With Unpublished Documents from National Archives of India, 1919-1924,* South Asia Books, 1971, p. 133.

46 The fulfilment of the Anglo-Soviet Accord of 16 March 1921 was subject to the following pre-condition:

> That each party refrains from hostile action or undertakings against the other and from conducting outside of its own borders any official propaganda direct or indirect against the institutions of the British Empire or the Russian Soviet Republic respectively, and more particularly that the Russian Soviet government refrains from any attempt by military or diplomatic or any other form of action or propaganda to encourage any of the peoples of Asia in any form of hostile action against British interests or the British Empire, especially in India and in the independent State of Afghanistan. The British Government gives a similar particular undertaking to the Russian Soviet Government in respect of the countries which formed part of the former Russian Empire and which have now become independent.

See: Ullman, R.H., *The Anglo-Soviet Accord*, Princeton University Press, 1972, p. 474.

47 Ibid. 9.

48 Forbes, Andrew D.W., *Warlords and Muslims in Chinese Central Asia: A Political History of Republican Xinjiang (1911-1949)*, Cambridge University Press, 1986, p. 65.

49 Ibid. 42.

50 Hasiotis, Arthur C., *Soviet Political, Economic and Military Involvement in Sinkiang from 1926 to 1949*, Garland Publishing, 1987, p. 76.

51 Forbes, Andrew D.W., *Warlords and Muslims in Chinese Central Asia:*

A Political History of Republican Xinjiang (1911-1949), Cambridge University Press, 1986, p. 98.

52 Ibid. 118.

53 *Ukrainska Pravda*, 15 August 1933.

54 Ibid; Whiting, Allen S., and Sheng Shih-ts'ai, *Sinkiang: Pawn or Pivot*, Michigan State University Press, 1958, p. 26.

55 Forbes, Andrew D.W., *Warlords and Muslims in Chinese Central Asia: A Political History of Republican Xinjiang (1911-1949)*, Cambridge University Press, 1986, pp. 136–37; Hasiotis, Arthur C., *Soviet Political, Economic and Military Involvement in Sinkiang from 1926 to 1949*, Garland Publishing, 1987, p. 100.

56 Whiting, Allen S., and Sheng Shih-ts'ai, *Sinkiang: Pawn or Pivot*, Michigan State University Press, 1958, p. 68.

57 Forbes, Andrew D.W., *Warlords and Muslims in Chinese Central Asia: A Political History of Republican Xinjiang (1911-1949)*, Cambridge University Press, 1986, pp. 148–49.

58 Whiting, Allen S., and Sheng Shih-ts'ai, *Sinkiang: Pawn or Pivot*, Michigan State University Press, 1958, p. 174.

59 Ibid. 157–58.

60 Ibid. 202.

61 Ibid.

62 *The Times*, London, 25 March 1939.

63 *The Times*, London, 1 June 1939.

64 Forbes, Andrew D.W., *Warlords and Muslims in Chinese Central Asia: A Political History of Republican Xinjiang (1911-1949)*, Cambridge University Press, 1986, p. 147.

65 Oglivie, G.D., Received by Resident in Kashmir, 18 December 1930, Foreign & Political Department, 67-X (Secret), National Archives of India, New Delhi, 1930, Nos 1–28.

66 Howell, E.B., Received by the Director, Frontier Circle, Survey of India, 12 January 1928, Foreign Political 71-X (Secret), National Archives of India, New Delhi, 1928.

67 Secretary of Chief Commissioner NWFP, Received by Director, Frontier Circle, Survey of India, 18 July 1927, National Archives of India, New Delhi.

Chapter 13

1 Malhotra, Iqbal Chand, and Maroof Raza, *Kashmir's Untold Story: Declassified*, Bloomsbury, 2019, p. 48.
2 Brown, William A., *The Gilgit Rebellion*, Ibex, 1998, p. 30.
3 Ibid. xi.
4 Ibid.
5 Malhotra, Iqbal Chand, and Maroof Raza, *Kashmir's Untold Story: Declassified*, Bloomsbury, 2019, pp. 40–41.
6 Brown, William A., *The Gilgit Rebellion*, Ibex, 1998, p. 30.
7 Ibid. 53.
8 Ibid.
9 Ibid. 55.
10 Singh Sarila, Narendra, *The Shadow of the Great Game: The Untold Story of India's Partition*, HarperCollins, 2005, p. 333; *Bulletin of Military Historical Society of Great Britain*, Vol. 46, No. 182, 1995.
11 Brown, William A., *The Gilgit Rebellion*, Ibex, 1998, p. 30.
12 Ibid. 66.
13 Ibid. 116.
14 Ibid. 97.
15 Ibid. 104.
16 Ibid. 138.
17 Ibid.
18 Ibid.
19 Ibid. 155.
20 Ibid.
21 Ibid. 284.
22 Ibid. 283.
23 Ibid. 285.
24 Ibid. 265.
25 Ibid. 237–38.
26 Ibid. 282.
27 Dani, A.H., *History of Northern Areas of Pakistan*, National Inst. of Historical and Cultural Research, 1991, pp. 354–55.
28 Brown, William A., *The Gilgit Rebellion*, Ibex, 1998, pp. 226, 285.

29 Ibid. 161.

30 Dani, A.H., *History of Northern Areas of Pakistan*, National Inst. of Historical and Cultural Research, 1991, p. 345.

31 Ibid. 327.

32 Ibid.

33 Ibid. 330.

34 Brown, William A., *The Gilgit Rebellion*, Ibex, 1998, pp. 175–77.

35 Dasgupta, C., *War and Diplomacy in Kashmir*, Sage Publications, 2002; Singh Sarila, Narendra, *The Shadow of the Great Game: The Untold Story of India's Partition*, HarperCollins, 2005; Malhotra, Iqbal Chand, and Maroof Raza, *Kashmir's Untold Story: Declassified*, Bloomsbury, 2019; Singh, Raghvendra, *India's Lost Frontier: The Story of the North-West Frontier Province of Pakistan*, Rupa Publications, 2019.

36 Dasgupta, C., *War and Diplomacy in Kashmir*, Sage Publications, 2002, p. 57.

37 Ibid.

38 Sarila, N.S., *The Shadow of the Great Game: The Untold Story of India's Partition*, HarperCollins, 2005, p. 336.

39 Ibid.

40 Ibid.

41 Ibid.

42 Brown, William A., *The Gilgit Rebellion*, Ibex, 1998, p. xii.

43 Stanley, H.S.H., Received by F.R. Bairett, 10 June 1958.

44 Brown, William A., *The Gilgit Rebellion*, Ibex, 1998, p. xiii.

Chapter 14

1 *Gilgit Agency Diaries*, National Archives of India, New Delhi, March and April 1933.

2 *Administration Report for Gilgit Agency*, 1934, National Archives of India, New Delhi.

3 *Administration Report for Gilgit Agency*, 1935, National Archives of India, New Delhi.

4 *Gilgit Agency Diary*, May 1934, National Archives of India, New Delhi.

5 *Administration Report for Gilgit Agency*, 1933, National Archives of India, New Delhi.

6 *Leh Treaty Road Administration Report*, 1934, National Archives of India, New Delhi.

7 Ibid.

8 Ibid.

9 L/P and S/12/2386, India Office Library & Records, No. 12/L5.

10 Telegram from Government of India, Received by British Minister, Kabul, 18 June 1936, L/P and S/12/2386, India Office Library & Records, No. 12/L5.

11 Forbes, Andrew D.W., *Warlords and Muslims in Chinese Central Asia: A Political History of Republican Xinjiang (1911-1949)*, Cambridge University Press, 1986, pp. 11, 124, 196, 304.

12 Radhu, Abdul Wahid, *Tibetan Caravans: Journey from Leh to Lhasa*, Speaking Tiger, 2017, p. 146.

13 Caroe, O.K., Received by L.E. Lang, 9 August 1935, National Archives of India, New Delhi.

14 Author's interview from 4 June 1986 at Srinagar with R.K. Kak, a senior journalist who was witness to the coming of Tungan refugees to Kashmir. Kak had also interviewed their chief in Srinagar.

15 L/P and S/12/2387, India Office Library & Records, No. 12/46.

16 Telegram from Government of India, Received by the Secretary of State for India, 29 April 1937, L/P and S/12/2387, India Office Library & Records, No. 12/46.

17 Mahmud Si Jang, Received by Chinese Consul General, Calcutta, 6 May 1937.

18 *Gist of Interview between Mahmud and Resident in Kashmir at Srinagar*, 20 July 1937.

19 Government of India, Received by Punjab Government, 21 December 1937.

20 Telegram from Government of India, Received by Secretary of State for India, 14 February 1938, National Archives of India, New Delhi.

21 *Kashgar Diary*, National Archives of India, New Delhi, September 1937.

22 Telegram from the British Consul General, Kashgar, Received by the

Government of India, 2 October 1937, National Archives of India, New Delhi.

23 Telegram from the Government of India, Received by the British Consul General, Kashgar, 6 October 1937, National Archives of India, New Delhi.

24 L/P and S/12/2387, India Office Library & Records, No. 12/46.

25 Telegram from Government of India, Received by the Resident in Kashmir, 8 October 1937.

26 Telegram from Resident in Kashmir, Received by Foreign Department, Government of India, 3 November 1937, National Archives of India, New Delhi.

27 82 rifles and 12 pistols were confiscated from these Tungan refugees.

28 Telegram from Resident in Kashmir, Received by Foreign Department, Government of India, 28 October 1937, National Archives of India, New Delhi.

29 Telegram from Government of India, Received by Secretary of State for India, London, 14 February 1938, National Archives of India, New Delhi.

30 Telegram from Government of India, Received by the British Consul General, Kashgar, 11 April 1938, National Archives of India, New Delhi.

31 British Embassy, Chungking, Received by the Chinese Ministry of Foreign Affairs, 23 April 1942, National Archives of India, New Delhi.

32 Ibid.

33 Ibid. The increase in its value was due to the rise in price of gold since 1937.

34 Telegram from British Consul General, Kashgar, Received by Government of India, 3 December 1937, National Archives of India, New Delhi.

35 After the communist victory in 1949, Ma Hu-shan led an anti-communist guerilla group in the hills in southern Kansu. He was captured and executed at Lanchow in 1954. See: Forbes, Andrew D.W., *Warlords and Muslims in Chinese Central Asia: A Political History of Republican Xinjiang (1911-1949)*, Cambridge University Press, 1986, p. 310.

36 Ogilvie, Mac I.G., Received by J.P. Gibson, 8 January 1945, National Archives of India, New Delhi.

37 Lias, Godfrey, 'Kazakh Nomads Struggle against Communists', *The Times,* London, 17 February 1955.

38 Ibid.

39 *Tribune*, 9 November 1941.

40 Ibid.

41 300 rifles and ammunition were recovered from the Kazakhs.

42 See also: *Hindustan Times,* 14 November 1941.

43 Ibid.

44 For instance, see editorials and commentaries in weeklies *Jamhoor, Khalid, Islah, Pasban,* etc. during 1941–42.

45 *An Appeal by the Working Committee of All J&K National Conference*, Jammu, 17 January 1942.

46 *Jammu and Kashmir Government Press Communiqué*, 4 and 5 January 1942.

47 Ibid.

48 *Statement of O.K. Caroe in the Central Assembly*, 16 February 1942.

49 D.O. letter N. F-745/43 dated Srinagar,17 August 1943 from Resident in Kashmir to Prime Minister, Jammu & Kashmir.

50 Ibid.

51 L/P & S/12/3302, India Office Library & Records, No. 24/19.

52 Ibid.

53 Ibid. This included the reimbursement of ₹114,708 to Jammu and Kashmir government.

54 Ibid.

55 Ibid.

56 Tao-Chih-yueh, the Kuomintang Garrison Commander in Xinjiang alongwith his 80,000 KMT troops surrendered to Peng Teh-huai's PLA forces on 25 September 1949. Next day, Burhan Shahidi, the provincial chairman of Xinjiang severed connection with the nationalist government at Canton, pledged allegiance to the communist government then being formed at Beijing and announced his acceptance of the peace terms offered by the CCP. Burhan Shahidi was appointed the first Chairman of the Chinese Communist

27 Ibid.

28 From: Foreign. Secret F., National Archives of India, New Delhi, July 1889, Nos 203–230.

29 Ibid.

30 Ibid.

31 Ibid.

32 Ramsay, H., Received by Resident in Kashmir, 25 May 1889, National Archives of India, New Delhi.

33 Ramsay, H., Received by Resident in Kashmir, 16 June 1889, National Archives of India, New Delhi.

34 Ibid.

35 Foreign. Secret F., National Archives of India, New Delhi, September 1889, No. 31.

36 Ibid.

37 Younghusband, F.E., *The Northern Frontier of Kashmir*, Oriental Publishers, 1890. pp. 13–17.

38 For further details about Grombchevsky's explorations in the area see: Warikoo, K., *Central Asia and Kashmir : A Study in the Context of Anglo-Russian Rivalry,* Gian, New Delhi, 1989, pp. 46–50.

39 *Proceedings of Imperial Russian Geographical Society,* Vol. 26, No. 1, 1890.

40 Cunninghan, W.J., Received by Captain F.E. Younghusband, 23 June 1890, Foreign. Secret F., National Archives of India, New Delhi, July 1890, Nos 214–224.

41 Ibid.

42 From: Foreign Secret. F., National Archives of India, New Delhi, October 1890, Nos 141–170.

43 Ibid.

44 From: Foreign Secret F., National Archives of India, New Delhi, July 1890, Nos 225–245.

45 Lansdowne, Received by Walsham, 17 July 1890, National Archives of India, New Delhi.

46 Ibid.

47 Ibid.

48 Alder, G.J., *British India's Northern Frontier*, Longmans, 1964, p. 278.

Xinjiang Provincial Government established at Urumchi on 18 December 1949. See: Forbes, Andrew D.W., *Warlords and Muslims in Chinese Central Asia: A Political History of Republican Xinjiang (1911-1949)*, Cambridge University Press, 1986, pp. 220–22.

57 Bughra, Mohammad Amin, Received by Under Secretary, Ministry of External Affairs, New Delhi, 26 March 1950, 253-CJK/50, Ministry of External Affairs, GoI, National Archives of India, New Delhi.

58 Ibid.

59 They arrived at Leh on 12 December 1949.

60 253-CJK/50, Ministry of External Affairs, GoI, National Archives of India, New Delhi.

61 Ibid.

62 Ibid.

63 Ibid.

64 Ibid.

65 Ibid.

66 Ibid.

67 *Jammu and Kashmir Government Press Communiqué*, 7 August 1951.

68 Ibid.

69 Forbes, Andrew D.W., *Warlords and Muslims in Chinese Central Asia: A Political History of Republican Xinjiang (1911-1949)*, Cambridge University Press, 1986, p. 224.

70 Ibid. 225.

71 Yulbaz Khan arrived at Taiwan on 1 May 1951.

72 Forbes, Andrew D.W., *Warlords and Muslims in Chinese Central Asia: A Political History of Republican Xinjiang (1911-1949)*, Cambridge University Press, 1986, p. 225.

73 *The Times*, London, 25 August 1951.

74 *The Times*, London, 22 September 1951.

75 *Hindustan Standard*, Calcutta, 20 October 1951.

76 Ibid.

77 *Amrita Bazar Patrika*, Calcutta, 23 September 1951.

78 Ibid.

79 *The Statesman*, 14 June 1954; *Leader*, Allahabad, 19 June 1954.

80 *The Times*, London reported on 27 October 1952 the departure of

102 Kazakh refugees from Kashmir for permanent settlement in Turkey.

81 According to a report by Office of the British High Commission in Pakistan, 828 Muslims from Xinjiang had entered Gilgit in 1948. See: Oliver, P.R., Received by R.W.D. Fowler, 20 April 1949, DO/42/533, India Office Library & Records, No. S/24.

Even as late as 1963, the Pakistan government was reported to have allotted 3,000 acres of land in Gilgit to some Muslim refugees from Kashgar for permanent settlement, See: *Hindustan Times*, 16 September 1963.

Chapter 15

1 Ispahani, Mehnaz Z., *Roads and Rivals: The Political Uses of Access in the Borderlands of Asia*, Cornell University Press, 1989, p. 159.

2 Ibid.

3 Kamal, Nazir A., 'Karakoram Highway: A Nation Building Effort', *Strategic Studies*, Vol. 2, No. 3, Spring 1979, pp. 18–31.

4 Ibid.

5 Ibid.

6 Ibid.

7 Ibid.

8 Ispahani, Mehnaz Z., *Roads and Rivals: The Political Uses of Access in the Borderlands of Asia*, Cornell University Press, 1989, p. 188.

9 Ibid.

10 Ibid. 189.

11 Ibid.

12 Topping, Seymour, 'Karakoram Highway', *The New York Times Magazine*, 3 December 1979, pp. 38–42.

13 Ibid.

14 Antia, S.N., 'Karakoram Highway: Military-Political Implications', *Mainstream*, 14 October 1978.

15 Ispahani, Mehnaz Z., *Roads and Rivals: The Political Uses of Access in the Borderlands of Asia*, Cornell University Press, 1989, p. 197.

16 Sering, Senge H., *Expansion of the Karakoram Corridor: Implications and Prospects*, IDSA, 2012, p. 20.

17 *The Express Tribune*, Karachi, 29 December 2019.
18 Sering, Senge H., *Expansion of the Karakoram Corridor: Implications and Prospects*, IDSA, 2012, p. 12.
19 Ibid.
20 Ibid. 10–11.
21 Wolf, Siegfried O., *The China-Pakistan Economic Corridor of the Belt and Road Initiative*, Springer, 2010, p. 13.
22 Sareen, Sushant, *Corridor Calculus: China Pakistan Economic Corridor & China's Comprador Investment Model in Pakistan*, VIF, 2015, pp. 12–13.
23 Aimin Deng and Qian Lui, 'Research on the Transportation Infrastructure Construction of China-Pakistan Economic Corridor', *World Journal of Research and Review*, Vol. 16, No. 3, March 2018, pp. 93–97.
24 Chinoy, Sujan R., *China-Pakistan Economic Corridor (CPEC): The Project and its Prospects*, IDSA, 2021, p. 4.
25 Sering, Senge H., *Expansion of the Karakoram Corridor: Implications and Prospects*, IDSA, 2012, p. 31.
26 Sareen, Sushant, *Corridor Calculus: China Pakistan Economic Corridor & China's Comprador Investment Model in Pakistan*, VIF, 2015, p. 43.
27 Sering, Senge H., *Expansion of the Karakoram Corridor: Implications and Prospects*, IDSA, 2012, p. 46.
28 Chinoy, Sujan R., *China-Pakistan Economic Corridor (CPEC): The Project and its Prospects*, IDSA, 2021, p. 27.
29 Ibid.
30 Ibid. 27–28.

Chapter 16

1 Harris, Lillian Craig, 'Xinjiang, Central Asia and the Implications for China's Policy in the Islamic World', *China Quarterly*, Vol. 133, March 1993, p. 115.
2 Ibid. 116.
3 Chew, Amy, 'How Syria's Civil War Drew Uyghur Fighters and Shaped the Separatist Group TIP in China's Crosshairs', *South China Morning Post*, 23 November 2020.

4 Ma Rong, 'The Soviet Model's Influence and the Current Debate on Ethnic Relations', *Global Asia*, Vol. 5, No. 2, 2010, pp. 50–55.

5 Ibid.

6 Ibid.

7 Ruser, Nathan, et al., 'Cultural Erasure: Tracing the Destruction of Uyghur and Islamic Spaces in Xinjiang' *Australian Strategic Policy Institute*, September 2020.

8 PTI, 'China announces new rules for Muslims visiting Saudi Arabia for Haj', *The Economic Times*, 12 October 2020, https://tinyurl.com/3duabuwc. Accessed on 31 August 2023.

9 Dake Kang, and Yanan Wang, 'China's Uighurs Assigned "Relatives" who Report to the State', *The Indian Express*, 1 December 2018.

10 Yajun Bao, 'Xinjiang Production and Construction Corps: An Insider's Perspective', *China: An International Journal*, Vol. 18, No. 2 May 2020, pp. 161–174.

11 Ibid.

12 Ibid.

13 'Dismantling China's Muslim Gulag in Xinjiang is Not Enough', *The Economist*, 14 January 2020.

14 'Joint Statement on Xinjiang at Third Committee Made by Belarus on Behalf of 54 Countries', *Permanent Mission of the People's Republic of China to the UN*, 29 October 2019, https://tinyurl.com/ysve3xn3. Accessed on 31 August 2023.

15 Buckley, Chris, 'Brushing Off Criticism, China's Xi Calls Policies in Xinjiang "Totally Correct"', *The New York Times*, 26 September 2020, https://tinyurl.com/bdz82s5s. Accessed on 31 August 2023.

16 Hu Yue, 'Hand in Hand', *Beijing Review*, 10 June 2010, pp. 30–31.

17 Warikoo, K., 'Genocide of Kashmiri Pandits', *Genocides and Xenophobia in South Asia and Beyond*, Rituparna Bhattacharya (ed.), Routledge, 2023.

18 Ashiq, Peerzadaq, '208 Temples Damaged in Kashmir', *Hindustan Times*, 4 October 2012.

19 'Lok Sabha Passes Jammu and Kashmir Official Languages Bill, 2020', *The Economic Times*, 23 September 2020.

20 Ibid.

21 Masood, Basharat, 'In Srinagar, Jeweller Killed Weeks After Domicile Nod, Militants Warn of More Attacks', *The Indian Express*, 2 January 2012.

22 Majid, Zulfikar, 'Kashmiri Pandits Prepare for Another Mass Migration Amid Targeted Killings', *Deccan Herald*, 2 June 2022, https://tinyurl.com/2266rnfw. Accessed on 11 July 2023.

23 PRC State Council, *White Paper on Development and Progress in Xinjiang*, Beijing Language Press, 2009, p. 10.

24 Ibid. 8.

25 Ibid. 6.

26 Li Woke, 'Xinjiang Reportedly to Pilot 5% Tax on Gas, Oil', *Global Times*, 27 May 2010.

27 'J&K's Dependence on Centre Alarming', *The Times of India*, 19 July 2010.

28 *Outlook (The News Scroll)*, 21 March 2020.

29 *The Hindu*, 20 May 2010.

30 'J&K Government Announcement', *Daily Excelsior*, 9 April 2010.

31 'Business Thrives Amidst Kashmir War', *Christian Science Monitor*, 11 April 2007.

32 Ahmed, Rashid, 'Despite Terror, J&K Economy is Shining', *Hindustan Times*, 12 September 2007.

33 'A Report on Freedom of Religion or Belief in Xinjiang', *Global Times*, 3 November 2020.

34 Warikoo, K., 'Genocide of Kashmiri Pandits', *Genocides and Xenophobia in South Asia and Beyond*, Rituparna Bhattacharya (ed.), Routledge, 2023.

35 Ibid.

Index